50 Treasures from
Winchester College

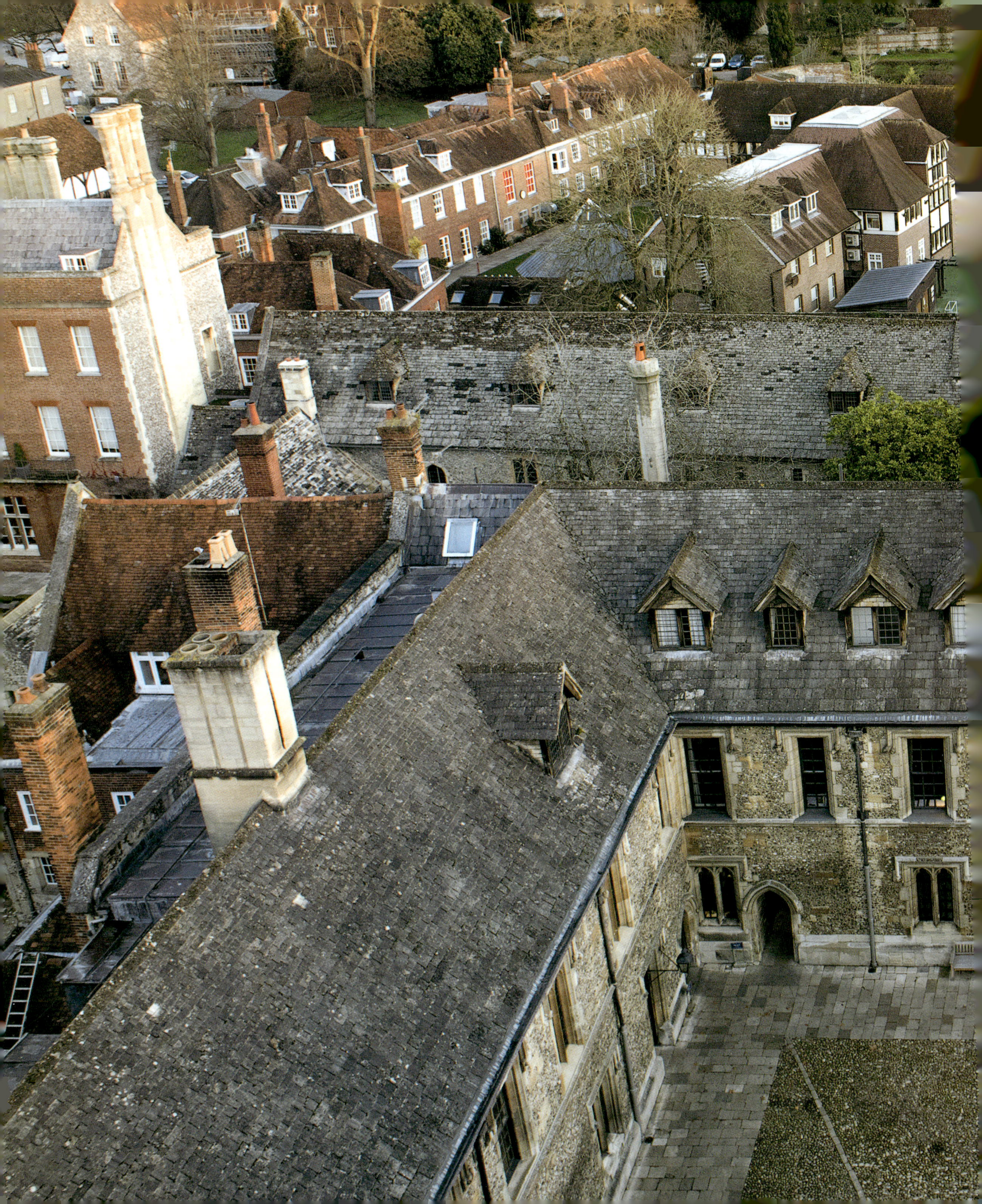

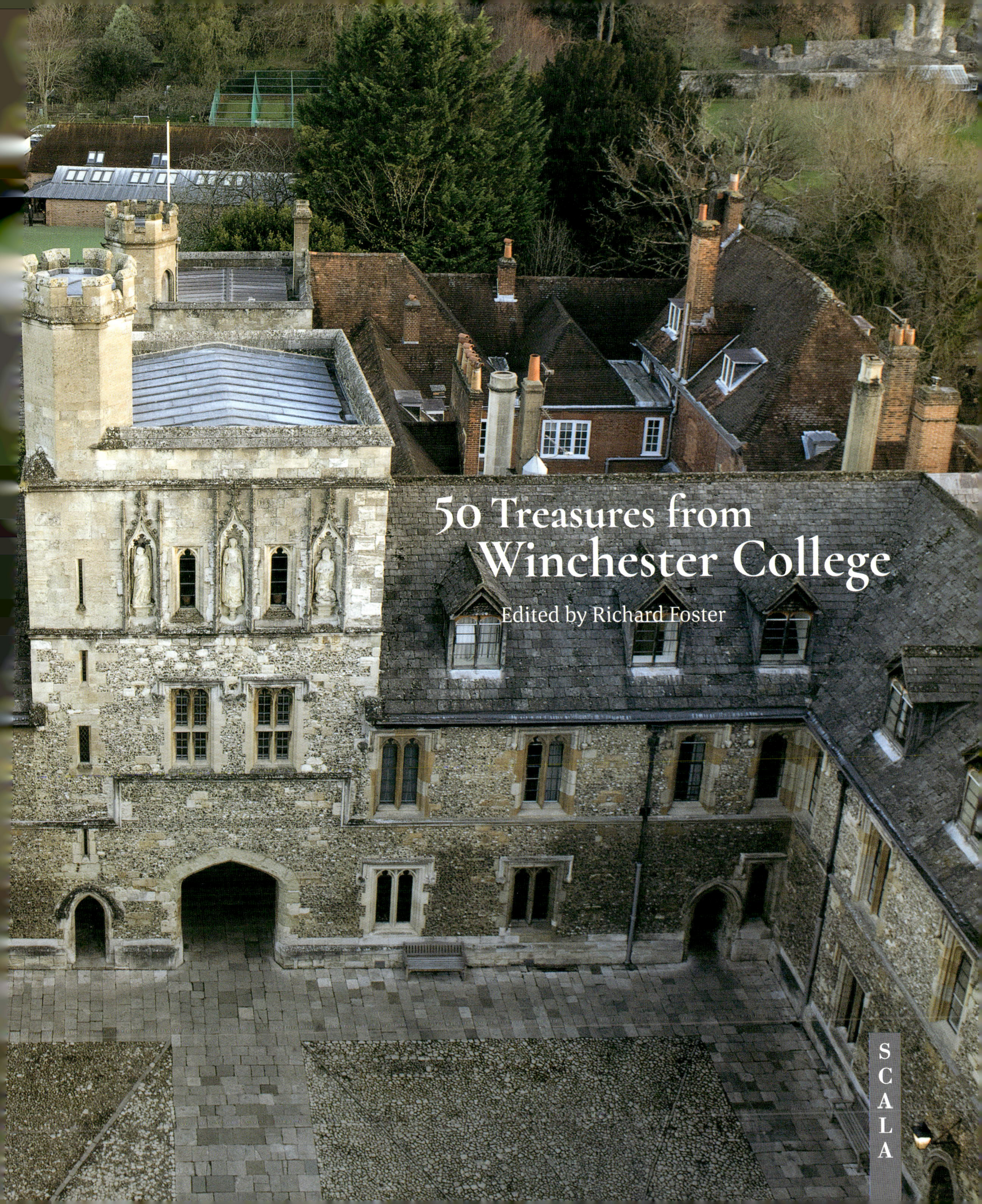

50 Treasures from
Winchester College
Edited by Richard Foster
SCALA

Preface

Winchester College has probably the longest unbroken history of any school in England. It was established by William of Wykeham in 1382 and tuition began in 1394. Most of the school's medieval buildings are still used for their original purpose, and the name of every Scholar educated here is recorded. For more than six centuries the pattern of learning, worship and daily life established at the College's foundation has continued, altered in its details but true to its essential character.

This book celebrates some of the works of art, books and documents that belong to this ancient institution. They are part of its identity. The depth and diversity of the College's collections are unique. Our treasures range from ancient Greek pottery to contemporary artists' books, from medieval silver to models of eighteenth-century warships. Some of the objects featured here are important and well known to scholars; others have a more local significance in the context of Winchester's history. All are part of the life of the school and contribute to the education of our pupils. The collections take a central place in Div, Winchester's unique cultural and historical curriculum. Pupils have the opportunity to curate their own exhibitions, and often become involved in the care and study of the collections.

The essays in this volume have all been written by members of the school community: pupils past and present, teachers, staff and Fellows (our governors). The authors have drawn on their own experience and expertise in a variety of fields, as academics, collectors, curators and gardeners, among many others. The result is a series of personal responses to the College's treasures. This publication has been funded by the Warden and Fellows of Winchester College, and for their collegial spirit I am most grateful. It is our intention that it will be the start of a series on the history of the College and its collections.

In recent years the school has made its heritage increasingly accessible. Since 2016 our collections of art and archaeology have been displayed in a purpose-built museum, once the Warden's Stables, now known to us as the Treasury, and a treasure in its own right.

We think the treasures featured in these pages are worth a visit. Do come and make up your own mind.

Charles Sinclair (Warden)

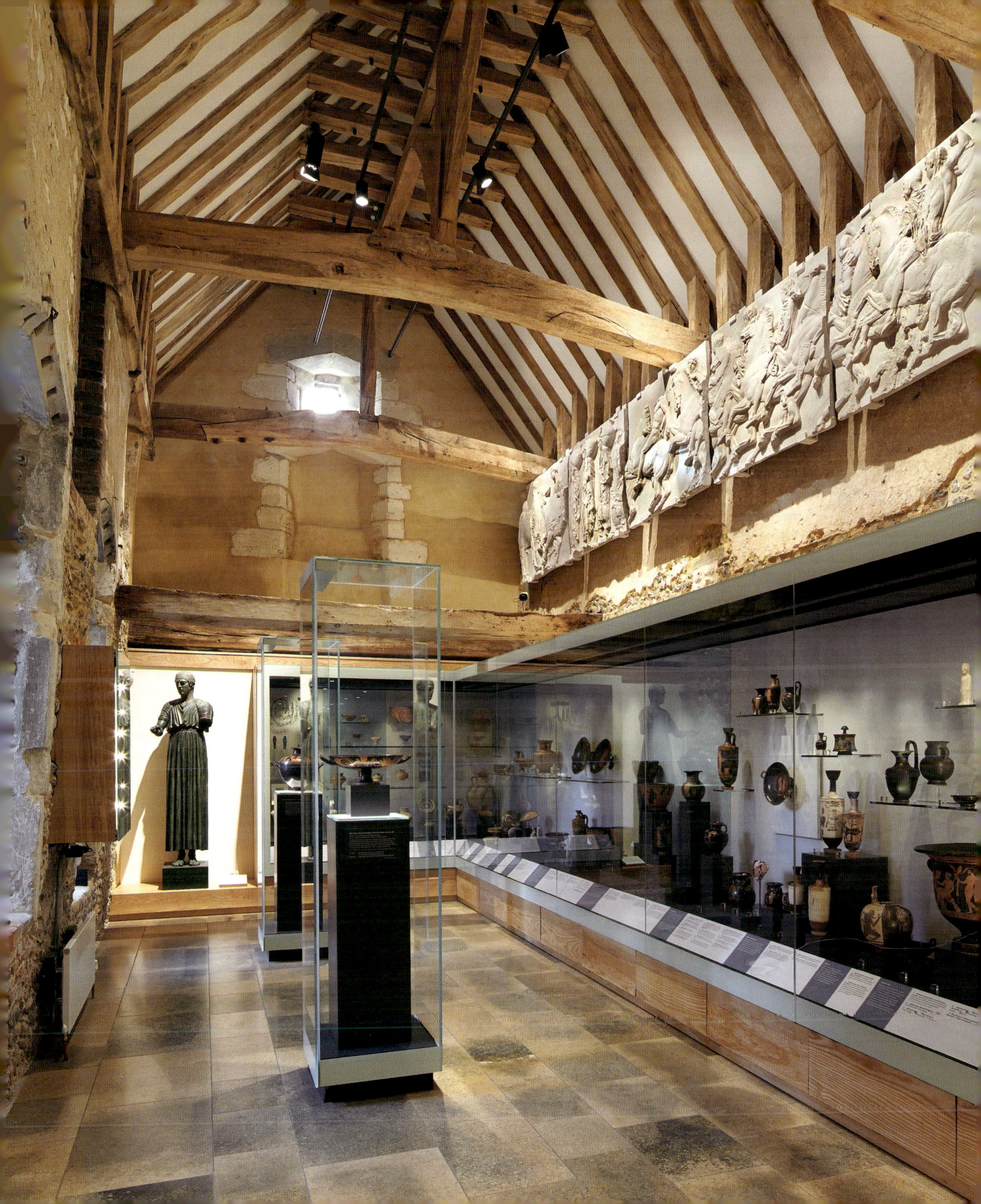

This edition © Scala Arts & Heritage Publishers Ltd, 2019
Text and photography © Winchester College, 2019

First published in 2019 by
Scala Arts & Heritage Publishers Ltd
10 Lion Yard
Tremadoc Road
London SW4 7NQ, UK
www.scalapublishers.com

In association with
Winchester College
College Street
Winchester SO23 9NA
www.winchestercollege.org

ISBN 978-1-78551-220-9

Edited by Robert Davies
Designed by Maggi Smith, Sixism
Printed and bound in Italy

10 9 8 7 6 5 4 3 2 1

Front cover: Rose Tapestries, 1480s

Contents

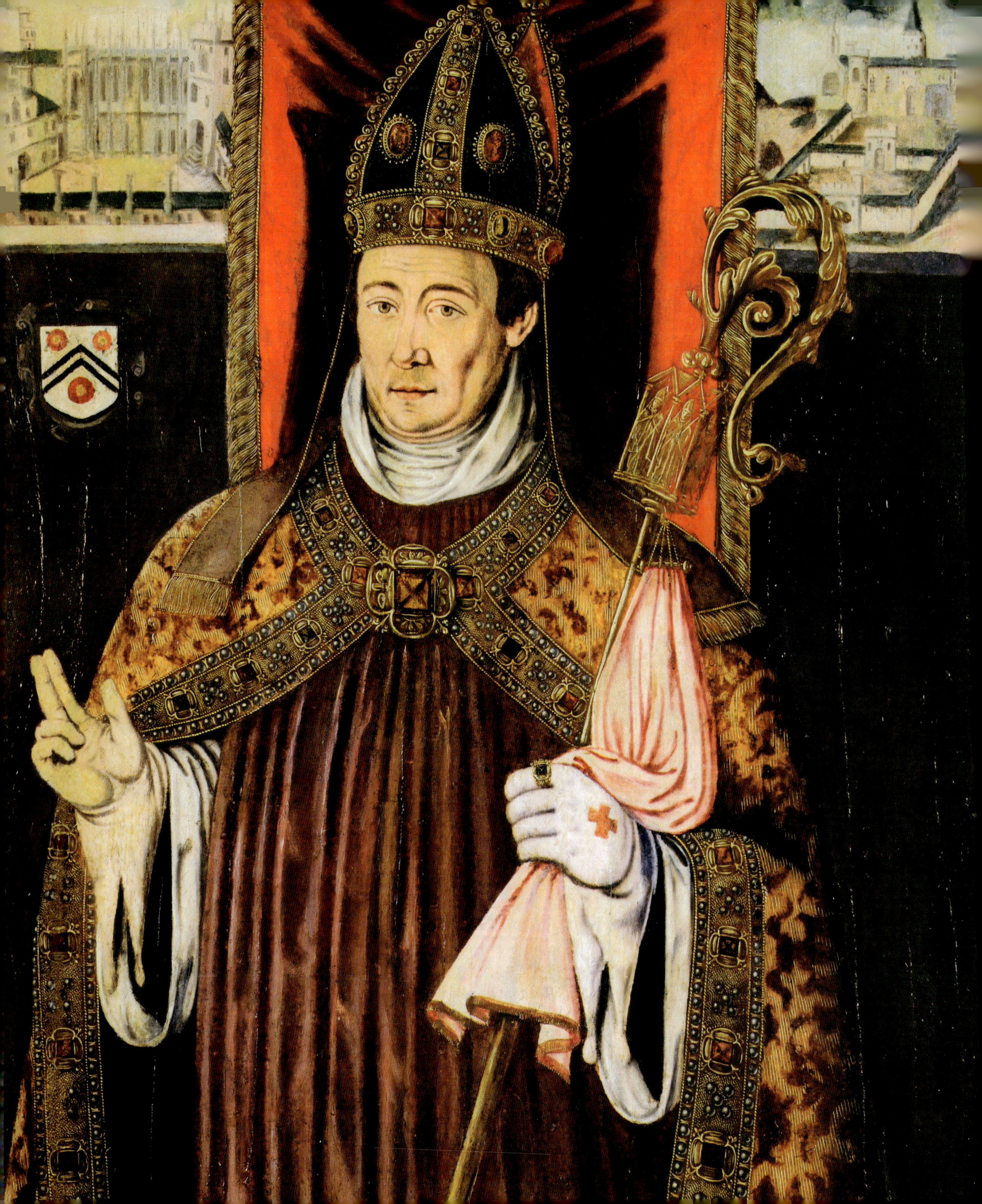

Introduction
The College and its Collections

William of Wykeham and the Medieval College

The history of Winchester's collections begins with the
works of art commissioned by its founder, William of
Wykeham (1324–1404).[1] He was born at Wickham in
Hampshire into a peasant family, and received some
education in Winchester, perhaps at the grammar
school attached to the Cathedral. As a young man
Wykeham obtained employment at the royal castle in
Winchester. In 1356 he was given an important post in
royal service as clerk of the works at Windsor Castle,
and in 1363 he became Lord Privy Seal. Edward III
came to rely on Wykeham, and he received a series of
coveted positions in the Church. In 1366 Wykeham was
appointed Bishop of Winchester, which brought with
it an enormous income of over £3,000 per annum.
The following year he became Chancellor, the most
senior of the king's ministers. A hundred years later
the contemporary French historian Froissart wrote:
'At this time there reigned a priest in England called
Sir William de Wican, and this Sir William de Wican was
so much in favour with the King, that by him everything
was done, and without him they did nothing.'[2]

Wykeham in fact spent only brief periods in
government. He resigned the Chancellorship in 1371,
and in 1373 was impeached and disgraced. Although
he was pardoned by Richard II in 1377, and served
again as Chancellor from 1389 to 1391, Wykeham
diverted his attention from politics to education and
artistic patronage. Much of his great wealth was used
to found colleges at Winchester and in Oxford. Both
were dedicated to the Virgin and are properly called
'The College of the Blessed Mary of Winchester, Near
Winchester', and 'The College of St Mary of Winchester,
in Oxford'. The Oxford foundation soon became known
as New College, probably because there already existed
a college (Oriel) dedicated to the Virgin, but it was also
'new' in being quite unlike the earlier colleges in its
size and wealth (its seventy scholars almost equalled
the total number at all the other colleges), and in being
the first college to admit undergraduates. Wykeham

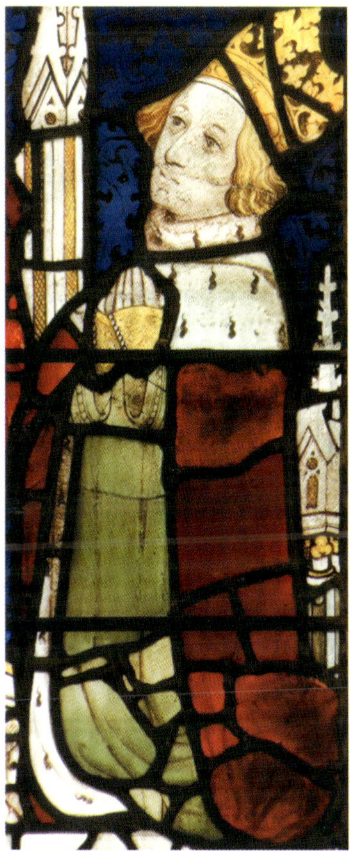

provided for tuition at New College in the faculties of
law, theology and arts. His professed intention was to
enhance the number of educated clergy embarking
upon careers in the Church. Winchester was intended
as a feeder school for Wykeham's College in Oxford,
and until the nineteenth century all fellowships at
New College were reserved for pupils coming up from
Winchester. Boys typically entered the school between
the ages of eight and twelve, and received a grounding
in Latin grammar over a period usually of four or five
years. Each year the Warden and two Fellows of New

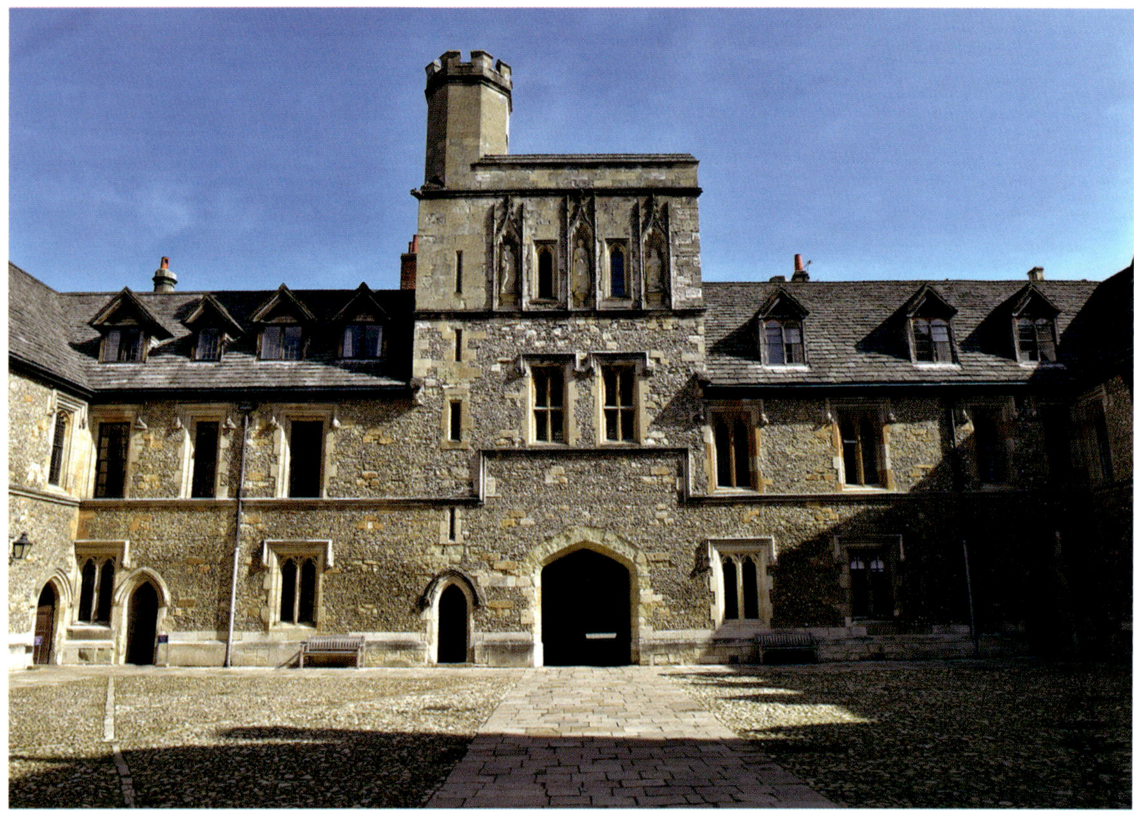

Chamber Court, built 1387–94.

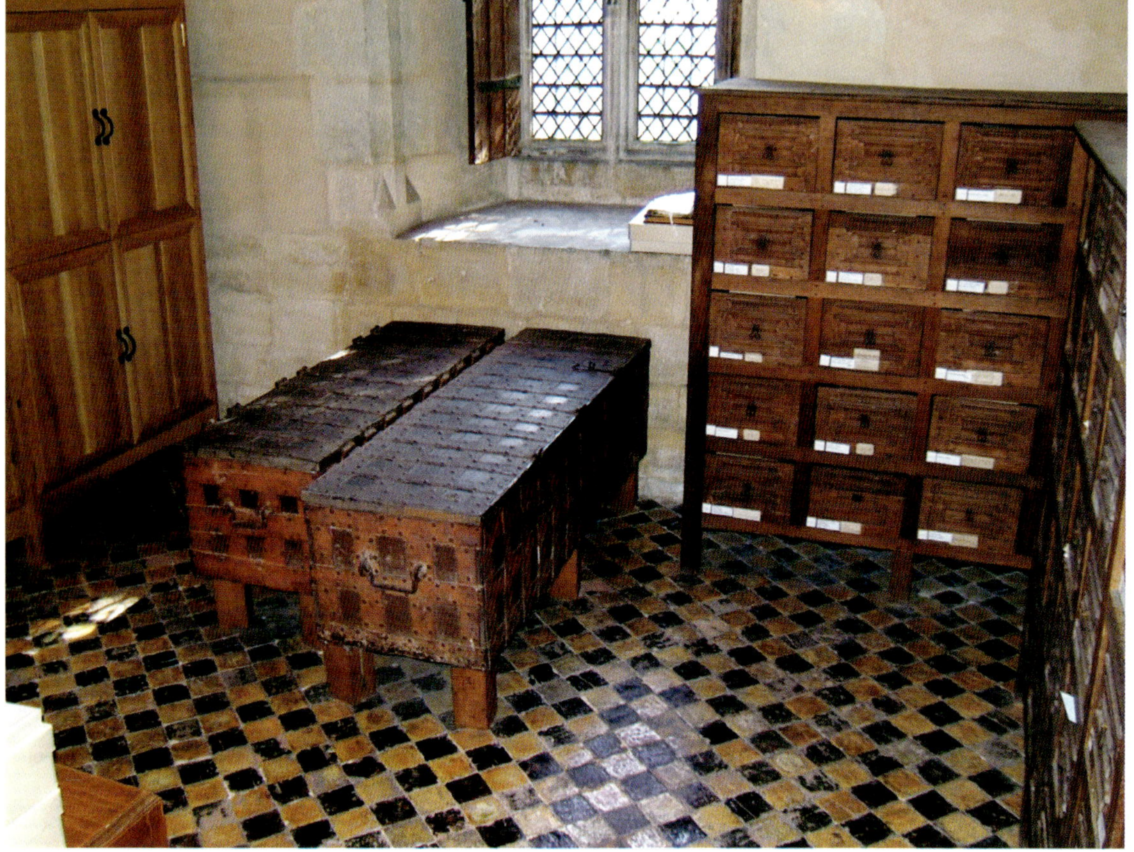

Muniment Room with two late 14th-century chests and 16th-century drawers.

College visited Winchester to choose pupils to fill the vacancies arising in Oxford.[3]

Wykeham's two foundations were pioneering in their conception as the first educational institutions to be designed as a complete entity. Earlier schools and colleges occupied smaller premises and developed piecemeal, whereas Wykeham's foundations were planned out in every detail and built on a grand scale.[4] They provided a model for other schools and university colleges, in particular for Henry VI's dual foundation of Eton College and King's College, Cambridge. In the early sixteenth century the curriculum of the new cathedral grammar schools founded by Henry VIII was based on those of Winchester and Eton, and several were led by Old Wykehamists.[5]

Winchester was established to provide free education to seventy Scholars chosen by examination. Wykeham made allowance for their number to be augmented by fee-paying pupils known as Commoners. Space was provided for ten Commoners living in College, but dozens more came in each day from lodgings in the town. Over time, and particularly from the eighteenth century onwards, the school began to provide more extensive accommodation for Commoners.[6] Today there are still seventy Scholars living in College, and just over six hundred Commoners in ten boarding houses. Whereas originally the Scholars were financially supported by the endowments of the College, and Commoners paid fees, today bursaries are applied equally across the school on the basis of need rather than according to academic standing.

Until the eighteenth century pupils were taught by just two masters: the Headmaster (Informator) and the Second Master (Hostiarius), although sometimes senior boys helped with the teaching of younger pupils. Services in Chapel were led by three priests and sixteen boy choristers (Quiristers). The College was governed by a Warden and ten Fellows, all of whom were priests. This community of about a hundred lived in chambers around three sides of the quadrangle known as Chamber Court. The fourth side comprised a chapel and hall set end to end, just as at New College and Windsor Castle. Underneath the hall was the schoolroom, now known as Seventh Chamber. Into this room, originally 46 feet by 29 feet, were often crammed more than a hundred pupils. The College was entered through a second quadrangle, Outer Court, which housed stables, brewery, granary and slaughterhouse. To the south of Chapel, as at New College, is a cloister where teaching once took place in the summer months.[7]

The maintenance of this community and its buildings, which were without precedent among English schools, required a large income. One of Wykeham's first priorities was to endow the College with the lands which would secure its future. As early as 1371, more than a decade before Winchester's foundation, Wykeham began to purchase estates which later passed to the College.[8] In the 1380s Wykeham bought extensive tracts of land in Hampshire, Wiltshire and Middlesex. As well as providing for the College financially, the founder took a close interest in its buildings and governance. The statutes, which were revised several times before taking their final form in 1400, show the careful attention Wykeham paid to the running of the school. Several rubrics relate to the keeping of records of the College's estates and the Bursars' annual expenditure, and a register of Scholars. This concern with detailed record-keeping, developed during Wykeham's years in royal service,

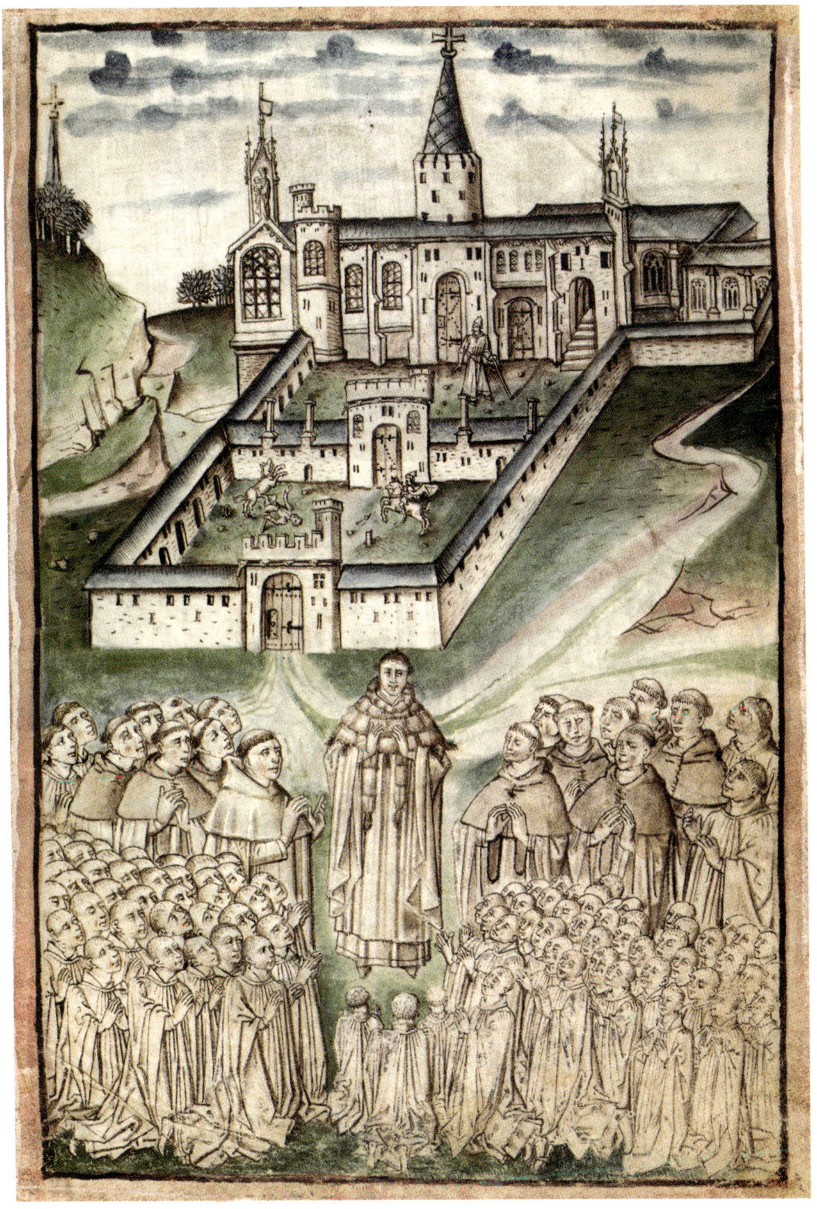

Winchester College in the 15th century with the Warden surrounded by members of the College. From Thomas Chaundler's *Life of William of Wykeham* (New College MS 288).

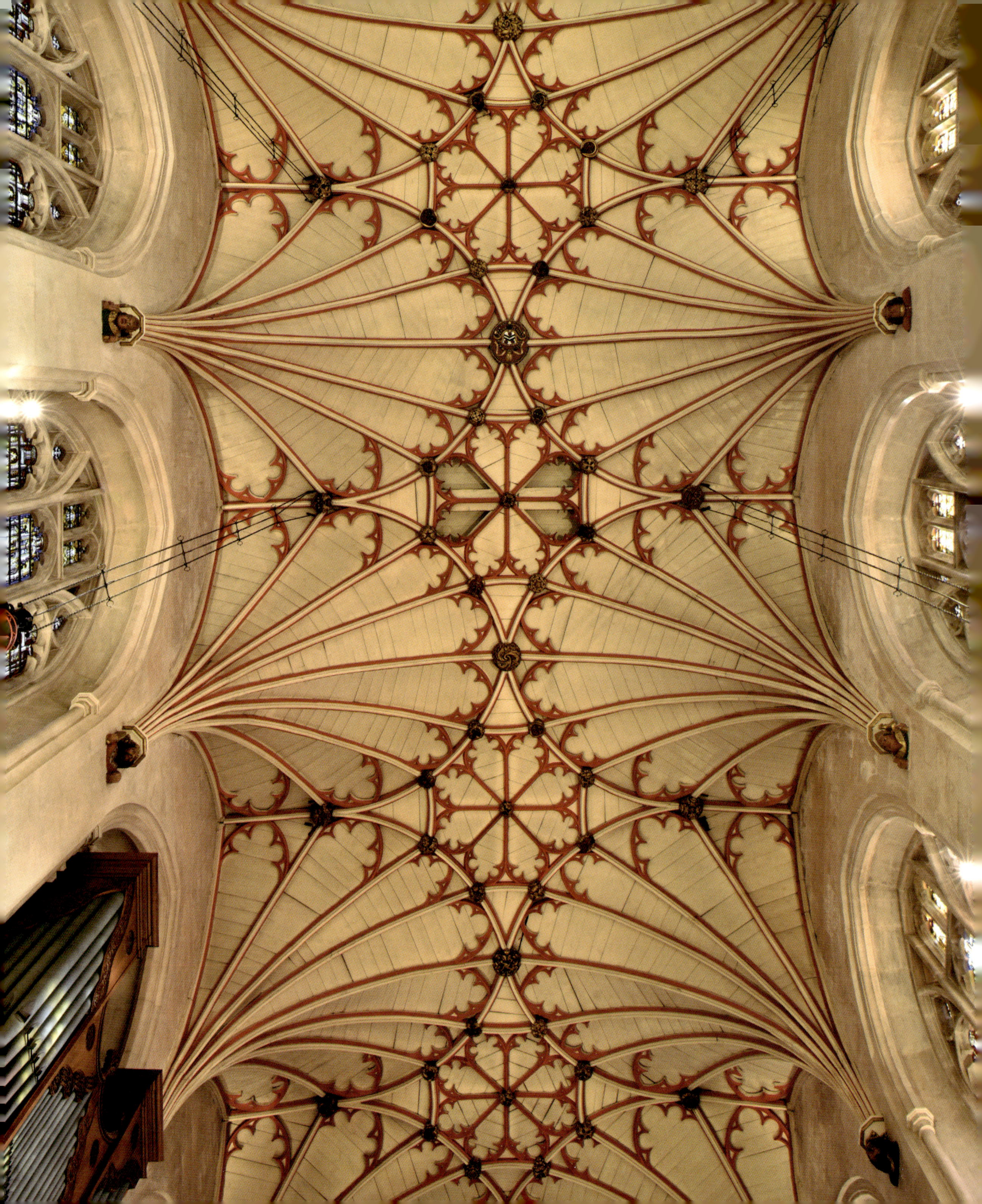

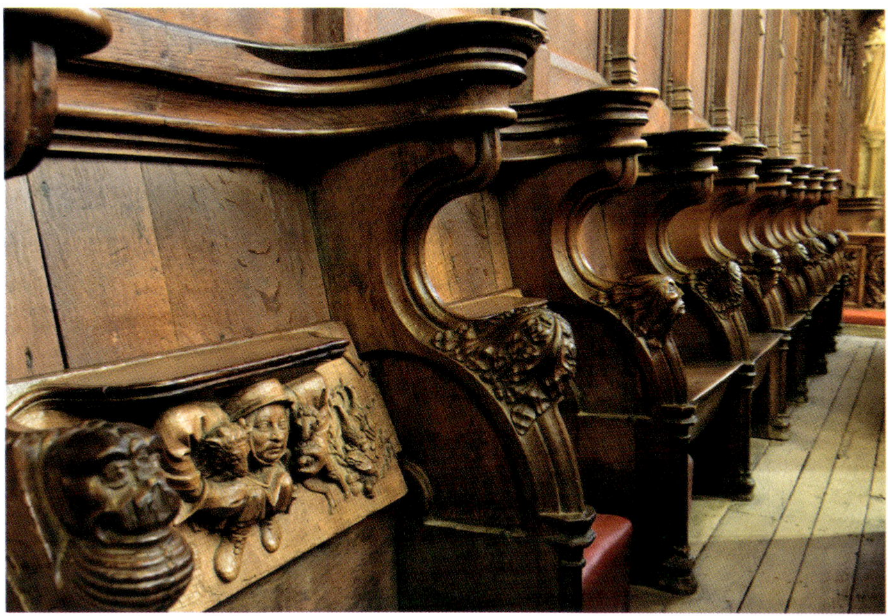

led to the establishment of one of the richest medieval archives in existence. The College's earliest documents remain in Muniment Tower, in the south-east corner of Chamber Court, still in the room built to house them at the end of the fourteenth century. Here Wykeham deposited copies of the Foundation Charter and the statutes of both his colleges. Administrative records, which soon began to accumulate in the muniment chests, provide vivid glimpses of the medieval past. The Bursars' account rolls contain fascinating details of College expenditure, while the Hall Books preserve a week-by-week record of all those who dined in the College. A wealth of material relating to the College estates includes medieval seals, sixteenth- and seventeenth-century estate maps, and one of the earliest watercolours of an English landscape.[9]

Much of Wykeham's career in royal service was spent overseeing architectural projects, and this experience must have been crucial when it came to planning his two colleges. As clerk of works at Windsor Castle in the late 1350s Wykeham was responsible for the building of new royal lodgings in the Upper Ward. This brought him into contact with the master mason William Wynford, who would design three great buildings for Wykeham: New College, Winchester College and the nave of Winchester Cathedral. Wykeham and Wynford tackled these projects one after another, bringing each to completion with extraordinary efficiency. New College was begun in 1379 and largely completed by 1386. Work at Winchester began in 1387 and the first pupils came into residence in 1394. Finally, in 1394, Wykeham turned his attention to Winchester Cathedral, where

he rebuilt the existing Romanesque nave. This last project was completed soon after Wykeham's death in 1404. Each of these buildings is an important example of the Perpendicular style of Gothic architecture, which was pioneered at Gloucester Cathedral in the early fourteenth century, and reached full maturity in the designs of Wynford and Henry Yevele, another mason in royal service well known to Wykeham. Their buildings are characterised by tall windows, large expanses of blank wall and elaborate fan-vaulted or hammer-beam roofs.[10]

Wykeham's architecture was of great sophistication and in the most up-to-date style. The same may be said of the work that he commissioned to ornament his new buildings. Much has been lost through exposure to the elements, to deliberate destruction during the Reformation, and to decay and changes in fashion. Nonetheless, important elements of Winchester's original stone sculpture, stained glass and woodwork remain. The statue of the Virgin and Child above Outer Gate has been described as 'the high-point of fourteenth-century sculpture in England',[11] while the misericords in the choir stalls are among the finest examples of woodcarving from this period.[12] The most important of the College's original works of art were the stained-glass windows of Chapel, of which only parts remain. The surviving remnants reveal the international character of late medieval art: made by the glazier Thomas of Oxford, the figures show many similarities with contemporary German book illumination and were probably designed by a painter in Wykeham's circle named Herebright of Cologne.[13]

13

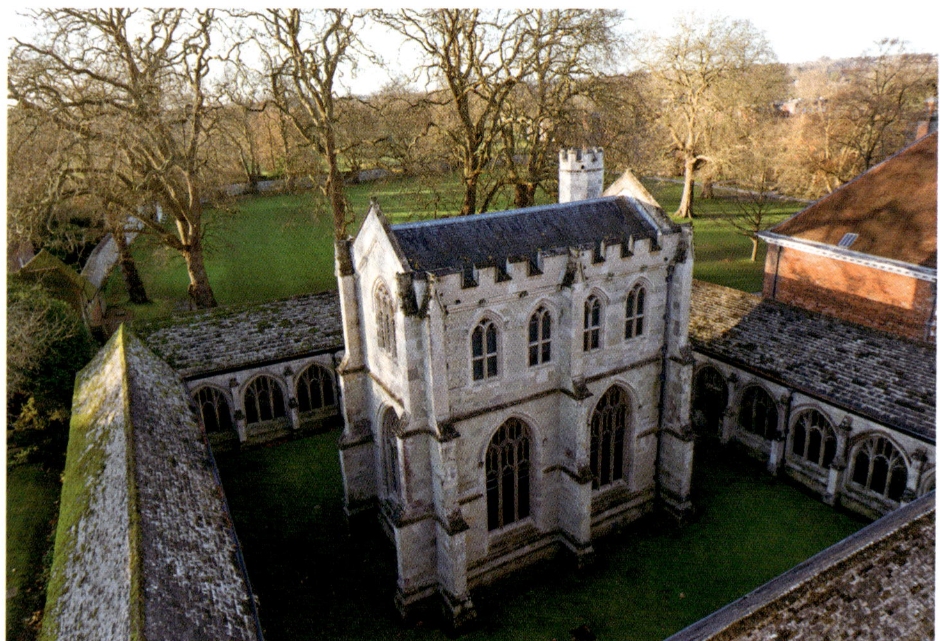

Fromond's Chantry, built 1425–45.

Nearly all of Wykeham's surviving personal possessions were bequeathed to New College, which preserves his mitre and crozier, and two dozen of his books.[14] Winchester was less favoured; two objects once associated with Wykeham, the 'Founder's spoon' and 'Founder's jewel', have not survived modern scrutiny, and it is clear that they both date from after his death. The only objects at Winchester once owned by the Founder are three manuscripts, from a total of nine which he gave to the College. These are poignant objects because of their tangible link with Wykeham, but they are also significant volumes in their own right. William of Canterbury's *Life of Thomas Becket* is the only source for some important incidents in the archbishop's life, while Higden's *Polychronicon* contains a rare medieval map of the world.

The gift of these books may indicate a change of heart by Wykeham, who did not originally intend for Winchester to have a library.[15] Unlike at New College, there is no place for a library in the plan of the College and no mention of library books in the statutes. While there must have been, from the beginning, rudimentary grammar books in the schoolroom, and service books for use in Chapel, it was perhaps assumed that the Fellows, having quit their studies in Oxford, would have little need of a library. From an early stage, however, they began to accumulate books that they held in common, and by 1410 a library room had been established in Exchequer Tower above College Hall. Following a common collegiate and monastic custom, some of these books were chained to desks, while others could be borrowed by the Fellows. The chest in which the circulating collection was kept survives in the original library room.

The College's book collection grew rapidly during the first few decades of the fifteenth century. A detailed inventory compiled in 1429 lists about 130 manuscripts in the Fellows' Library and dozens more in Chapel.[16] Some of these had been purchased by the College, but most were gifts from men in Wykeham's circle and from early alumni. Only seven or eight of the books listed in the medieval inventories remain at the College today, but Winchester is nonetheless one of only about two dozen English institutions to have survived with any part of its medieval library *in situ*. It also has one of the country's earliest purpose-built library buildings, the upper chamber of a free-standing chantry chapel in the cloister, built between 1425 and 1445. This was intended as a replacement for the earlier library in Audit Room, which was small and poorly lit.

As well as books, the medieval College attracted numerous gifts of silver, some from illustrious donors. In 1449 Henry VI gave a gold tabernacle, and his wife, Margaret of Anjou, presented a large pair of silver-gilt basins. An inventory drawn up in 1521 lists dozens of silver cups, ewers, salts and spoons.[17] With the possible exception of the so-called 'Founder's spoon', none of these survive. Other medieval possessions have also disappeared without trace: the vestments worn by priests; the fabrics that must once have adorned Chapel; the various wall paintings referred to in early documents; wooden statues and devotional objects. While important objects from the College's early collections survive, they give only a hint of former riches.

Reformation to Restoration, 1500–1700

The middle decades of the sixteenth century saw the destruction of many of the College's possessions, but also the acquisition of some of its greatest treasures. Winchester's collections were transformed by the Reformation, which brought about a movement of wealth and goods from which the College both suffered and benefited, and by the Renaissance, which shaped the education offered by the school and the tastes of those commissioning works of art.

The Henrician Reformation of the 1530s had little effect on Winchester.[18] Services were still said and sung in Latin, the souls of the dead in Purgatory were prayed for and the richly decorated interior of the chapel was left unchanged. Much more considerable was the impact of Edward's reforms in the years around 1550. It was at this point that the service books in Chapel became obsolete and must have been discarded, and the images of saints on the chapel rood screen were pulled down. Wall paintings were destroyed or covered up. Only the stained glass, misericords and stone sculptures survived. It was at this time that Winchester suffered the loss of its medieval chapel plate, although this was really an unfortunate accident.[19] The College was exempt from the levy on church silver introduced by the Privy Council in 1553, but when commissioners were sent to raid the Cathedral they also took the opportunity to seize plate from the College. The complaints of Warden White arrived too late to save the silver, although it is possible that he received monetary compensation for it. White went some way to making good the loss when he presented a magnificent standing cup in 1555, although this was for secular rather than ecclesiastical use.[20]

Not all the significant losses of this period were a direct result of religious turmoil. Changing tastes, along with economic and technological developments, also had an important part to play. Most of the College's medieval secular silver seems to have disappeared in the 1530s, and it is likely that many pieces were converted to cash to help fund some of the extensive land purchases made at this time. In the 1550s and 1560s several old pieces of silver were beaten out and refashioned in Renaissance style: recycling the original metal but destroying all evidence of its medieval form. The Henslowe Ewer and Basin, perhaps the finest pieces of silver in the College's possession, are an example of this practice.[21]

The loss of most of the College's medieval manuscripts seems to have taken place at about the same time as the removal or refashioning of its medieval silver, in the middle decades of the sixteenth

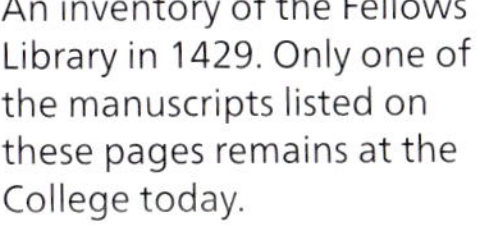

An inventory of the Fellows' Library in 1429. Only one of the manuscripts listed on these pages remains at the College today.

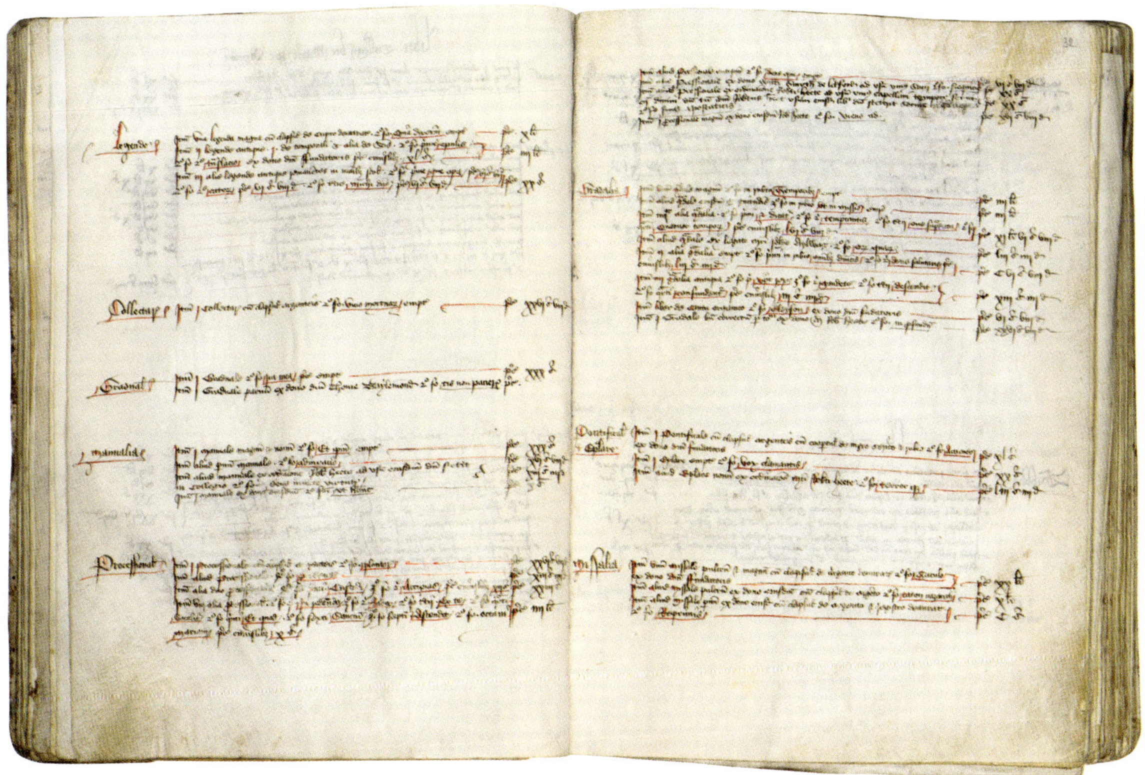

century. The library's donations register, and two sixteenth-century inventories, show that the 1540s to 1570s was a period of sustained growth.[22] Many, although not quite all, of the newly acquired books were printed works, and they seem to have displaced the existing manuscripts. At this time, books were usually kept chained to sloping desks and even a large library room could hold only a few hundred volumes. As a result, the acquisition of new books put pressure on space and often led to the discarding of older stock. It is telling that several of the Bursars' account books from the 1560s to 1580s are bound with manuscript fragments apparently cannibalised from the College's own books.[23] When a detailed catalogue of the library was made in 1634, it included about thirty manuscripts: while some of these were survivors from the medieval library, almost half had been acquired by the College since 1543.

Several of the books that entered the library in the sixteenth century now count among the College's greatest treasures. The gift of William Moryn in 1543 included a substantial group of scientific and geographical texts, including the 1482 edition of Ptolemy. In 1558 George Greswold gave a number of modern theological books, and one outstanding manuscript: a late eleventh- or early twelfth-century copy of Paschasius on Lamentations, almost certainly made at Winchester Cathedral Priory. It had presumably remained in a monastic library until the dissolution and is therefore one of several treasures gained by the College as a result of the Reformation. Similarly, Winchester's Saxon charters came to the College following the dissolution of Hyde Abbey.[24] The Tudor Rose tapestries, perhaps made for the baptism of Prince Arthur in the Cathedral, may well have belonged to one of Winchester's religious houses before being used at the College in the sixteenth century.[25] In various other practical ways the College benefited from the Reformation: the income once spent on Masses for the dead (about £50 per annum) could now be put to other uses,[26] and monastic lands bordering the school were purchased.[27] Fromond's Chantry was converted from a chapel into a library.[28]

As well as having obvious material effects, the Renaissance and Reformation shaped the teaching and culture of the school over the course of the sixteenth century. The early decades of the century saw the introduction of new teaching methods, exemplified by the grammar books of John Stanbridge (1463–1510), an Old Wykehamist.[29] Christopher Johnson, Headmaster from 1561 to 1571, was remarkable for teaching pupils about scientific topics, including the latest theories about comets and the use of mice in medical experiments, and for his lenient approach to corporal punishment.[30] Yet while he was

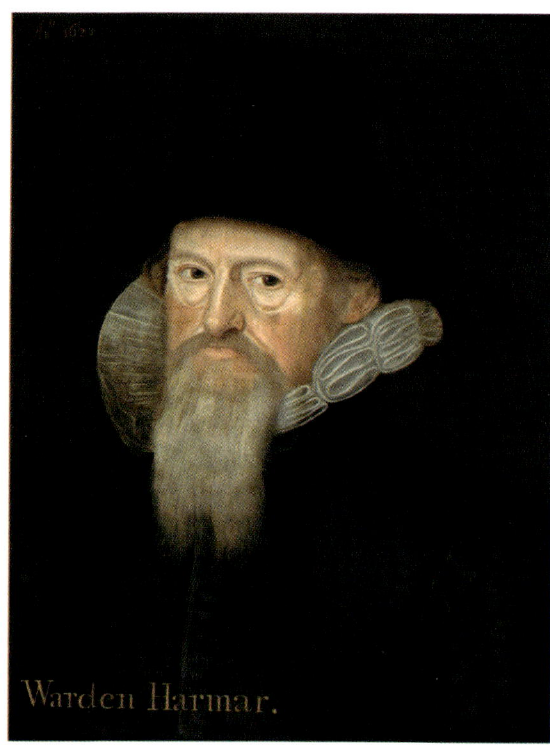

John Harmar (Warden, 1596–1613), by an unknown artist, c. 1600.

progressive in educational matters, Johnson seems to have been conservative in religion. Several of his pupils would go on to become prominent recusants, including Henry Garnett, executed for his role in the Gunpowder Plot. In 1571, more than a decade after Elizabeth came to the throne, the Bishop of Winchester issued the College with forty injunctions to bring it into conformity with the new religion.[31]

Under Johnson's successors the character of the College changed markedly. Thomas Bilson (Headmaster, 1572–79, Warden, 1581–96) and John Harmar (Headmaster, 1588–95, Warden, 1596–1613) were both Protestant scholars of considerable renown. Bilson wrote two significant defences of the Elizabethan Settlement during his time as Warden, and later became Bishop of Worcester and then Winchester. As a young man Harmar travelled to Geneva and came under the influence of Theodore Beza. In 1585 he became Regius Professor of Greek at Oxford, for several years holding the post concurrently with his headmastership. He published translations of the sermons of Calvin, Beza and Chrysostom.

It was this confluence of Renaissance learning and Protestant faith that led to Winchester's prominent involvement in one of the major cultural achievements of Early Modern England: the King James Bible.[32] Harmar was a member of the Second Oxford Company, responsible for the Gospels, Acts of the Apostles and Apocalypse, and at least four other Wykehamists were

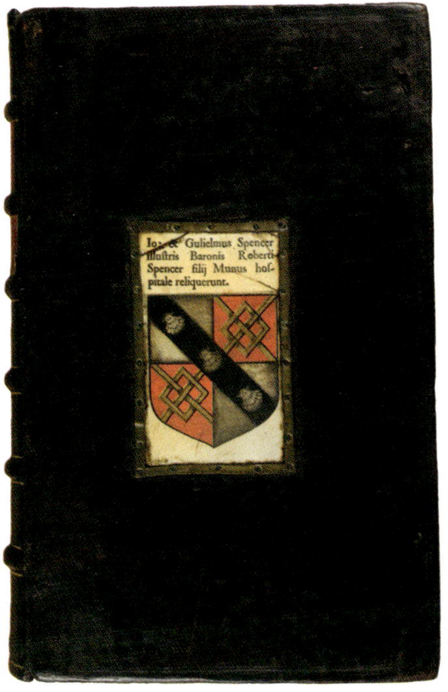

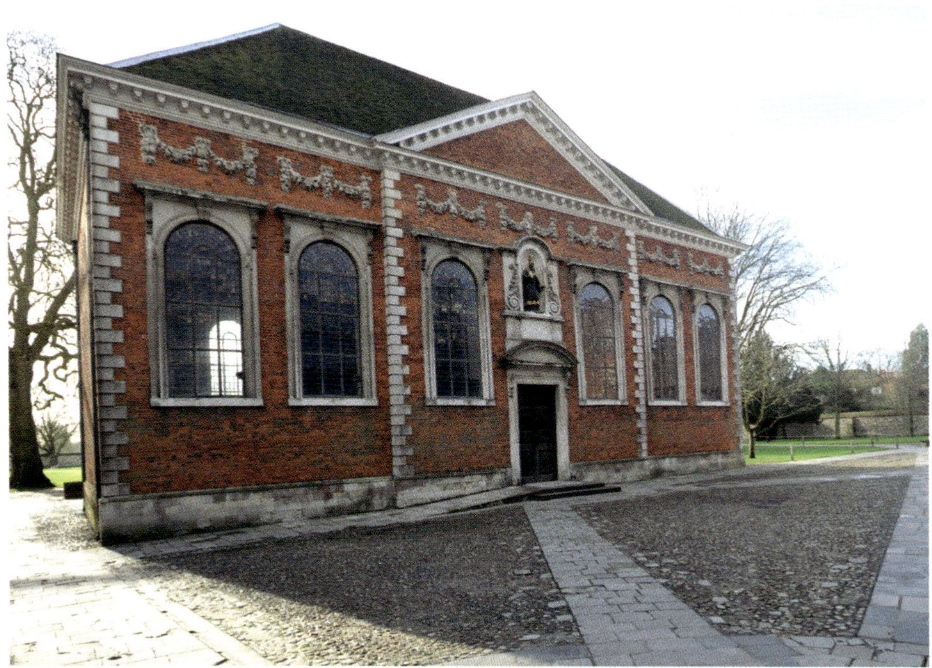

among the translators. During his time as Warden, Harmar encouraged numerous donations to the Fellows' Library. Many of the works of theology and biblical scholarship acquired in this period would have been of great use to the translators. On his death in 1613 Harmar's own working books, including Bibles in French, Dutch, Spanish, German and Italian, were bequeathed to the College. It was around this time that the Fellows' Library also received a number of medieval manuscripts, increasingly regarded as objects of antiquarian interest and prized by collectors for their antiquity and beauty. One particularly appropriate acquisition was an early manuscript of Wycliffe's translation of the New Testament, given by one of the Fellows in 1609, two years before the publication of Harmar's own work as a translator.

Unlike the Reformation, the Civil Wars did not bring about any significant changes to the character of the College nor any destruction of its collections.[33] On several occasions fighting came to the outskirts of the city, and in 1642 parliamentary officers lodged in the College. Despite this, none of the school's medieval religious imagery was defaced. Winchester, like Eton, was exempt from most forms of parliamentary taxation. Although a parliamentary visitation questioned Warden Harris's religious sympathies, the College community was otherwise left untouched. Indeed, the English Revolution was a period of prosperity for the College, in which Winchester's collections were significantly augmented. The library

continued to grow and to support the scholarly activities of the Fellows. In 1652 the Council of State ordered that the surviving remnant of Winchester Cathedral Library, consisting of fifteen medieval manuscripts and about 170 printed volumes, should be removed to the College. All except one of these books was returned to the Cathedral in 1669. During the 1640s and 1650s a number of fine pieces of silver were acquired, including the Capel Cup.[34] This period also saw the building of the College Sickhouse, known as Bethesda, the first significant addition to the school's medieval architecture.

The College's prosperity continued into the late seventeenth century. The journal of William Emes, Fellow from 1670 to 1703, provides an idiosyncratic account of contemporary events. He records the significant alterations to the fabric of the College undertaken by John Nicholas (Warden, 1679–1711), a wealthy and well-connected man.[35] The interior of Chapel was reordered and a fine reredos and screen carved by Edward Pierce were installed. A new schoolroom was completed in 1687 at a cost of £2,600, towards which Nicholas contributed more than half from his pocket. A number of spectacular pieces of silver were acquired in this period, including the Marquess of Winchester's Cup, which weighs an extraordinary 115 ounces.[36] It was in the late seventeenth century that the College attracted its first recorded foreign tourist, the American Samuel Sewall, who donated to the Fellows' Library his Algonquian Bible.[37]

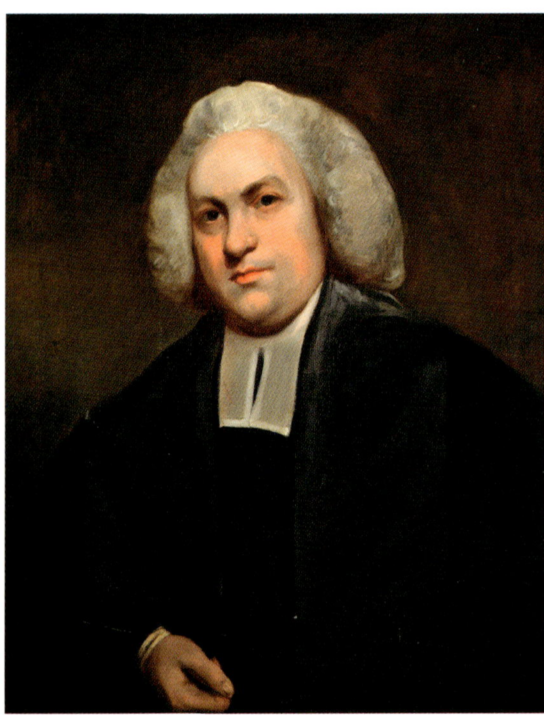

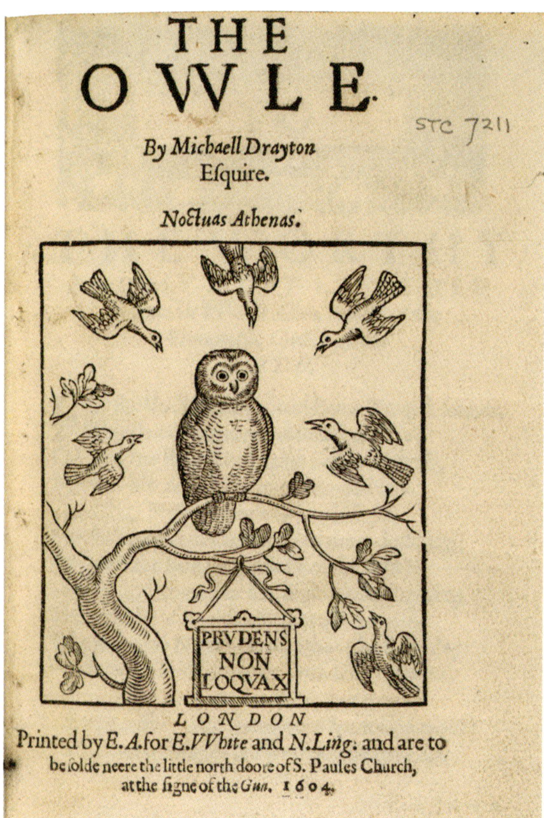

Reason, Romanticism and Reform, 1700–1900

Dr John Burton, Headmaster from 1724 to 1766, was the College's most important patron since William of Wykeham. The altarpiece he commissioned for Chapel remains one of the finest eighteenth-century French paintings in Britain.[38] His portraits of twelve Commoners reflect his concern with improving provision for the fee-paying pupils, particularly those of higher social status than earlier Wykehamists, which set the school on the path it was to follow in the next century.[39]

In the eighteenth century pupils and Fellows engaged in a broader range of scholarly pursuits than in earlier periods. In 1750 and 1762 the Fellows' Library received significant gifts of mathematical and scientific texts. It was then that the school acquired first editions of Hooke's *Micrographia* and Newton's *Principia*, as well as works by Kepler, Galileo and Boyle.[40] Soon afterwards the Fellows purchased a telescope, microscope and a pair of globes.[41] In 1767 the school received its largest single donation of books, more than a thousand volumes from the library of Alexander Thistlethwayte, a local MP.[42] Most of these were works of literature in Greek and Latin, English and modern foreign languages. Among the many highlights are volumes of rare Elizabethan pamphlets, Lewis Theobald's copy-texts for his editions of nine Shakespeare plays, and the library of two French Huguenots. Thistlethwayte's gift transformed overnight a scholarly collection that had consisted largely of theology, history and classical texts, into something that more closely resembled a gentleman's library. This direction continued with gifts in 1811 and 1815 from Nathaniel Atcheson, a local landowner, who gave incunabula and examples of fine printing.

A third significant group of books came in the 1830s and 1840s from the Reverend Peter Hall, a former pupil who assembled a large library of literary works by Wykehamist authors.[43] From the sixteenth century onwards Winchester had produced many notable writers (among them Henry Wotton, Thomas Browne, Thomas Otway and Edward Young), but it made an especially notable contribution to the development of English literature in the eighteenth century. William Collins, Joseph Warton and Thomas Warton all began their poetical careers as pupils around 1740. Joseph Warton (Headmaster, 1766–93) gained a national reputation as a critic, and encouraged literary pursuits among his pupils. He introduced prizes for English verse; early winners included Sydney Smith and William Lisle Bowles, whose work was much admired by Wordsworth and Coleridge. The writings of all these Winchester authors are well represented in Hall's collection.

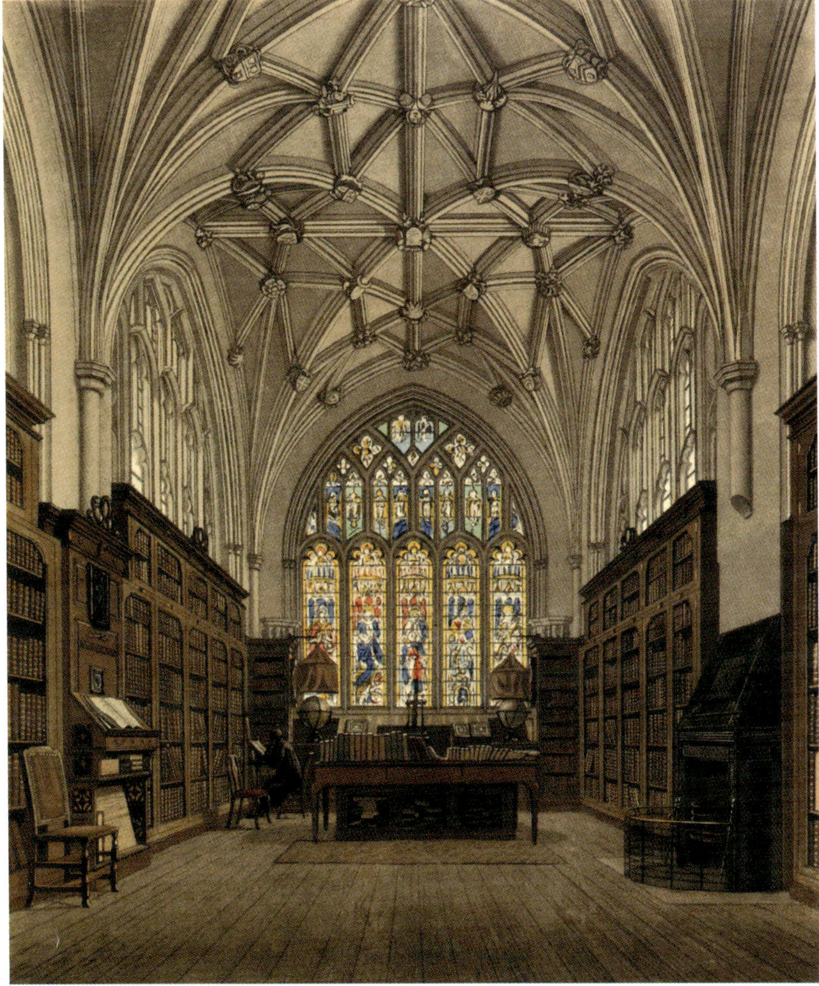

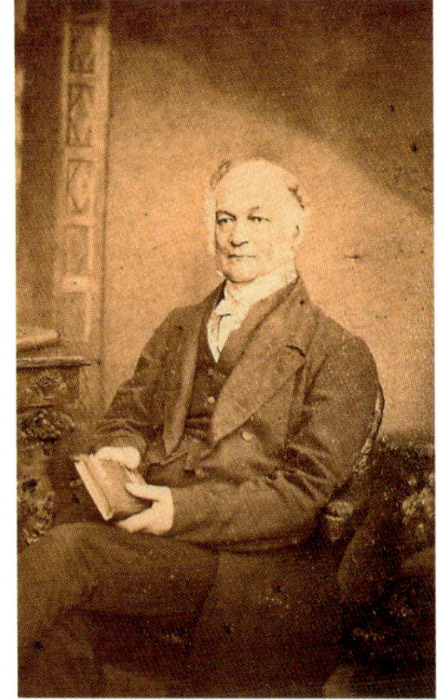

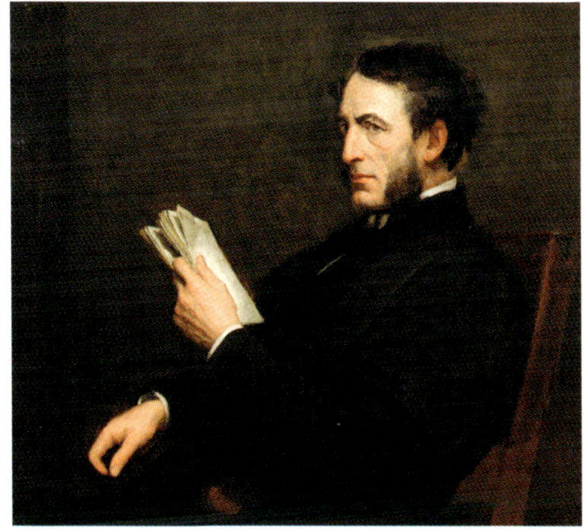

In the nineteenth century, Winchester was swept up in the great movement of reform in English public schools.[44] After tentative beginnings under George Moberly (Headmaster, 1836–66), the comprehensive changes effected by George Ridding (Headmaster, 1867–84) amounted to a second foundation. The school grew considerably in size, from about two hundred pupils in the first half of the nineteenth century to more than four hundred by its end. While seventy scholars remained in College, nine boarding houses were constructed in the 1860s and 1870s to house the increased number of Commoners, and a tenth followed in 1905. As in other public schools, organised games were established over the course of the nineteenth century. A distinctive version of football had developed by 1825 and is still played today. The history of Winchester Fives goes back at least to the construction of the first courts in 1862.

Under Moberly and Ridding the curriculum was broadened to include teaching in subjects other than Latin and Greek. The number of masters (known as 'Dons' at Winchester) increased steadily. A mathematics Don was appointed in 1834, and formal science teaching began in the 1860s. A new building with purpose-built science laboratories was completed in 1904. Following the establishment of a Natural History Society in 1870, the College began to accumulate a scientific collection. At first this consisted largely of birds, insects and geological specimens, many of them collected by members of the Society, but it later came also to encompass historic examples of the apparatus used in Science lessons.

The fact that none of the fifty treasures featured in this volume was acquired during the nineteenth century is indicative of a declining interest within the College in commissioning and collecting works of art. This must have been due, in part, to the rapid pace of reform during this period, but it also reflects the absence of the Governing Body from the day-to-day life of the school. Although one Fellow remained resident until 1893, and Warden Lee a decade beyond that, most of the nineteenth-century Fellows made only

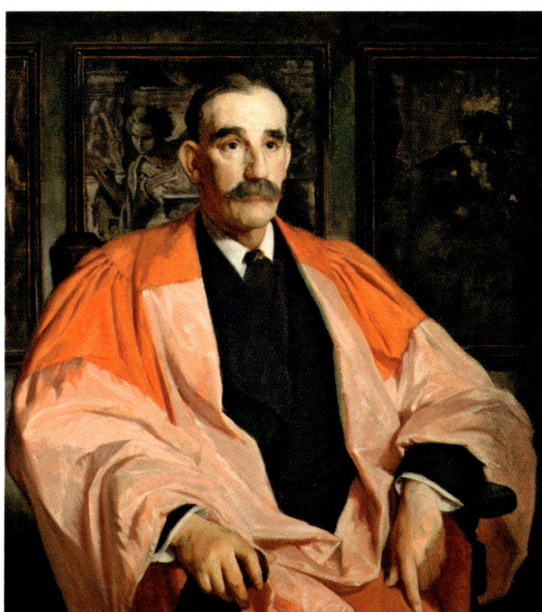

occasional visits to the College.[45] This development undermined the tradition among the fellowship of commissioning silver, and removed any impulse to augment the collections of the Fellows' Library, which seems to have become virtually moribund between the 1860s and the 1930s. The story would have been very different, however, had more come of the negotiations between the Fellows and Sir Thomas Philipps, who in 1853 promised the College a large part of his extraordinary library.[46]

Teaching and Collecting, 1900–2019

In the years around 1900, after decades of neglect, considerable attention was devoted to Winchester's collections. Unlike in earlier periods, however, the emphasis was now in making them accessible to pupils and acquiring items that would be useful in teaching. Montague (Monty) Rendall (Headmaster, 1911–24), who joined the staff of Winchester College in 1887, played a crucial role in the revitalisation of the school's collections. He believed, unusually for the time, that study of the visual arts had an important part to play in education. He was himself a collector and had travelled extensively in Italy.[47] Although he was not the originator of the project, Rendall was closely involved in the establishment of the school's first museum, which was commissioned to commemorate the school's quincentenary and opened in 1897. The ground floor of the new building, which subsequently became known as Musā (short for Museum), contained rooms for the Natural History Society and Photography Society, a herbarium and a fossil collection. In the galleries upstairs were displays of natural history specimens, ancient Greek vases and plaster casts of classical and Renaissance statues.[48]

Most of the exhibits were purchased especially for the new museum. Arthur Bather, one of the Dons, travelled to Greece and probably also to Italy to acquire classical antiquities. A collection of stuffed birds was purchased by William Fearon (Headmaster, 1884–1901) and presented by him in 1900. Rendall provided the museum with casts and photographs of Italian works of art, and he gave regular lectures on art history at a time when the subject was not generally thought worthy of serious study. Musā was built for 'the preservation of Wykehamical antiquities, and the encouragement of Art, Architecture, Natural History and other Sciences.'[49] Its main audience was pupils, and from this point onwards nearly all of the items added to the school's collections were intended to inspire and to educate. It was in this spirit that C.H. Hawkins, one of the early housemasters and founder of the Shakespeare Society, gave to the school a copy of the First Folio. His gift was soon followed by a fifteenth-century Book of Hours from Frederick Morshead (Housemaster of E, 1868–1905) and two fine Greek vases from Arthur Cook (Housemaster of C, 1893–1909).

After Musā, Rendall's second great project was a memorial to Wykehamists killed in the First World War. He began planning War Cloister in 1917 and it was completed to designs by Sir Herbert Baker in 1924. Later, Rendall left to the school a more personal reminder of the war through his bequest of C.R.W. Nevinson's painting *Twilight*. He had already commemorated an earlier European conflict in which many Wykehamists served, by giving to the school a scrapbook compiled during the Crimean War.

In the 1920s and 1930s the influence of Rendall continued through Reginald Gleadowe (Art Master, 1922–39). He designed new stained glass for College Hall and for Chantry, as well as a medal to mark Rendall's retirement and several pieces of silver. Gleadowe also commissioned a wooden carving of St Sebastian, designed by Eric Gill and carved by Donald Potter.[50] Rendall made a final contribution to Winchester's collections long after his retirement, persuading Harry Collison to present over a hundred English watercolours to the College in 1940. Further gifts of watercolours from Colonel Arthur Brooke (1954), General Sir John Anderson (1993) and Adam Crick (2016) have created a wide-ranging collection with works by most of the leading watercolourists of the eighteenth and nineteenth centuries. Collison's hope that pupils would 'admire works of art in the original and by using their own eyes, gain help and inspiration' was entirely in accordance with Rendall's vision for the place of the collections within the school.[51]

Montague Rendall (Headmaster, 1911–24), portrait by Glyn Philpot (1925).

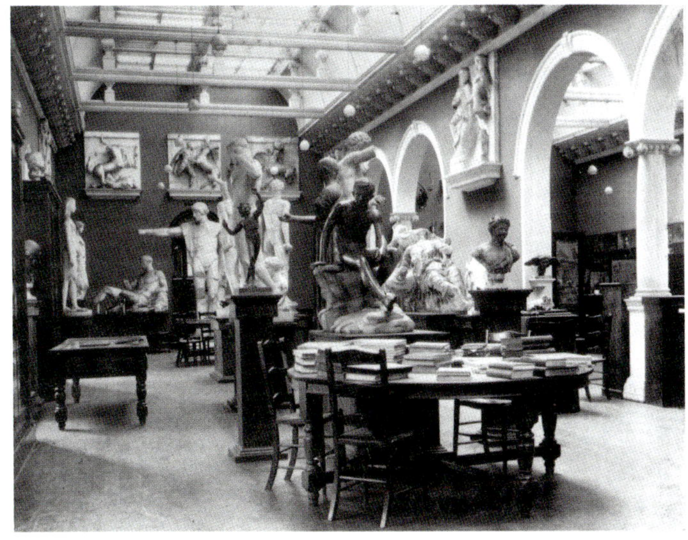

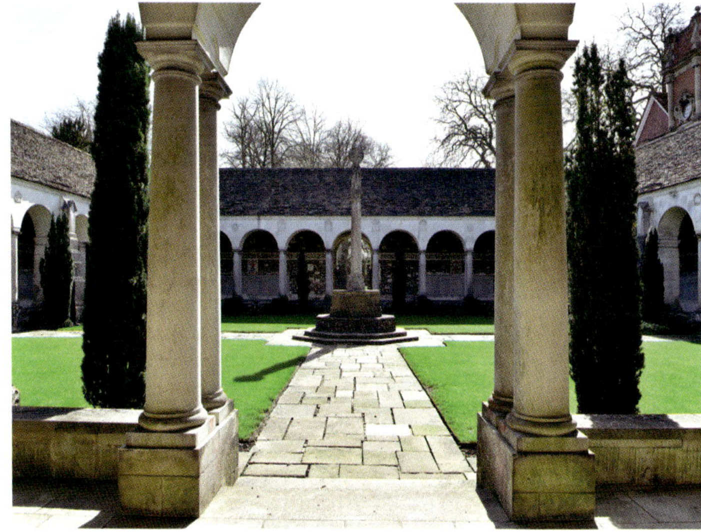

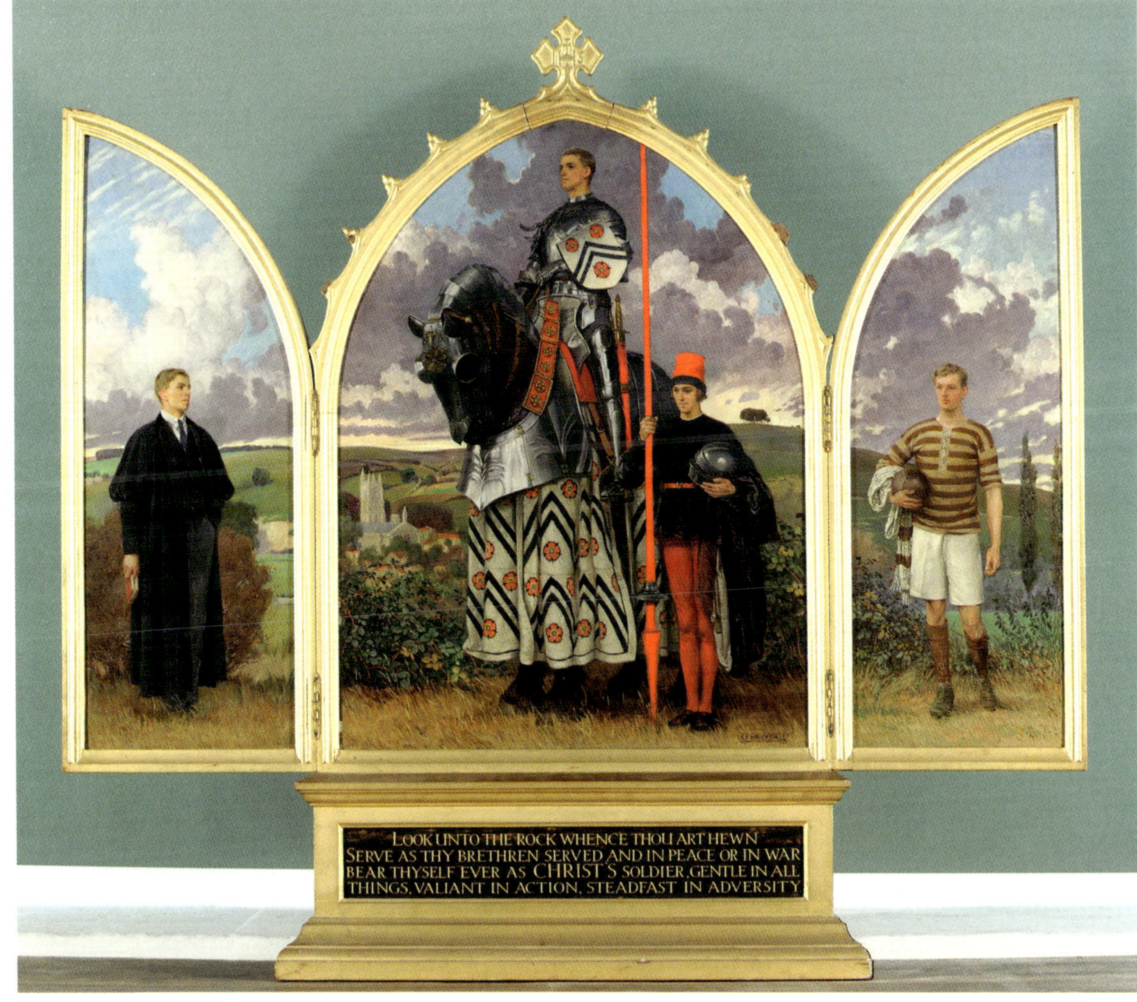

above left
Musā in the early
20th century.

above right
War Cloister, designed by
Sir Herbert Baker, 1922–24.

right
Eleanor Fortescue-Brickdale,
Winchester Triptych (1926),
commissioned by
Montague Rendall.

The Fellows' Library also experienced a revival in the early twentieth century. The key figure here was Walter Oakeshott, who as a young History teacher in the 1930s organised exhibitions of rare books for pupils, and used them extensively in lessons.[52] It was in preparation for one exhibition that he discovered in the Warden's Lodgings the only surviving medieval manuscript of Sir Thomas Malory's *Morte d'Arthur*, subsequently sold to the British Library.[53] Oakeshott returned to Winchester as Headmaster in 1946 and continued to take a close interest in the Fellows' Library. He donated a number of books from his own library, which were almost the first additions to the collection since the 1860s.

The momentum established by Rendall, Gleadowe and Oakeshott was not fully sustained in the decades after the Second World War. Musā was taken over for art lessons and many of its contents dispersed around the school. Several of the Greek vases were stolen, and a number of sculpture casts and other items were disposed of. It was the gift in 1978 of the Duberly Collection of Chinese Art that refocused attention on the College's collections. To display this new acquisition an exhibition space, known as Treasury, was created in the medieval beer cellar under College Hall. Here Chinese ceramics and Greek vases were displayed side by side, along with other ancient artefacts and changing selections from the watercolour collection.

While there have been few significant additions to the Treasury collections since the 1970s, the Fellows' Library has grown considerably over the last half century. In 1972, H.A. Jackson (Housemaster of Moberly's) bequeathed some outstanding sixteenth- and seventeenth-century books, including first editions of Aristophanes and Hobbes' *Leviathan*. The library has been a beneficiary of book-collecting alumni, notably John Sparrow (College, 1919–25), Warden of All Souls, Oxford. On his death in 1992, Sparrow gave twenty-five volumes to the library and left a portion of his estate as an endowment for new acquisitions. This has enabled the library to make regular purchases of antiquarian books that may be used in teaching, or that relate to the history of the school. Sparrow's bequest was followed two years later by Viscount Eccles' (G, 1918–23) gift of modern fine printing and artists' books. More recently, Viscount Gough (G, 1955–59) has presented a magnificent set of Joseph Banks' *Florilegium*. One of the most significant modern acquisitions, the Gordon Trollope Collection, came not from a former pupil, but the father and grandfather of Wykehamists.

Over the past few decades, the school has invested considerable resources in the care of its collections. Oil paintings, ship models and tapestries have undergone extensive conservation. Parts of the collection, notably the Greek vases, have recently been the subject of scholarly publications.[54] Several

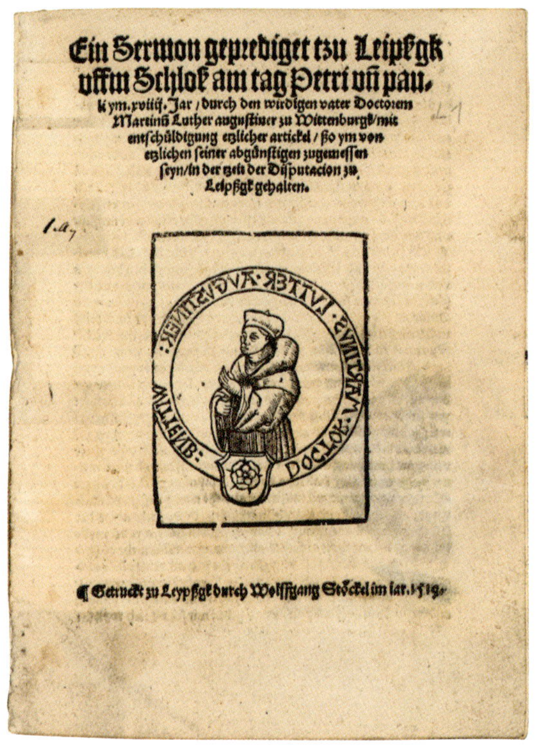

Martin Luther, *A Sermon Preached at Leipzig* (Wittenberg, 1519).

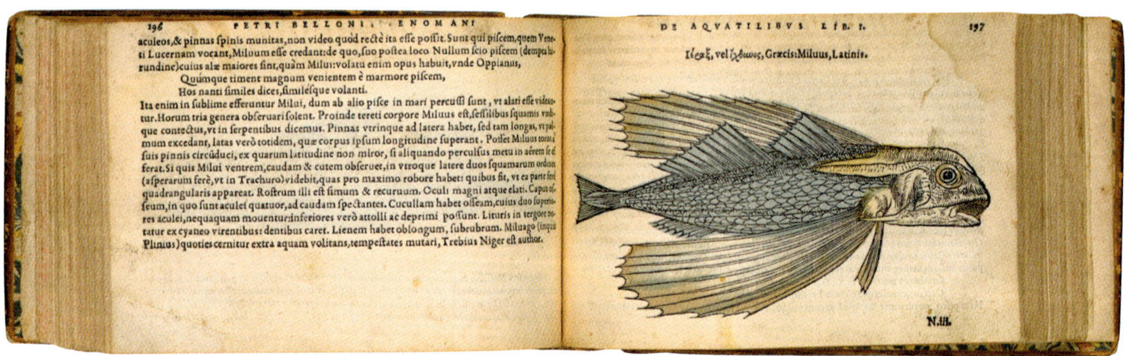

Pierre Belon, *De Aquatilibus* (Paris, 1553), purchased from the Sparrow Fund in 2016.

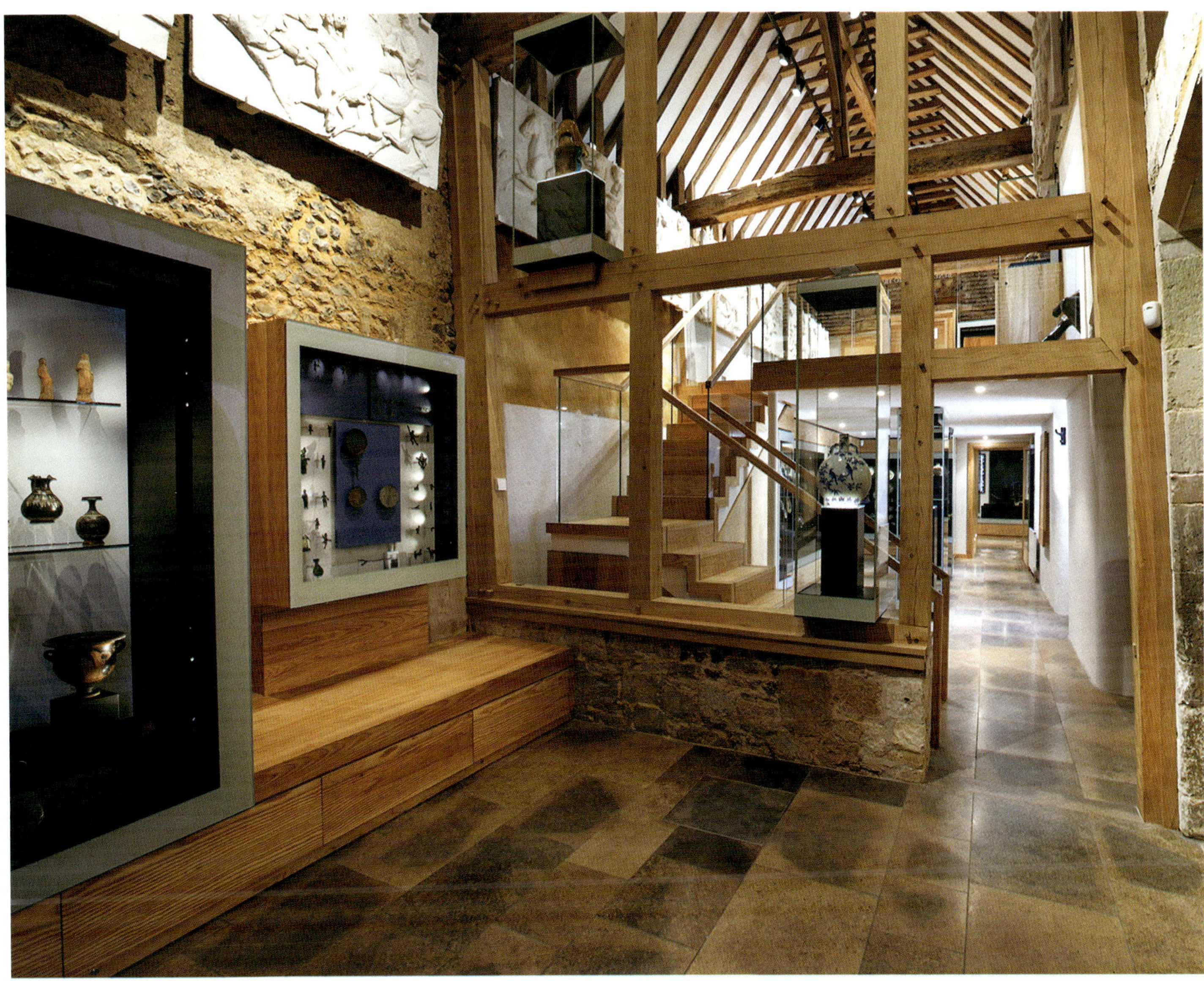

items have been exhibited outside the school for the first time. The Fellows' Library was fully catalogued between 2005 and 2014, a process that brought about many new discoveries. Since 1999 the College has employed a professional archivist.

In recent years Winchester has begun to make its collections more accessible to the public. In 2015–16 the College's medieval stables were converted into a museum. This replaced the Treasury of the 1980s and is known by the same name. Here the best of the school's art and archaeology collections are on permanent display and may be seen by visitors to the College.[55] Temporary exhibition space in the new museum allows for a changing selection of items from the Fellows' Library, Archives and Science School.

Attention has now turned to giving our collections a greater online presence, making them available for other educational institutions to use, and a programme of publications.

Meanwhile, the school's collections continue to grow. Five of the fifty treasures featured in this book have been acquired in the twenty-first century. Most of the Greek coins that constitute the third of our treasures were bought in the last two years, thanks to a generous gift from Lowell Libson Ltd. The most significant acquisition of the past few months – a collection of Reformation pamphlets purchased with a donation from the Alta Foundation – must wait to appear in some future selection of Winchester's treasures.

Richard Foster

Notes to the Introduction

1 Virginia David, *William of Wykeham: A Life* (London, 2007).

2 Robert Lowth, *The Life of William of Wykeham, Bishop of Winchester* (London, 1777), pp. 33–34.

3 On the early history of the College see T.F. Kirby, *Annals of Winchester College from its Foundation in the Year 1382 to the Present Time* (London and Winchester, 1892); A.F. Leach, *A History of Winchester College* (London, 1899); R. Custance (ed.), *Winchester College, Sixth-Centenary Essays* (Oxford, 1982).

4 Nicholas Orme, *English Schools in the Middle Ages* (London, 1973), pp. 187–88.

5 Leach, *A History of Winchester College*, pp. 198–214.

6 James Sabben-Clare, *Winchester College after 600 Years, 1382–1982* (Southampton, 1981), pp. 14–18.

7 On the College buildings see Winchester Archaeological Society, *Winchester College: Its History, Buildings and Customs* (Winchester, 1926); John Harvey, 'The Buildings of Winchester College', in Custance (ed.), *Sixth-Centenary Essays*, pp. 77–127.

8 Leach, *A History of Winchester College*, pp. 143–49.

9 Sheila Himsworth (ed.), *Winchester College Muniments: A Descriptive List*, 3 vols (Chichester, 1976–84); Maurice Keen, *Winchester College Archives* (Winchester, 2000); P.D.A. Harvey, *Maps in Tudor England* (London, 1993), pp. 21, 79, 95.

10 William Hayter, *William of Wykeham: Patron of the Arts* (London, 1970), pp. 33–91.

11 Jonathan Alexander and Paul Binski (eds), *Age of Chivalry: Art in Plantagenet England, 1200–1400* (London, 1987), p. 470.

12 A number are reproduced and discussed in Marshall Laird, *English Misericords* (London, 1986).

13 J. Buxton and P. Williams (eds) *New College Oxford, 1379–1979* (Oxford, 1979), pp. 163–64; Harvey, 'The Buildings of Winchester College', p. 85; J.H. Harvey and D.G. King, 'Winchester College Stained Glass', *Archaeologia*, 53 (1971).

14 Hayter, *William of Wykeham*, pp. 102–07.

15 Walter Oakeshott, 'Winchester College Library before 1750', *The Library*, 5th series, 9:1 (1954), pp. 1–16; James M.W. Willoughby, 'College of St Mary the Virgin of Winchester', in *The Libraries of Collegiate Churches*, Corpus of British Medieval Library Catalogues, 15, 2 vols (London, 2013), vol. 2, pp. 595–861.

16 Willoughby, 'Winchester', pp. 691–731.

17 Charles Oman, 'The Winchester College Plate', *The Connoisseur*, 149 (1962), pp. 24–25.

18 Patrick McGrath, 'Winchester College and the Old Religion in the Sixteenth Century', in Custance (ed.), *Sixth-Centenary Essays*, pp. 233–38.

19 Oman, 'The Winchester College Plate', p. 25; McGrath, 'Winchester College and the Old Religion', pp. 238–39.

20 On Election Cup see John K.D. Cooper, 'A Re-Assessment of Some English Late Gothic and Early "Renaissance" Plate – II', *The Burlington Magazine*, 119 (1977), p. 473; Philippa Glanville, *Silver in Tudor and Early Stuart England* (London, 1997), pp. 147, 248; R. Marks and P. Williamson (eds), *Gothic: Art for England* (London, 2003), pp. 316–17.

21 Oman, 'The Winchester College Plate', p. 27; Glanville, *Silver in Tudor and Early Stuart England*, pp. 62, 471.

22 Willoughby, 'Winchester', pp. 810–61.

23 For example, WCM 22213 (1556–58); WCM 22215 (1564–72).

24 N.P. Brookes, 'The Oldest Document in the College Archives? The Micheldever Forgery', in Custance (ed.), *Sixth-Centenary Essays*, pp. 189–228.

25 H. Chitty, *The Winchester College Tapestries* (Winchester, 1912); Thomas P. Campbell, *Henry VIII and the Art of Majesty: Tapestries at the Tudor Court* (New Haven and London, 2007), pp. 80–81.

26 McGrath, 'Winchester College and the Old Religion', p. 238.

27 Derek Keene, 'Town into Gown: The Site of the College and Other College Lands in Winchester before the Reformation', in Custance (ed.), *Sixth-Centenary Essays*, pp. 69–70.

28 Willoughby, 'Winchester', p. 606.

29 Orme, *English Schools*, pp. 107–09.

30 Geoffrey Day, *John Harmar, Translator* (Winchester, 2016), pp. 8–9, 30–31.

31 McGrath, 'Winchester College and the Old Religion', pp. 253–54, 261–62.

32 Paul Quarrie, *Winchester College and the King James Bible* (Winchester, 2011); Day, *John Harmar, Translator*.

33 G.E. Aylmer, 'Seventeenth-Century Wykehamists', in Custance (ed.), *Sixth-Centenary Essays*, pp. 281–311.

34 Oman, 'The Winchester College Plate', p. 29; E.J.G. Smith, 'Richard Blackwell & Son', *The Silver Society Journal*, 15 (2003), pp. 19–45.

35 Harvey, 'The Buildings of Winchester College', pp. 98–99.

36 Oman, 'The Winchester College Plate', pp. 30–32; many of the College's seventeenth-century pieces are further discussed in Charles Oman, *Caroline Silver, 1625–1688* (London, 1970).

37 Eve LaPlante, *Salem Witch Judge: The Life and Repentance of Samuel Sewall* (New York, 2007).

38 Christopher Rowell, 'François Lemoyne's "Annunciation" (1727) rediscovered at Winchester College', *The Burlington Magazine*, 154:1308 (March 2012), pp. 177–181.

39 Christopher Rowell, 'Portraits of "Dr Burton's Commoners" at Winchester College', *The British Art Journal*, 14:1 (Spring/Summer 2013), pp. 3–17.

40 J.M.G. Blakiston, 'Winchester College Library in the Eighteenth and Early Nineteenth Centuries', *The Library*, 5th series, 17 (1962), pp. 32–33.

41 Fellows' Library MS 225, p. 124.

42 Blakiston, 'Winchester College Library', pp. 34–37; Carly Emma Watson, 'The Legacy of an Eighteenth-Century Gentleman: Alexander Thistlethwayte's Books in Winchester College Fellows' Library', PhD thesis, University of Birmingham, 2013.

43 Blakiston, 'Winchester College Library', pp. 41–43.

44 On the school in the nineteenth century see Sabben-Clare, *Winchester College*.

45 Sabben-Clare, *Winchester College*, pp. 31–35.

46 J.M.G. Blakiston, 'The Fellows' Library: Sir Thomas Phillips and After', in Custance (ed.), *Sixth-Centenary Essays*, pp. 403–29.

47 J.D.E. Firth, *Rendall of Winchester: The Life and Witness of a Teacher* (Oxford, 1954); Kenneth Clark, *Another Part of the Wood* (London, 1974), pp. 60–65.

48 Winchester College Muniments M/27/2.

49 Sabben-Clare, *Winchester College*, p. 20.

50 Judith Collins, *Eric Gill: The Sculpture. A Catalogue Raisonné* (London, 1998), pp. 55, 196–97 (where it is incorrectly said to have been carved by Gill).

51 *The Wykehamist*, 9 July, 1940.

52 John Dancy, *Walter Oakeshott: A Diversity of Gifts* (Norwich, 1995), pp. 59–60, 64–68.

53 Paul Yeats-Edwards, 'The Winchester Malory Manuscript: An Attempted History', in B. Wheeler, R.L. Kindrick and M.N. Salda (eds) *The Malory Debate: Essays on the Texts of Le Morte Darthur* (Woodbridge, 2000), pp. 367–90.

54 John Falconer and Thomas Mannack, *Corpus Vasorum Antiquorum: Great Britain. Winchester College* (Oxford, 2002).

55 Richard Foster, *Winchester College Treasury: A Guide to the Collections* (Winchester, 2016).

A note on abbreviations

The boarding houses at Winchester are referred to by letter as follows:
A: Chernocke House (Furley's)
B: Moberly's (Toye's)
C: Du Boulay's (Cook's)
D: Fearon's (Kenny's)
E: Morshead's (Freddie's)
F: Hawkin's (Chawker's)
G: Sergeant's (Phil's)
H: Bramston's (Trant's)
I: Turner's (Hopper's)
K: Kingsgate House (Beloe's)

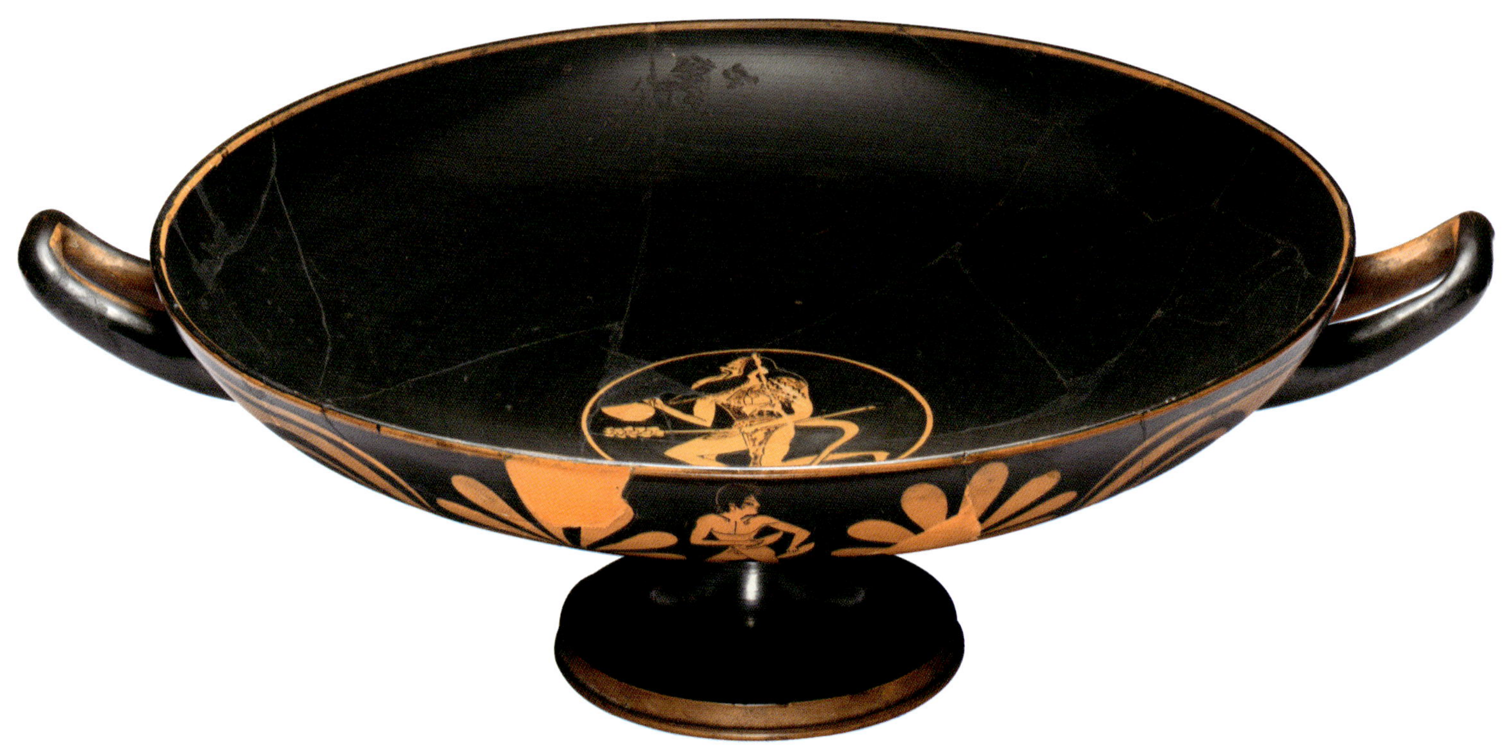

Greek Cup by the Winchester Painter, 515–510 BC

Painted pottery (H. 13 cm, W. 41 cm across handles)

In the early twentieth century archaeologists made a careful study of ancient Greek vases and identified the hands of hundreds of individual painters. Where a Greek name could not be found through an inscription, Sir John Beazley, the scholar behind much of the enterprise, often chose to name the painter after the location of one particular vase that provided a clear representation of the painter's style. The Winchester Painter takes his name from this cup. Seven other vases, in the museums of Florence, Dresden, Paris, Bourges, Oxford and London, are attributed to the same hand. The Winchester Painter worked in the late sixth century when Greek pottery underwent its most dramatic technical change, from the black-figure technique, which had been dominant for more than two hundred years, to the red-figure technique.

This vase is a shallow drinking cup, known as a kylix. In the centre of the interior, and placed within a tondo, is painted a satyr holding a wine jug and thyrsus, the staff associated with the worship of Dionysus. The exterior features two athletes holding *halteres* (jumping weights) and a pattern of palmettes and eyes. Around both athletes there is the inscription 'ΗΟ ΠΑΙΣ ΚΑΛΟΣ' (the boy is beautiful), often found on Athenian vases and a reminder of Greek ideals of beauty and athleticism. The vase shows many of the artistic preoccupations of the late Archaic period. The painter takes advantage of the red-figure technique to show the human body in various positions. One of the athletes turns his head to look behind him, twisting his torso almost at a right angle to his legs. A variety of brush lines are used in the precise depiction of muscles, tendons and hair.

The College has a collection of nearly a hundred Greek vases. Most of these were made in Athens, but there are also Mycenaean, Corinthian and South Italian vases, and a substantial group of Cypriot vessels. Many of these were purchased for the College in the 1890s when one of the dons, Arthur Bather, travelled to Greece and probably also to Italy to build a collection. This vase, however, was not one of Bather's purchases, but was given some years later by Arthur K. Cook (Housemaster of C, 1893–1909). Before that it was part of the large collection of antiquities formed by William Henry Forman (d. 1869), from whom it passed by descent to his nephew Major Henry Alexander Browne. The vase was then sold at Sotheby's (19 June 1899), which was probably where Cook bought it. There is evidence to suggest that Forman purchased the vase when the collection of the poet Samuel Rogers was sold in 1856, but this is not certain. Like most of the better-quality Greek vases on the English market in the middle of the nineteenth century, it was probably excavated in Etruria, perhaps at Vulci, but unfortunately we cannot be sure.

Henry Berry (B, 2012–2017)

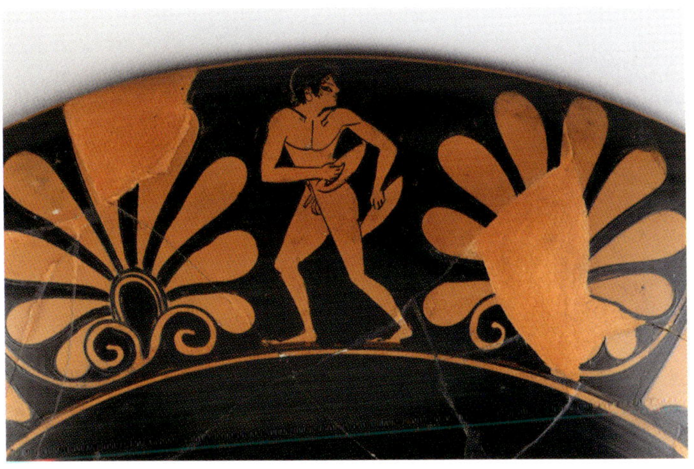

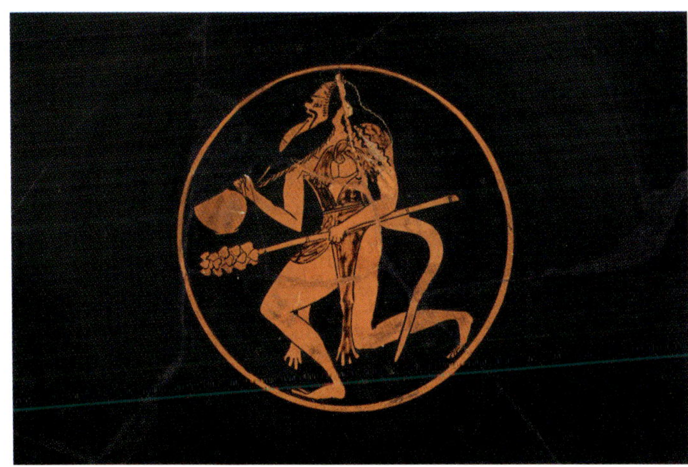

Parthenon Frieze Casts, 443–437 BC

Plaster casts, late 19th century, after marble originals (H. 104 cm, W. 124–149 cm)

Winchester's fifteen Parthenon frieze casts are thought to have been made by the firm of Domenico Brucciani (established 1837 in Covent Garden), shortly after his death in 1880. They were made from moulds owned by the British Museum; these moulds themselves were taken from casts made for Lord Elgin in 1802, and so the casts at Winchester are at two removes from the original marbles. Nonetheless, they are of a high quality, faithfully reproducing the fine detail of the ancient sculptures. Indeed, they preserve some details that are no longer visible on the originals, having been lost through the British Museum's controversial cleaning of the frieze's surface in the 1930s or the erosion of the sections that remained on the Parthenon until 1993.

The Parthenon is a temple of Athena constructed on the Acropolis in Athens between 447 and 442 BC. The building work was directed by the Athenian statesman Pericles and involved the best craftsmen and artists in Greece, most notably the sculptor Pheidias who supervised the artistic side of the whole project. The frieze ran along the top of the sanctuary wall, behind the columns that supported the roof. It is thought to depict the Panathenaic procession, an annual religious festival at Athens in which the citizens would parade through the city and offer a new *peplos* (robe) to their patron goddess.

Most of the Winchester casts are from the west and north walls of the temple, and mainly show the parade of horsemen and water carriers, as well as the famous and charming vignette of a frisky cow. The frieze is remarkable for the naturalistic details of the bulging muscles and veins in the running horses, the anatomical realism in the muscles and sinews of their riders, and the flowing drapery of the clothing of humans and gods. The energy of the procession is captured by the dynamic and varied poses of the horses, some of which are shown rearing as their riders' cloaks billow in the wind.

The casts were purchased as part of a visionary project to civilise the rather spartan corridors and classrooms of the late Victorian school: a special edition of *The Wykehamist* (16 June 1897) refers to 'a bold experiment, to decorate our class-room passages with casts and photographs', and indeed a photograph taken in August 1914 shows the Parthenon casts on the walls of Flint Court alongside members of the Royal Wiltshire Yeomanry taking a break from their duties. Until their recent conservation, some of the casts still bore the signs of graffiti done by boys waiting for their next lesson. Despite these occasional acts of vandalism, the experiment was judged a success, at least by the author of *The Wykehamist* article, who continues, 'how admirably it has justified itself! Something good, which you will never be made to look at but can always look at if you will, has turned our formerly squalid and still tumultuous passages into a state of civilization which makes the memory of the old condition seem like a dismal dream'.

At some stage in their history the casts were taken down and moved to the Warden's Stables (now refurbished as the Treasury) and stored in damp conditions in the then semi-derelict building. From there they were rescued in 2010 and treated by professional conservators, and have now been installed high on the walls in the museum. This new location allows the casts to be enjoyed by visitors to the College and by pupils, who regularly use them in Art lessons as well as studying them in Classics and Div.

Sarah Harden (Head of Classics)

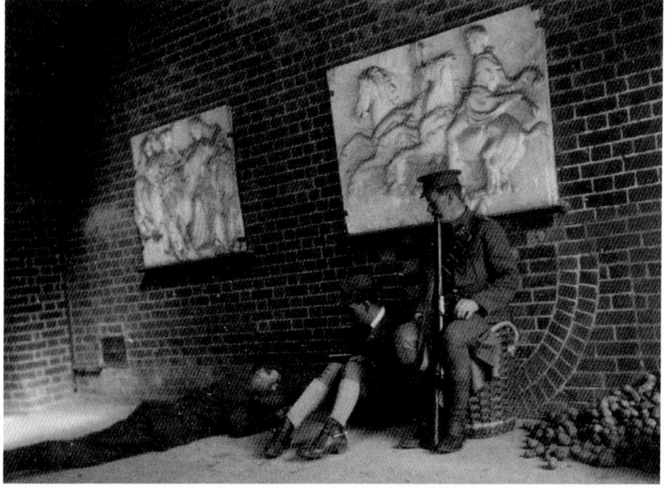

Members of the Royal Wiltshire Yeomanry outside one of the Flint Court classrooms in 1914.

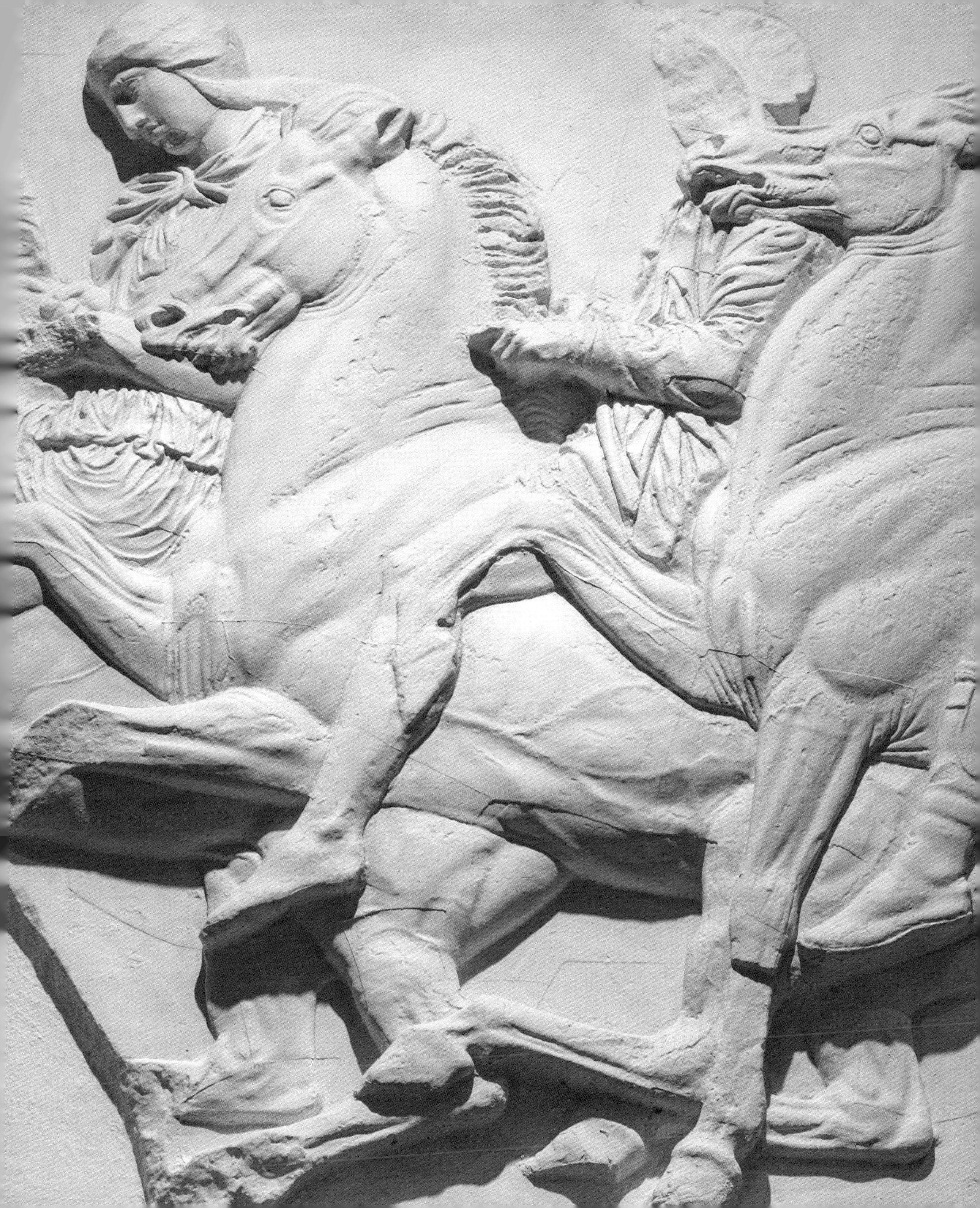

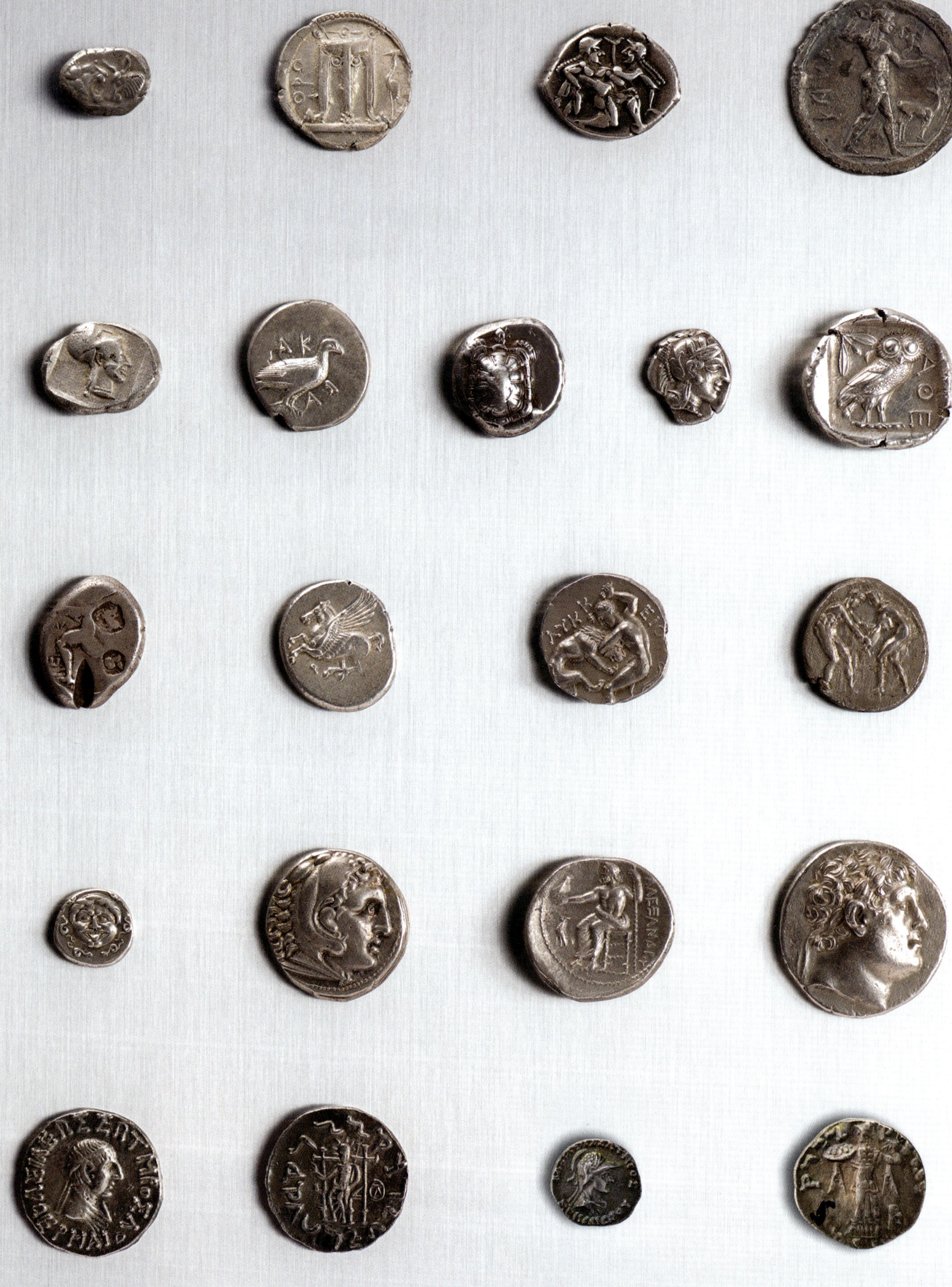

Ancient Greek Coins

Silver, 6th century BC to 1st century BC (various sizes)

The school's collection of Greek coins ranges from the earliest silver issues of the sixth century BC to Hellenistic coins of the third century onwards. There are examples from across the ancient Greek world, from Southern Italy to Bactria. Among the highlights of the collection are a group of Indo-Greek coins acquired by Brigadier Evelyn Cobb, an Old Wykehamist who served in the Indian Political Service during the 1930s. These coins are a result of the campaigns of Alexander III of Macedon, who in the space of a decade demolished the Achaemenid Empire and advanced with his army into Egypt, Mesopotamia, and even as far as Punjab. In his lifetime ninety million silver tetradrachms were issued. This resulted in a great projection of the Greek economic system into regions previously lacking a reliable coinage system. The new kingdoms established in the wake of Alexander's conquests soon adopted their own coinages based upon the Macedonian royal coinage already in circulation.

The monumental spread of Greek culture in the fourth century BC led to Hellenisation beyond the Mediterranean world, and resulted in a fusion of cultures in the kingdoms established by Alexander. This influence went both ways: one of its major legacies was the adoption by Greeks of the Eastern idea of divine kingship. In earlier periods Greek coins bore images not of rulers, but of gods and heroes, along with emblems of the issuing state, often in the form of animals or birds. But in the Hellenistic period, when kings began to be regarded as gods (especially in the East), it was acceptable for them to appear on coins. Even on the coins of Alexander the boundaries were blurred. Their obverse bears an image of the hero Heracles, but one that was made to resemble Alexander himself.

Portrait coins became widespread in the Greek world from the third century BC, the best types exhibiting a brilliant blend of realism and idealisation. The coins of the Indo-Greek kingdom, created through the eastward expansion of the Bactrian kings who succeeded Alexander, are particularly interesting for their unique combination of local elements with the newly imposed culture of Greece. While the coins are essentially Greek in weight and style, they include legends in the local language as well as iconographical types not associated with traditional mythology, and are sometimes square in shape.

A good example of the cultural amalgamation typical of these coins is a drachma of Menander I (155–130 BC), a Bactrian ruler whose conquests created a new kingdom in the north-western part of the Indian subcontinent. The obverse is clearly Greek in conception, with a realistic portrait bust of Hellenistic style. The reverse too draws on Greek models, with a spirited representation of Athena Alkidemos (her epithet when associated with the Macedonian capital of Pella). However, the coin's legend, which is given in both Greek and the local Karosthi language, has a distinctly eastern feel: 'ΒΑΣΙΛΕΩΣ ΣΩΤΗΡΟΣ ΜΕΝΑΝΔΡΟΥ/*maharajasa tratarasa Menandrasa*' ('of the saviour king Menander').

Perhaps even more striking is a tetradrachm of Hermaeus, who ruled the Hindu-Kush region around 90 to 70 BC. It represents a development from Greek-influenced coinage to something more stylised and localised. While the fundamental form remains Hellenistic (profile bust, Greek legend, a realistic portrait with distinctive hooked nose), the letter forms, and the representation of Zeus on the reverse, are quite different in style from the original type of Alexander from which it ultimately derives.

Alfred Deahl (H, 2014–19)

Coins of Alexander the Great (*c.* 324 BC), obverse and reverse; Menander I (155–130 BC) and Hermaeus (90–70 BC).

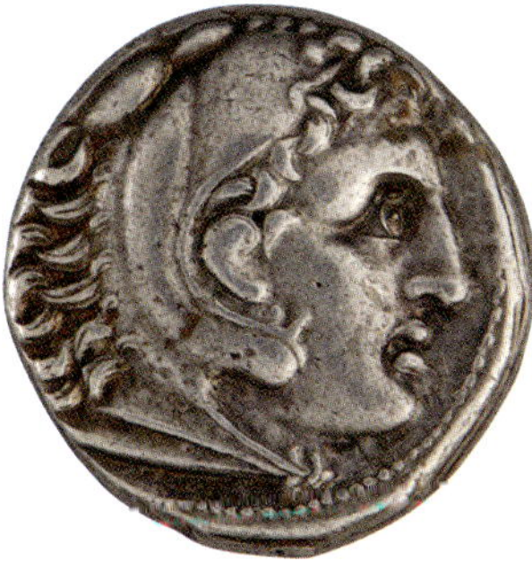

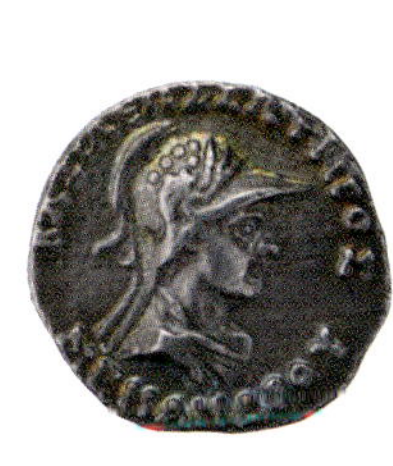
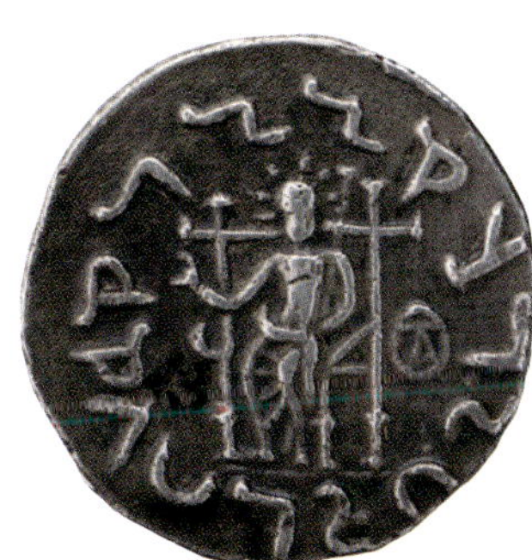

In Xpo ihu saluatore nostro uero & summo do in unitate trino · in trinitate uno · atq; incomprehensibili natiuitate omousios

Pacoeterno patre genito qui pulcherrimus rerum pulchrum profunda mente gerens empyrium · ante materialem olimpi telluris

& oceani specificationem luminosam angeloru ierarchiam · ac preclara solis & lunae astrorumq; igneorum uasa limpida · uarigenumq;

cosmi quadrifidi ornatu ac specimen · atq; squamigeram neptunice procellositatis copiam inexcogitabile · solo dum taxat uerbi ptulit

imperio · indeficienter regnante · ac triumphante · ppetualiterq; omnia moderante · Ego cnuto inclite ac speciosae gentis anglorum reg

nator basileius coenobio qued nouellu dicitur · famosa ac pop'losa munitate uuintonia situm · Inquo & preclarorum confessoru iudoci

atq; grimbaldi mirifica decenter hodietenus pollent somata · hanc membranulam grammatum care_eribus canna sulcante incepi exarari

adfundum · v · cassatorum amplitudinem inse continentem · quem indigenaru lingula drægtun uocitare assol& · quatinus haec terra mona

chorum inprefato monasterio degentium utilitatib; deseruiat · quemadmodu ante multa deseruiebat tempora · Hanc quippe terrã quidam

preface ciuitatis inhabitator adolescens animosus & instabilis · callidicate & mendacio sibi ame adquisiuit · dicens terram meam fuisse · meq; facile

eam sibi m& tradere posse · qued & feci · At ubi ueritatem agnoui · hereditatem dī dignis heredib; ocius restitui feci · & ad testimonium & con

firmationem hoc inpresenti cartula manifestari precepi · Et quia penes prescriptum adolescentem litteras huic libertati contrarias · &

callidicatis indagine adquisitas haberi comperimus · & illas sub anachemate dampnamus · & quascumq; alias si alicubi sunt pronibilo du

cimus · hancq; dum taxat litteraturam libertate perhenni dicamus ac corroboramus · Consentientibus insup huic libertati · benedictione

& misericordiam xpi u'   _desse desideramus · & contradicentib; inter_ ni poenas ppetuas imminere obtamus nisi a malitiae suae praui

tate & iniustitia celerius resipiscant · Prefatae quippe telluris latera · sic sua rurigenis dilatant confinia · Ærest of humtunan east be middel

hæma meapice to tidan byrig · of tidan byrig nyþer into micel defer · 7 spa andlang micel defer to leofpinne meapice · of leofpynne meapice to þam hæþenan beorge ·

7 of þam hæþenan beorge est into þuæg tune · Enim uero huius inscriptionis dictionalis paginula anno dnicae incarnationis millesimo · xix ·

prima paschali ebdomada inpresentia regis adconfirmationem & testimonium heroum illustrium quorum hic& subsequuntur

onomata digesta sunt · ✝ Ego cnuto rex anglorum hoc_____m libenti animo concessi atque roboraui ·

✝ Ego lyfing dorobernensis aecclesiae archi eps stabilitatem testimonii confirmaui · ✝ Ego pulfstan eboracensis archi eps consensi ·

<table>
<tr><td>✝ Ego ælfgyfu eiusdem regis conlateranea adiuui ·</td><td></td><td></td><td>✝ Ego þegnold</td><td>dux ·</td><td>✝ Ego þlitþuic</td><td>m̄ ·</td><td>✝ Ego þupkil</td><td>minist̄ ·</td></tr>
<tr><td>✝ Ego ælfrige</td><td></td><td>imp̄ sui ·</td><td>✝ Ego þupkil</td><td>dux ·</td><td>✝ Ego æþelrige</td><td>abb ·</td><td>✝ Ego hacun m̄ · ✝ Ego byþlitþuic</td><td>minist̄ ·</td></tr>
<tr><td>✝ Ego byþlitpold</td><td>eps</td><td>stabiliui ·</td><td>✝ Ego _____c</td><td>dux ·</td><td>✝ Ego byþlitrig</td><td>abb ·</td><td>✝ Ego healden m̄ · ✝ Ego æþelþend</td><td>minist̄ ·</td></tr>
<tr><td>✝ Ego ælfmæn</td><td>eps</td><td>adnotaui ·</td><td>✝ Ego goopine</td><td>dux ·</td><td>✝ Ego byþlitmæn</td><td>abb ·</td><td>✝ Ego þuned m̄ · ✝ Ego riþed</td><td>minist̄ ·</td></tr>
<tr><td>✝ Ego eadnoþ</td><td>eps</td><td>impressi ·</td><td>✝ Ego elaf</td><td>dux ·</td><td>✝ Ego æluuie</td><td>abb ·</td><td>✝ Ego atsene m̄ · ✝ Ego oflac</td><td>minist̄ ·</td></tr>
<tr><td>✝ Ego goopine</td><td>eps</td><td>adquieui ·</td><td>✝ Ego leofpine</td><td>dux ·</td><td>✝ Ego byþlitpold</td><td>abb ·</td><td>✝ Ego ælfgan m̄ · ✝ Ego leoffpine</td><td>minist̄ ·</td></tr>
</table>

Gloria & diuitiae & felicitas & beatitudo cunctas huic libertati fauentibus intabernaculis donetur iustorum ·

The Drayton Charter, 1019

Manuscript on parchment (28 × 36 cm)

This is an extremely rare survival, an original royal charter of King Cnut. It was drawn up one thousand years ago in the first week of Easter 1019 in the presence of Cnut, the archbishops of Canterbury and York, his consort Aelgifu (the old English name used for Queen Emma), five bishops, six earls, five abbots and twelve thegns. It is not as large as some royal charters, but at around 28 by 36 cm it was still designed to impress. As with other royal charters its use of Latin subtly associates the authority of God with that of the king; revealingly in lines 16–18 it switches to the vernacular, which everyone could understand, when it comes to record the boundaries of the land conveyed (here notably including a heathen burial mound, *Hæþenan beorge*, as one of the markers). And its script, a beautiful Anglo-Caroline minuscule (one of the ancestors of our modern typefaces), is easily accessible, in marked contrast to later medieval documents.

What does it record? The striking chi-rho extending over the first six lines sets a high religious tone at the outset. The subsequent preamble displays the full rhetorical and literary power of insular Latin as it describes how the Word brought forth heaven, earth and the ocean, and evokes a hierarchy of angels through to an unimaginable abundance of fish in Neptune's tempestuous domain. Only at the end of line 5 do we come to the name of Cnut (highlighted in rustic capitals) and his description as the ruler and *basileus* of the noble and fair race of the English. There follows an account of how he restored land at Drayton (now a hamlet of Barton Stacey by the A303) to the New Minster in the populous and famous city of Winchester. The linkage of God's word and the king's word could

not be neater. But what follows reveals a murkier reality. Cnut had previously given the land to someone else, but was now revoking his earlier gift by a veritable tour de force of character assassination: the previous recipient was a mere youth and, as if that was not enough on its own, he was headstrong, inconstant and had used cunning and fraud to persuade Cnut to give it to him.

What is this charter dating from 363 years before the College's foundation doing amid the thousands of later charters and deeds in its archives? When land was gifted or conveyed it commonly came with bundles of older deeds, so the archives of medieval monastic and collegiate foundations often contain older hinterlands, and Winchester's are no exception; the College gained a mass of older documents from Hyde Abbey (the post-conquest successor to New Minster) when it acquired the abbey's estate of Woodmancott in 1543 following the dissolution of the monasteries. But Cnut's charter and three other Anglo-Saxon royal charters from New Minster (one of which is an eleventh-century forgery) do not directly relate to any of the College's later landholdings. Instead, it looks as if they were purloined by Woodmancott's former tenant, John Fisher, who signed his name in the bottom right-hand corner of Cnut's charter and the three others – he clearly felt these were documents worth having and retaining. Fisher was related to Richard Bethel, who had been granted the site of Hyde Abbey in 1538, and it seems likely that this enabled the two of them to help themselves to its archives. Tempting as it is to be censorious, one should be grateful that the collecting instinct of John Fisher saved this charter from destruction.

John Nightingale (D, 1973–77, Fellow, 2002–17)

Song Dynasty Bowl, 11th century

Stoneware with incised decoration under a green glaze (D. 22 cm)

This bowl is from the Duberly Collection of Chinese porcelain, one of three pieces now in the school museum that were made in or near Yaozhou, some fifty miles north of Xi'an and the Yellow River in Shaanxi Province, during the Northern Song period (AD 960–1127). This group of celadon ceramics was mainly made to be used in the court of the emperors. The colour was produced by iron in the feldspathic glaze over a fine grey stoneware body. The word celadon to describe this colour is European and not used by the Chinese, who just called them green wares. The name comes from the colour of the cloak worn by Céladon, a shepherd in a pastoral romance of the seventeenth century by the French writer Honoré d'Urfé.

Major Montagu Duberly OBE JP married Lady Eileen Stopford, daughter of the 6th Earl of Courtoun, in 1924. Their only son James was killed aged eighteen in the German bombing of the Guards' Chapel on 18 June 1944. In 1947, when they decided to start collecting Chinese porcelain, they agreed that on their deaths it should be left to Winchester College in James's memory. As a result, their collection of nearly two hundred works of Chinese art is now displayed in the College Treasury. Until 1953 this bowl was in the collection of Alfred Chester Beatty. The Duberlys bought it for only £150 through the agency of the famous Chinese art dealer Peter Sparks, who was their principal adviser in the purchase of their Chinese collection.

Early Chinese ceramics have been collected by scholars throughout the centuries, in particular by the Qing Emperor Qianlong (r. 1735–96). Song ceramics were exported as far as the Middle East, and some reached Europe from the thirteenth century onwards, but most arrived in the twentieth century and by the middle of the century scholars were able to classify most pieces. Later in the century, after the end of warfare in China, Chinese scholars were able to make far more excavations of sites and knowledge has recently been greatly extended. The complexity of certain kiln sites has been discovered and it has been proved that many of them made brown and other wares as well as celadon wares. Song ceramics are now quite common on the market, and only the particularly rare and beautiful examples are sought after by museums and rich collectors. Of the olive-coloured pieces from the north, this bowl is of particularly fine quality with its carved and combed design of a lily spray and other flowers.

Anthony du Boulay (C, 1943–46)

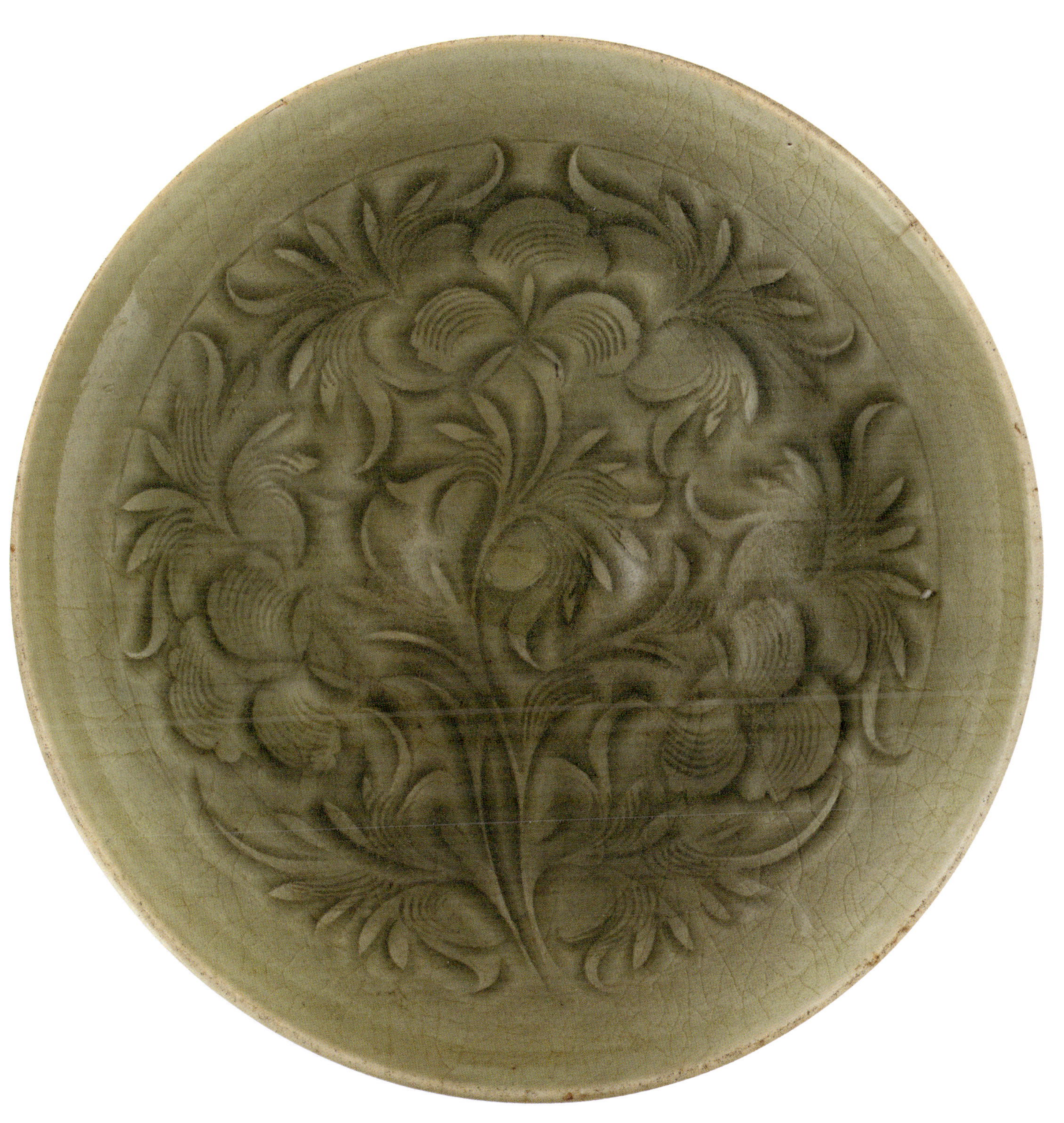

Paschasius on Lamentations, *c.* 1100

MS 5: Manuscript on parchment, ff. 126, bound in 20th-century alum-tawed pigskin over wooden boards by Roger Powell
(31.4 × 23.6 cm)

This manuscript of Paschasius Radbertus's commentary on the Book of Lamentations appears from its writing and other evidence to date from around 1100. It is the oldest complete manuscript in the Fellows' Library and was probably written at Winchester in the Cathedral Priory. It was given by one George Greswold, who in 1558 presented a number of books to the Library, from Bede's *Ecclesiastical History of the English People* to a contemporary commentary on the Gospels.

Paschasius's text (written between 849 and 857) is an exercise in what the Benedictine monks called *lectio divina,* a reading which dwells on phrases of the biblical text, allowing their associations to build in the silence of the mind. The script of this manuscript is a late form of Carolingian minuscule, the hand invented in eighth-century Francia to give a clear rendering of the foundation texts of Charlemagne's political ordering of Europe. It is a style of writing which has acted as an instrument of power. But its clarity and steady austerity are the fitting inscription of what the monastic tradition calls the *regula vitae*: the 'rule of life', a way of ordering life which in the handling of the individual impulse and the unpredictability of events makes a balance between discipline and suppleness, and gives freedom within a pattern of ritual. The regularity of the script bears this out. If one ceases to read it for its sense and sees it as a complex relation of lines, it becomes an endless choreography of brief linear possibilities: an intricate yet simple drawing.

The initials are coloured, never illuminated, but there are two marginal drawings (on folios 71v and 103v). The medieval image is shadowed by, sometimes defiant of, Plato's disdain for image as a distraction from truth. How though can I pray, asks the monk in the desert, without images? I cannot avoid them. The two drawings show a head straight on, long-haired, staring out; and three other heads, possibly with a satirical edge, caricatural and accomplished in execution. Their presence is a riddle. Was the discipline of no-image too much for the scribe (he nearly managed it)?

Should we say, then, that the drawings are witness to the individual mind in a society devoted to the collective? Or are they attempts to reimagine the narrative of the words above them? The words above the male head speak of Judgement, and the drawing is perhaps the judging Christ; and the three figures in dispute are perhaps representations of the discord mentioned in the nearby text. It may be that stylistically these three heads are related to the tradition of the Winchester Psalter, with its interest in the relation of the grotesque and grace in caricature. But it might also be that these figurative asides, very likely the work of the scribe, are of interest chiefly because they are an unconscious moment in writing – and in reading. They are sketches in the sense that they do not aim at anything. They are a lapse from word into image, only to go back to word. There is no reading without distraction, but distraction reaffirms the text.

Peter Cramer (History, 1993–2018)

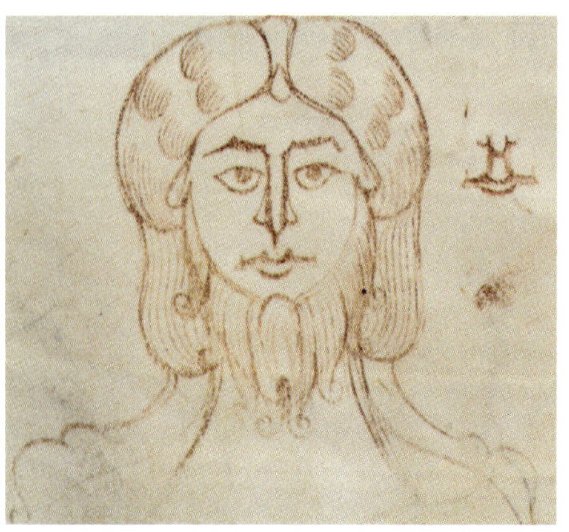

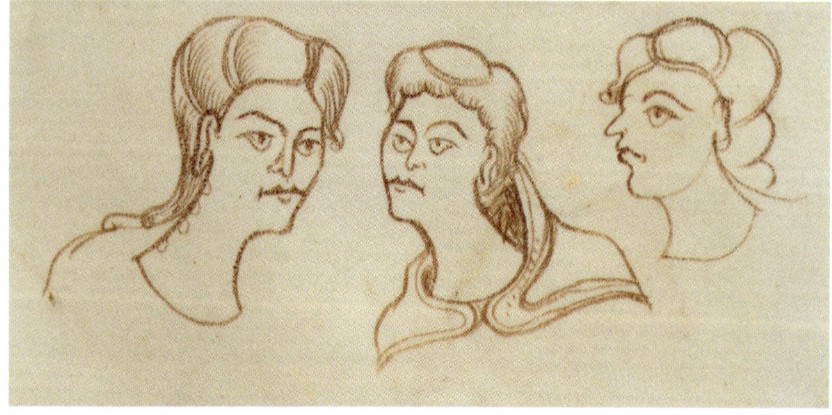

PASCHASIVS RADBERTVS MONACHORVM OMNIVM P IPSEMA
SENI ODILMANNO SEVERO PLVRIMAM ET SEMPITERNĀ
SALUTEM

MULTO COGOR LONGOQ: CONFECT
uitae tedio tristes lacrimarū intremodos. Geme
bunda iam quia pfecto meis pregrauata malis. in-
opinate senectus nonuocata uenit. Quādū inspicio
specie deformatus aliena p horresco. eo quod me
subito animo non mutat quod fui noninuenio.
Euadere tamen nequeo illa decipiente quę adimisi.

Vnde congelatus usu longiori durior effectus nullis iam emolliri
queo fletib; quā uis multas miseriarū mearū intus fousue premar dolo-
ribus. Quib; cotidie saltem ad suspiria ppulsus. ieremię pphę inter
discrimina ultimę uitę threnos explanare decreui. Siquidem eius
ut emolliar lamtus. quatin uel sic addiscā fragilis uitę excidia deplo-
rare qm scs ille plangit aliena. Et quia hęc aetas alios poscit mores.
licet sero hortante scriptura quia semel domū luce intraui. proposui
tanti operis studia nonindiscussa transire. licet neminem latinozum
legerim explanasse threnos quos propheta syn phonizando metro
uoluit legentibus commendare. Inquo nimirū opere siquippiam
posteris condignum litteris enodauero. tuo frater iudicio decernendū
trans mitto. Quia nulli magis nra congruere putaui ad quoscun q;
oculos direxi quam tibi: qui & senectute coequaris. & cotidianis
precum fletibus ante cellis. INCIPIT IN LAMENTATIONIBUS HIEREMIE
PASCHASII RADBERTI MONACHORVM OMNIVM PIPSEMA.
VOTORVM LIBER PRIMVS. FLETIBVS EXPLICANDVS SENI ODILMAN
NO SEVERO OPERE PRETIO CONSECRATVS.

H. di gra Wint eps Archid Decanis 7 vniuso clero 7 populo Wint epatus.
salt. Nouerit vniuersitas vra quod petitione Walteri clerici mei qui ecclesie beati petri de Waltam psonatu obtinuit. 7 assensu xpofori clerici mei
qui pdicto Walto in eiusdem ecclesie psonatu nra largitione canonice suc-
cessit. concessi in ppetuu monachis de hamela oms decimas 7 obuentiones
tam de uiuis qm de mortuis illius hide terre que ipsoru monachorum
est. et alterius hide de byredond. excepta decima salis. Ita tamen quod
pdicti monachi. iiij. sol. annuati p recognitione soluent ecclesie beati
petri de Walta. Denariu q; beati petri dabunt parrochiani dicta-
rum hidaru ecclesie de Walta. Et pcessione pentecostes. et una uisita-
tionem ad uincula sca pet facient ecclesie de Walta. Monachis quoq;
pdictis apud byredona p commodo parrochianor capellam construere
concessi. Quam bene deseruire 7 quociens opus fuerit: monachi repa-
rare debebunt. Crisma etia pcipient a psona ecclie de Walta. Et
psbiter quem ibi deseruiturum pdicti monachi psentabunt psone
de Walta. ipsi psone ecclesie de Walta sicut ei placuerit fidelitate
faciet. T. his. Rad Archid Wint. Rob archid Surrie. Witto pore Hos-
pitalis. Rob Elemosin. Rob de Clatford. Albto Sumano. Rob de Lime-
sta. Mag Ghb. Mag Nicholao. Witto Tisello. Bern Capell. Joseph. Alano.
Martino Lacharre. clerici.

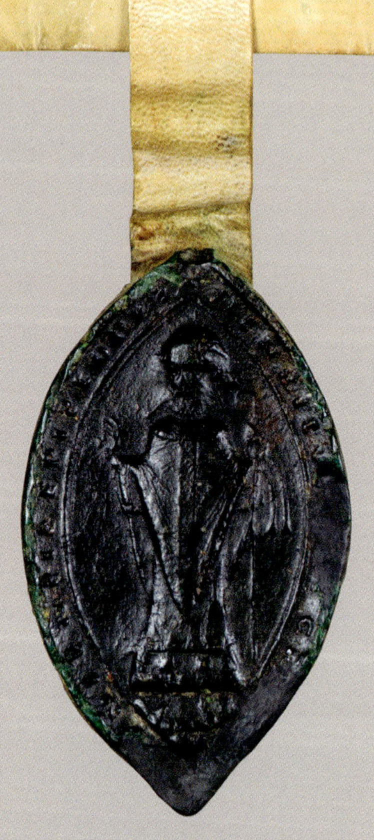

Seals of Henry of Blois, mid-12th century

Wax seals (L. 9 cm, W. 5.5 cm)

There are four charters issued by Henry of Blois in the College Archives. Two of these retain the personal seal he devised for himself as Bishop of Winchester and papal legate. Both examples are worn, but we can still make out a full-length portrait of Henry as bishop, with his right hand raised in benediction and his left holding a pastoral staff. The legend surrounding the figure on the obverse of the seal reads '+HENRICUS DEI GRATIA WINTONIENSIS EPISCOPUS' (Henry by the grace of God, Bishop of Winchester). On the reverse, somewhat surprisingly, a Roman intaglio has been used as a counterseal. Both these seals came into the College in 1391, when William of Wykeham purchased the Benedictine priory of Hamble. That acquisition, and the land that came with it, was just one of many investments he made for his new foundation.

The two charters are difficult to date precisely. It is thought the earliest surviving impression of the seal is attached to a letter sent by Henry to Pope Eugenius III between 1145 and 1148, but one of the College's examples may be earlier. In the portrait on the obverse Henry wears the *pallium*, to which he was entitled as papal legate, an office he held from 1139 to 1143. Both charters concern grants of land to Hamble Priory, which had been founded by Henry's predecessor, William Giffard. The document illustrated here is a confirmation of Giffard's original grant of one hide of land called 'Hamela'. The list of witnesses suggests it was issued before 1140. For the historian Dom David Knowles, Henry of Blois was 'unquestionably the most powerful agency in England both in secular and ecclesiastical politics'. This seal was probably cut when Henry's influence was greatest, both as a powerful ecclesiastic and the younger brother of King Stephen.

Henry's choice of counterseal was consistent with his artistic patronage and interest in classical art. The use of an ancient gem as a counterseal was fashionable in the 1140s, but they were often reinterpreted, with surrounding inscriptions showing how the pagan images had been given Christian significance. Henry's gem shows Zeus Sarapis wearing the distinctive *modius* headdress and facing the goddess Isis, and was probably made in the eastern Mediterranean. It is possible that Henry picked it up during one of his visits to Rome. He may have noticed the resemblance to papal bulls, which had an image of the confronted heads of Saints Peter and Paul, communicating papal authority and the *concordia apostolorum*. If so, it may have evoked Winchester as well as the abbey of Cluny, where Henry was brought up, since both were dedicated to Peter and Paul.

The choices open to seal-cutters in the twelfth century were few, since the prescribed form was necessarily conservative: it was important the seal looked like an episcopal seal. This meant that even subtle adjustments in the form were potentially significant. Henry's appearance on his personal seal resembles the famous image of him in the Winchester Bible, where he is found playing the part of Pope Desiderius. It also reminds us of John of Salisbury's *Historia Pontificalis*, in which John pokes fun at Henry's 'long beard and philosophical solemnity'. To contemporaries, however, the seal conferred Henry's authority as Bishop of Winchester. Its symbolism and counterseal suggest his deep religious sensibility and interest in ideas.

Nicholas Townson (History)

A Life of Thomas Becket, *c.* 1190–1200

MS 4: Manuscript on parchment, ff. 211, bound in 20th-century alum-tawed pigskin over wooden boards by Roger Powell
(30.5 × 21 cm)

This is the only manuscript to contain the complete Life of Thomas Becket by the monk William of Canterbury. Copied in the late twelfth or early thirteenth century, it was bequeathed by William of Wykeham to the College in his will, written at his manor of South Waltham – now Bishop's Waltham – on 24 July 1404, and has been in the College's possession ever since. An inventory of the library drawn up in 1428/29 describes it as '*ex dono domini Fundatoris*'.

William joined the monks of Canterbury after Becket had fled England in 1164 and only met the archbishop – who ordained him as deacon – on his return in November 1170. Of the nine authors who wrote full lives of Becket, William was one of only four who witnessed his murder in Canterbury Cathedral on 29 December 1170 by the knights Reginald FitzUrse, Hugh de Morville, William de Tracy and Richard le Breton. In life Becket had been post-conquest England's most controversial prelate; in death he instantly became England's best-selling saint. William of Canterbury wrote his *Passion of the Glorious Martyr Thomas, Archbishop of Canterbury* in 1173–74, as a preface to his own collection of Becket's miracles, which is nearly three times longer than the biography and forms the second component of this manuscript.

William of Wykeham would doubtless have been pleased to read of the bravery of his distant predecessor in office, Henry of Blois, whose refusal to take part in a council of bishops and abbots, summoned by the king to London in order to appeal to the papal court against Becket's excommunication of several prelates in the royal camp, is relayed in detail by William of Canterbury. Becket had already been canonised by Pope Alexander III by the time William wrote his *Passion*, although not before he began editing the collection of miracles, so the biography cannot have been conceived as part of a forensic dossier to persuade an ecclesiastical commission of Thomas's claims to sanctity. William sets out his purpose in writing at the end of the prologue, immediately before the illuminated initial which may represent Becket himself. Readers were to be inspired by the struggle of this 'strong athlete', presented here as an example for all to follow such that, having seen where, how and why Thomas ran his race, they too would not flee the challenge should the Lord call them into the stadium. One of the first to receive the message was the king from whose court the four assassins had begun their journey to Canterbury: William presented the book to Henry II in 1174.

Appropriately for a book bequeathed to a medieval foundation whose motto is in English, this manuscript contains several precious passages in early Middle English.

Magnus Ryan (G, 1980–84, Fellow)

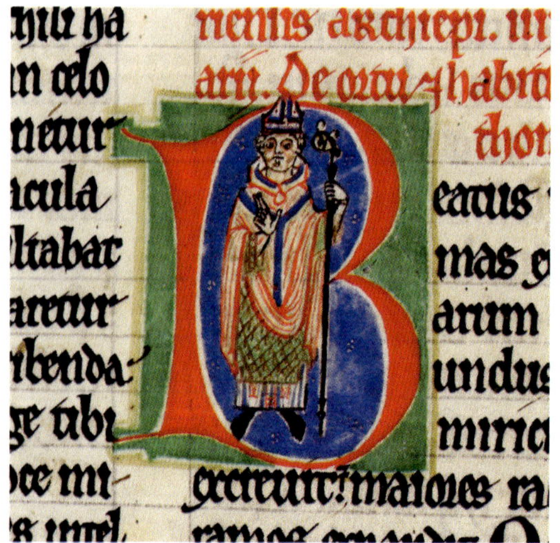

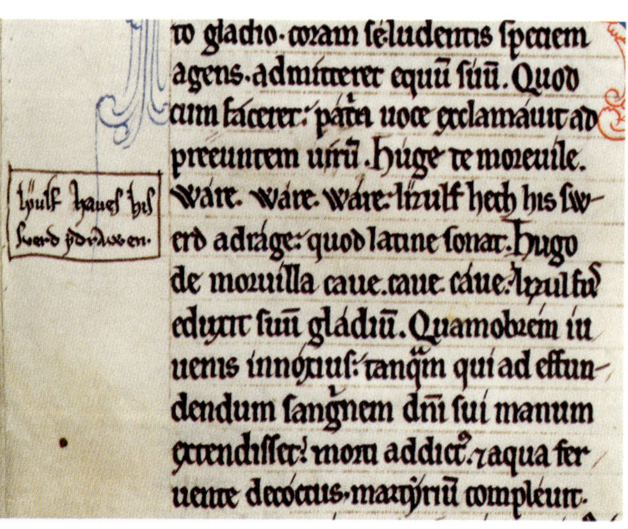

viliter p modu
lo suo tabnacu
lum dñi donis
suis exornat. ali
us auro. alius
argento. lapidi
bus preciosis. bysso. purpura.
cocco. iacincto. Si nichil istoru
potest: offert pelles oe caprarum
pilos. reputans contemptibi
lia sua necessaria ee: quibz to
ta tabnaculi pulchritudo con
tegatur. ut ardor solis + ymbri
um phibeantur iniurie. Hinc
nre paruitatis admonitu. qd
temp obtulit oe dñs contulit
offerim. glosum martyre tho
mam que uidim + audiuim
oe manus nre contrectauerut
i medio pponentes. oe ppinan
tes si q in tertiu uias transffusa
coacuerunt: sz q statim de pu
rissimo prelo comendata teste:
siuu sapiem seruauerunt Dig
nus quidem ore rotundo e
rat. oe maiori stilo: quia qd mai
habuit: impendit ecclie. Sed
quia q agnu ñ possum. colum

bas uel turtures offerunt. oe
dñs ignobilia mundi oe con
temptibilia eligit. ut fortia qoq
confundat. oe ea que non sunt
ut ea que sunt destruat: sagu
nrm ad opimentu tabnaculi
conferre cure sunt. Causaq pnci
palis dñs est oe martyr. q dño
similis e in passione. Nam sic
dñs imminente passione sua
loco passionis appropinquit:
ita thomas sciens futuror. ad
locu quo pateretur accessit. Si
cut thm. ita thomã querebant
apprehendere: sz nemo misit
in eum manum. quia ñ dum
uenerat hora el. Dñs triumpha
uit ante passionem suã. tho
mas ante suam: dñs passus e
post cenam. thomas passus e
+ p cenam: dñs a iudeis triduo
ierosolimis custoditus: thomã
diebz aliquot intra septa ecclie
sue custodit. Dominu querentibz
eum occurrens ait. Quem que
ritis: Ego sum. Thomas que
rentibz eum: ecce ego. Dñs. Si
me queritis sinite hos abire.
Thomas. nulli circumstantiu
noceatis. Cuius ibi uri hic uult

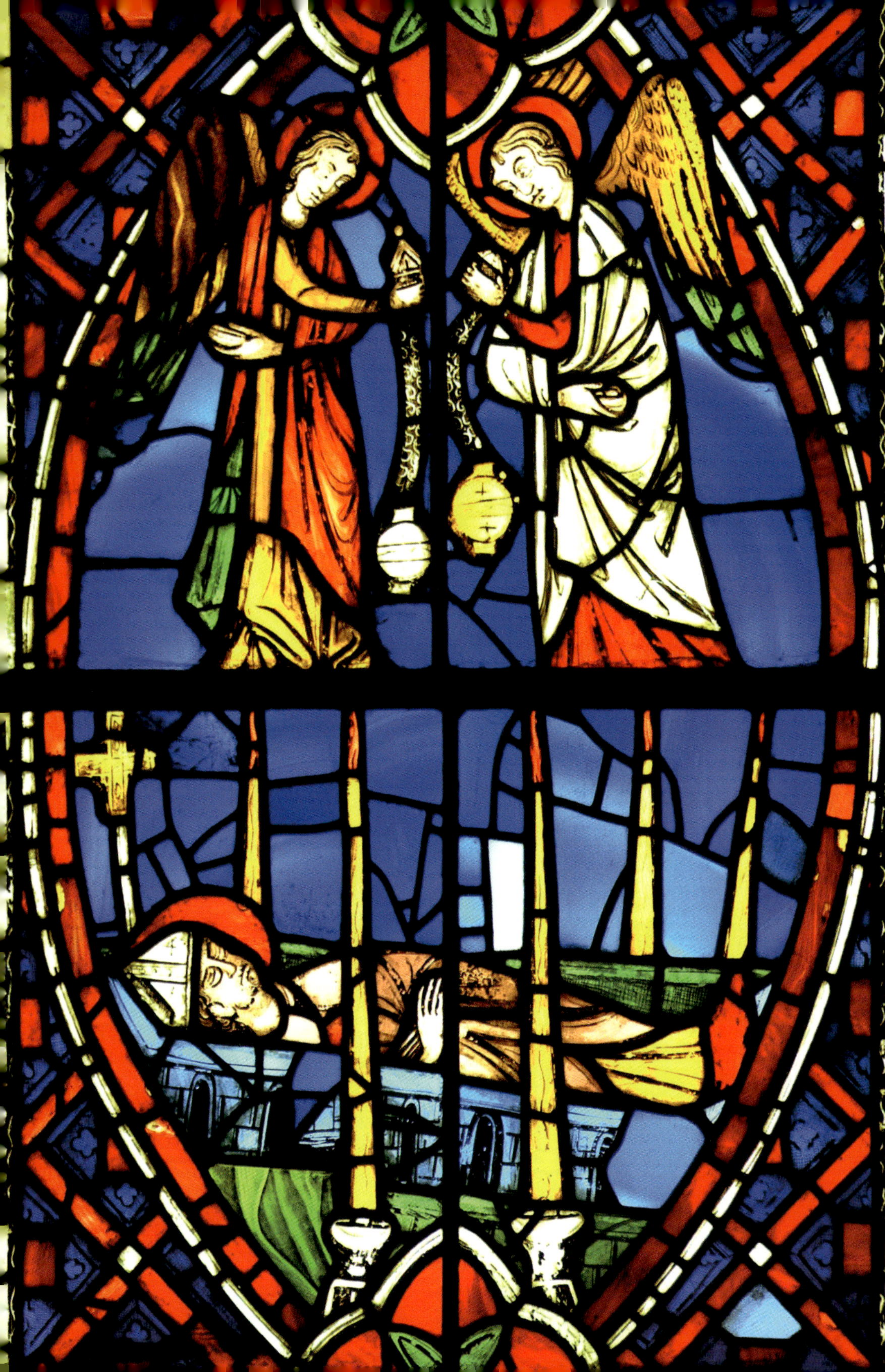

The Death of St Germain, 1240s

Stained glass with added paint (130 × 90 cm)

The scene takes place in an oval, enclosing a rich blue. In the lower half a bishop is laid out, candles around him and a processional cross at his head. Above are two angelic figures, looking down intently. They lean inwards – a dramatic use of the oval form. Each angel swings a censer in one hand while the other is crossed over, gathering up the splendid heavy mantles.

Scholars identify the deceased as Germanus (*c.* 496–576), Bishop of Paris under King Childebert I. Among his other acts, Germanus urged the king to build a church to house the relics of saints, and when he himself was canonised in the eighth century, the church was reconsecrated in his name, becoming the Benedictine abbey of St Germain-des-Prés. Centuries later, a Lady Chapel was built (*c.* 1244–47). The apse of this chapel was glazed with windows showing scenes from the lives of the Virgin Mary, St Vincent of Saragossa and St Germain himself. The Lady Chapel is gone, demolished after the French Revolution. Some of the glass was no doubt destroyed, but some was preserved in a museum in Paris. And from there the stained-glass windows, sometimes in fragments, were dispersed to international buyers, with little or no documentation to prove where they came from. But masters and workshops in the Gothic style have distinctive thumbprints, and certain common features suggest that a group of surviving fragments originated in the St Germain Lady Chapel: those staring eyes, the crossed arms, the heavy draperies.

But how did this window end up in Winchester College? The trail seems to run as follows. From Paris, the glass was sold in the early nineteenth century to a German agent in Norwich, who acquired it for Sir William Jerningham of Costessey Hall in Norfolk. The contents of the Hall were sold in 1918, and the Hall itself was demolished. Our glass next turns up in the possession of Sir Bruce Ingram, who offered it to Winchester College in memory of his father Sir William (both Ingrams were Old Wykehamists). The school accepted the gift but clearly did not know what to do with it, and the glass toured the campus in its search for a suitable home. Eventually it ended up in a far corner of Moberly Library. From there it was moved into the previous Treasury and now it rests in the new museum, in a modern light box, a relic among relics.

Ideally it would be lit by natural light, bringing out the gorgeous tones with the changing days and seasons. But against this loss, there are gains: we can see the wonderful detail close up, which is not always the case with medieval glass *in situ*. And the setting is suitably medieval. Lean in, like the angels. Listen carefully and you can hear the jingling censer chains, the rustling drapery and the candles flickering against the ocean of that deep blue night.

Malcolm Hebron (English)

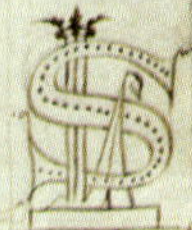
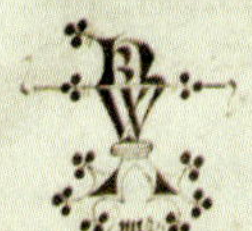
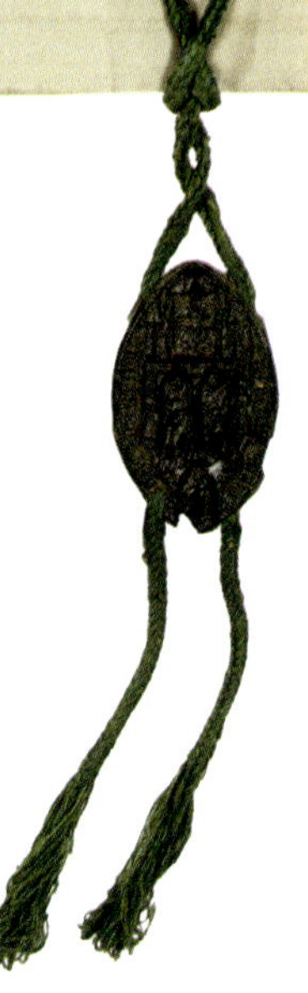

The Foundation Charter, 1382

Manuscript on parchment with wax seal (45 × 62 cm)

William of Wykeham surfed the crisis of the Middle Ages as successfully as Roman Abramovich did the fall of Communism. Born as the Little Ice Age began, Wykeham rode out the Black Death, Peasants' Revolt, demographic collapse and the Hundred Years' War. His oligarchical methods included huge bribes, speculation in commodities, the discounting of government debt, pressure on hostages, and rivals kept in fear and terror. 'Everything was done by him, and without him nothing was done.'

The Foundation Charter was issued on 20 October 1382. It begins in praise of God who 'thought fit to bring us forth from the womb of our mother into this vale of misery', which Wykehamists on boggy Itchen-side pitches take to be the Founder's small joke. 'Grammar is the foundation, gateway and mainspring of the liberal arts', and without it students 'often fall into the danger of failure when they have given up their enthusiasm for progress.' Wykeham spoke and wrote French, and understood administrative Latin, but 'deficiency, penury and indigence' had deprived him of the 'proper means for continuing in the art of Grammar'. Later his unremitting labours in finance and administration cost him 'the time and leisure for the study of letters' that his College would give its Scholars. Wykeham's insistence on generative grammar – and algebra and chemical valence are grammars too – rather than rote learning, still distinguishes a Winchester education.

The charter does all that words can do to ensure the independence of the College from Church and king: 'We confirm all the aforesaid messuages, land and meadow, to be held communally and in common by the Warden and Scholar Clerks for the time that they live there in free, pure, and perpetual alms.' Wykeham keeps an eye on the proper expenditure of his bounty: there shall be 'seventy poor and needy scholars leading a collegiate life, making progress in the grammar of art and science, to endure for all time'. In 1868 the Clarendon commissioners found that Harrow had dwindled to nine scholars while the Fellows lived high on the hog. At Winchester they found the seventy, all still making progress in grammar.

The charter concludes with a list of witnesses summoned to headquarters in Southwark. It is signed with the complex marks of two public notaries, dated to the fifth year of the pontificate of Urban VI and the sixth of Richard II's reign, sealed with Wykeham's green lozenge, and has rested for six centuries in the specified 'coffer or communal chest' that was built *in situ*, for it is much too wide for the Muniment Tower staircase. Space was left for a decorated initial, but with nearly two thousand pounds of building ahead, this was one corner that could be cut.

Oligarchs crave legitimate legacy, and Wykeham's at Winchester and Oxford should prove more significant than Abramovich's at Stamford Bridge. To date, Chelsea have won thirteen major trophies for their Russian; by 1430 Wykehamists were running Church and State in England.

Nick MacKinnon (Mathematics and English)

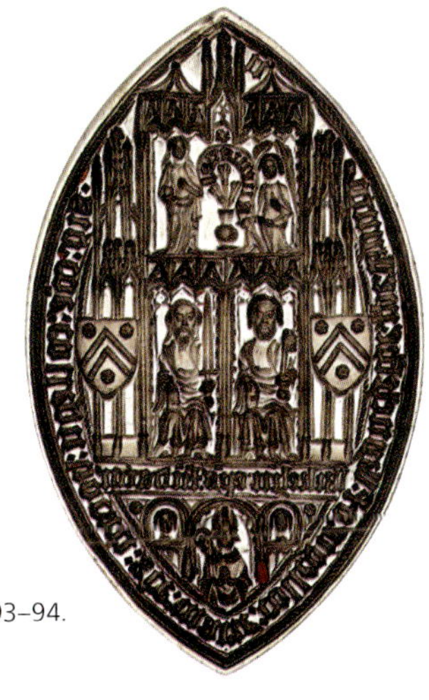

College seal matrix, c. 1393–94.

niuersis sancte matris ecclie filiis ad quos psentes lie nre puenerint Willimus de Wykeham pmissione diuina Wynton
celestis dispositione consilii nos ab vtero matris nre in hanc vallem miserie pduxe dignatus est miserni atq̧ in
condignum ad gradus et dignitates varios sublimauit hec nempe interna medriacione pensantes quondam co-
gerimus ac fundauimus Deo concedente ad laudem glam et honorem nois eiusuersi ac gliosissime marie vg̈ꝯ
existit sine qua artes huiusmodi sciri non possunt nec ad eaz pfeconem quisquam poterit puenire Consideran-
tientes etiam hatine in gramatica in deficiendi plurimŋ incedunt puculum vbi z faciendi posuerant appetitum
continuandum z pficiendum in arte gramatica supradca ꝥpe non suppetunt facultates nec suppetent in futurum huiusmodi scolarib3 elias p̃
valeant eas scienias seu artes alias liberales fiant vt expedit apciores ad oim scieniaz facultatum z artium liberalium titulum amphi-
mifiascripta diuina nobis assistente clemencia manus nras apponere adiutrices z caritatis subsidium impirn Ea pe nos Willimus z
Illustrissimi principis dni nri dm Ricardi secundi Regis Angle z efflante adquisimus nobis z successorib3 nris Epis Wynton vtʒlicet
carteri Wyntonie de Thoma Tannere de Soka Wynton vnum mesnagium cum ptinencs in eadem Soka z de Thoma Sanynton vnum
certis eius gliosis q̧ parcenere ecclie nre Wynton beatoz Aploz Petri z Pauli beatozq̧ vium Ecc̄e Switham z Arheldwold eiusdem ecclie de-
certis eius gliosis q̧ parcenere ecclie nre Wynton beatoz Aploz Petri z Pauli beatozq̧ vium Ecc̄e Switham z Arheldwold eiusdem ecclie de-
ciuitatum huiusmodi incrementum gratum p hoc deo obsequium pstaze sperantes de licenia z auctte sedis aplice dote p nos primitus a
ppte de nre seu alias momo doliber requisitis quozdam collegium ppetuum paupm scolarium clicoz pe cuitatem Wynton Pecan-
numero Septuaginta paupm z indigencium scolarium clicoz collegiale puenirimus in eodem stuprauimus q̧ pstciencium in gramaticalibus siue
efficiam manupage magrm Thomam de Claule in Theologia vacalaurm vium prudem z diseretum in spualib3 z temporalib3 circumspectum
arte facultate seu scienia gramaticali studere debentes admittimꝰ ipos q̧ eidem Custodi adiungimꝠ z in eodem nro Collegio r̃ealiter po-
nomen imponere pir decr̄ ipum sancte marie collegium vulgaris scinte marie Collegie ofꝰ Wynchestre notam at eciam nuncupam z illi
collegio collegialiter vt puinitus Aggregatis damus iuramus ac eciam Assignamus Statuimus eciam ordinamꝠ volumus q̧ dcꝰ custos
collegiali steint z viuant Statuies insup pdcos psentes Annos omnes z singulos ac ceros officianos z uincos imostimus eidem nro colle-
manere iuxta statim z ordinatoes nri collegii memorati Et sic custos z scolayes dci collegii z successores eozdem Custodis z scolarium clicoz
incontusse ad oinia z singula statuta z ordmacoes pmissa bene integre z fideli in omnib3 tenenda z inuiolabilit obseruanda pdca custos z su-
soribꝰ nuppetuum nihat nra pimaria fundacoe eiusdem collegii nri damus z concedimus ac psenti carta nra confirmamꝠ omia pdca mesnag̃
z inbitacione sins in collegio nro pdco de nobis z successorib3 nris Epis Wynton in liberam pinam z pperuam elemosinam nuppetuum lib-
artinium scolasticoz vicarias faciendis z extndi statita z ordinatoes de z sup legitime gubernacoe ac statu ipius nri Collegii z psonaz et
ciuntarat porestatem plenariam z liberam resernamus Iu quoz oin testimonium atq̧ fidem psentes has nras p Notarium publicum in-
tomens doc Anno ab incarnatoe dni sedm cursum z compurtacoem ecclie Anglicane millesimo Trecentesimo Octogesimosecundo Indiccione
Ricardi secundi post conquestum sexto Et nre consecracois anno Sextodecimo psentibz venerabilibz z discretis viris magris Johanne de Bloxham
ad pmissa vocatis spititer z rogatis ꝯ

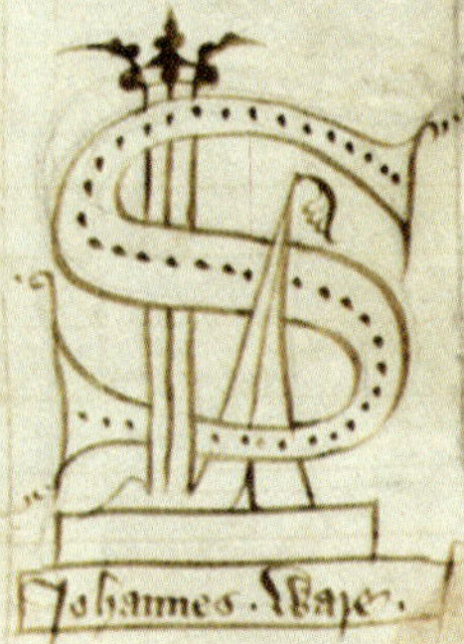

Et ego Johannes Baye clicus londoñ dioc publicus auctte aplica Notarius supdca Collegii Separazim
confirmacoi resernatoi ceterisq̧ omnibz z singtis que pdcam Reneendum patrm dnm Willm dei gra Epm Wyn
eaq̧ omia z onista sic fieri vidi z audiui ac de mandato dci venerabt pris p alium scribi feci publicam
testimonium oinm pmissoz Constat etiam michi Notario pdco de interlinia illius vbi imuero in ser

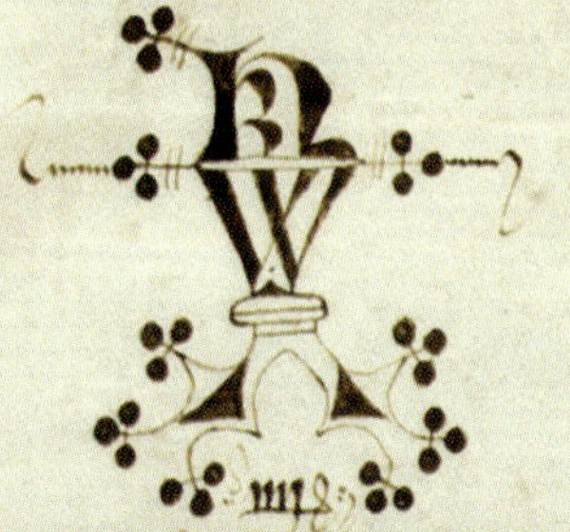

Et ego Johannes dnus de Walkhuni clicus Wellen dioc p
ac fundacoi eiusdem ac custodis pdca psenti z noialici concessioe
dm Iudiciis pontificatu meie die z loco cupri reciratis nge
z testiꝰ piuctanis psonalit psens imtfui in ea q̧ omia z singla
testiem pmissoz Et constat michi Notario antedicto de r̃
tatiuo cupradicto ꝯ IIIj ꝯ

cem in eo qui est omnium vera salus. Gloriosissimus et omnipotens deus noster eterni triumphator imperii qui sua potencia ineffabili et
... licet iuuenes qui nomnuncquam ponit humiles in sublime sua prudencia infallibili et gracie liberate amplis dicant honoribz et sublia
... Septuaginta pauperum scolarium clicos in Theologia Canonico et Ciuili iuribz et in Artibz in vniuersitate Oxonie studere debencium nuper
... hedium quia per magistra rerum experiencia edocet manifeste Gramatica fundamentum ianua et origo oim liberalium arcium aliarum
... scienciam iusticia colit et hospitas humane condicois auget quoque nonnulli studentes in scienciis aliis pro defectum bone doctrine suffi
... erunt imposterum ut hedii plerique scolares pauperes disciplinis scolasticis insistentes defectum penuriam et indigenciam pacientes quibz ad
... tuibz presentibz et futuris ut hac studio innorari seu vacare aut in facultate et sciencia gramaticali fecta per dei graciam ubertius et liberius proficere
... cium et proficiencium in eisdem quantum in nobis est minuerum dilatandum de facultatibz et bonis nobis a deo collatis sub forma preuium
... ctorum Epis autectis Diuisa mesuagia terras et pratum cum pertinencis in Soka Wyntonie nostre Wynton diocz et per ipsam ciuitatem de licencia
... tunc sancti Swithum Wynton vnum mesuagium vnam acram terre et dimidiam et tres acras prati cum pertinencis in Soka Wyntonie et iuxta ciui
... pertinencis in Soka fecta Ju et sup quibz tribz mesuagiis terra et prato cum pertinencis sic per nos ut prius adquisitis necnon in et super
... nostris Ju noie siue et indiuidue trinitatis patris et filii et spiritus sancti ad laudem gloriam et honorem nois inuocari gloriosissime virginis marie ma
... et pontificum instructorum et exaltacoem fidei xpiane eccle et perfeccium et honorem cultus diuini arciumque scienciarum liberalium et fa
... formam hanc apticam in hac pte concessam necnon et licencia tunc diui nostri Regis illustrissimi concedentis et omnibz aliis et singulis in ea
... ctualiter insistunt fundamus stabilimus et eciam ordinamus quod quidem collegium consistere volumus imperpetuum atque debet in et de
... cate seu sciencia gramaticali per dei graciam temporibz preteritis imaginum Dolentes et institucoem fundacoem et ordinacoem dicti nostri collegii virginis
... sciencia typhanum eiusdem nostri collegii proficientur in custodem. Septuaginta et pauperes et indigentes scolares clicos in gramaticalibz siue in
... collegialiter aggregamus quos scolarium clicos nora in munimentis dicti nostri collegii plenius sunt descripta Et volentes eidem nostro collegio
... seu nuncupato volumus imperpetuum nonari ac eciam nuncupari Archam et siue cistam communem dicti custodi et scolaribz clicis in eodem nostro
... ta ac alii sumus templis loco ipsorum perpetuo in eodem nostro collegio assumencium tanquam personae collegiales et collegiate simul comicent ac in eodem
... os sub custodia dispocione et regimine dicti custodis et successorum suorum custodum qui pro tempore fuerint volumus et disponimus et perpetuo per
... per fuerint omnes et singuli eciam suis successuris templis oimia et singula statuta et ordinacoes inca huiusmodi imperpetuum obseruent et teneant
... in cor perfectum tactis sacrosanctis Euangeliis corporale teneant et prestare debeant iuramentum/ Eisdem et custodi et scolaribz clicis et cor succes
... natu cum omnibz suis pertinencis tenens et possidens videlicet cois et in comuni eisdem custodi et scolaribz clicis ac successoribz eorundem per moca
... pacifice prius quiete Tenore tamen presentium virginis ordinandi et statuendi scolaribz et clicis dicti nostri collegii regulas vite scolastice et
... xem et regulis ordinacoibz et statutis assensi et muniuendi ipsaque oimia et singula in parte vel in toto mutandi innouandi et eciam declarandi nobis
... scribi et publicari mandauimus nisi et sigilli appensione fecimus communi Dat et Act in capella nostra manerium nostri de Suthewerk nostre Wyn
... pontificatus nostrum Catissimi in xpo patris et domini nostri dui Urbani diuina prudencia pape sexti anno quinto/ mensis Octobris die vicesima Anno regni Regis
... acono Wynton Johanne de Buryngham ebor Johanne de Chexeford exon et Johanne de Campeden Suthwellen ecclesiarum canonias et aliis testibz

Scolarium clicos pro ciuitatem Wynton in gramaticalibus studere debencium institucoes ac fundacoes perfeccioni nomincacoes concessioni
no diui Judicione Pontificatu mensis die a loco suprams geritatis agebant et fiebant vna cum pnominatis testibus personalis presens insiru
ane publicam formam redigendo presentes quasque lias meis noie et signo solitis et consuetis signaui rogatus et requisitus in fidem et
... linea presentis instrumenti a capite eiusdem compurando quam jasinam approbo ego Notarius supradictus +Ey

... uplice Notarius Presenti collegii Septuaginta clicos scolarium pro ciuitatem Wynton in gramaticalibz studere debencium Institucoes
... fimacoes ut resinacoes cotis et omnibz et singulis que per diu resinendum presentem dominum William de Wykeham dei gracia epm Wynton anno
... et fiebant vnum ipsa die ut subscribuntur agerent et fierent vna cum districto cortio vnisque Johne Seate Notario publico
... et coidi et audiui ut vigilii mei me presentis subscribendo Presentibz apposui consueti per diu redendum presentem requisitus in fidem et
... in deo immero scripius in sextradecim linea istius instrui ab ipsius capite compurando quam jasinam approbo ego No

Higden's *Polychronicon*, late 14th century

MS 15: Manuscript on parchment, ff. 220, in 20th-century deerskin chemise binding by Tim Wiltshire (34 × 24 cm)

William of Wykeham left the vast majority of the books in his personal library to the Fellows of New College, Oxford. To his Winchester foundation he gave but a handful. Some of these, it is reasonable to suppose, were to be read out loud, as was custom, during feast days when eating gave way to recreation time in Hall. Among those books for general edification was the wonderfully named *Ranulphi Castrensis, cognomine Higden, Polychronicon (sive Historia Polycratica) ab initio mundi usque ad mortem regis Edwardi III in septem libros dispositum*, or *Polychronicon* for short, a work started by Ranulf Higden (d. 1364), a Benedictine from Chester. His text became a staple compendium of world history framed within a biblical reference (the seven books echo the seven days of creation, for example) but recounting secular events, specifically concerning the history of England.

Higden's work survives in many copies from the fourteenth and fifteenth centuries, often with additions that bring the narrative up to date. Wykeham's copy continues with events to the accession of Richard II in 1377, and it is therefore likely to have been written within a few years of the College's foundation in 1382. What gives this manuscript special significance, and often brings scholars to study it, is a map of the world drawn on the leaf immediately before the beginning of Higden's text. Such maps are found in twenty-one copies of the *Polychronicon*, together accounting for almost one quarter of all surviving medieval *mappae mundi*.

Enclosed within a mandorla of bright sea-green are the places of the known world, broadly following the T–O division common in medieval world maps: placing Asia in the top half and Europe and Africa in the lower quadrants, left and right. The mandorla enclosure to this map is not insignificant. In Christian iconography in the Middle Ages it is a shape used to surround Christ and indicate his divine authority. Likewise, the T–O shape conveys both the Cross of Christ and the tripartite division of the world among the three sons of Noah. The map has perhaps a similar purpose to the rest of the *Polychronicon*: a compendium of knowledge, illustrating where the places of the world are situated in relation to each other. The vast majority of medieval maps were, as the historian P.D.A. Harvey puts it, 'diagrams of the world – and are best understood as an open framework where all kinds of information might be placed in the relevant spatial position ... the geographical element was only one of many: the map was a vehicle for conveying every kind of information – zoological, anthropological, moral, theological, historical....'

And so it is with the Winchester copy of the Higden world map, a wonderfully heteroclite composite. In the axis running top to bottom on the map we find the inaccessible earthly Paradise, but also labels for Babylon, Mesopotamia, their rivers the Tigris and Euphrates, and then on to Armenia, Jerusalem, Rome, Corsica, the Balearics and Spain. A red line at the top right denotes Sinai, the Arabian Peninsula and the Red Sea, roughly where we might hope to find them, and likewise our eyes are caught by the red outline of the Atlas mountains – home of the earth-supporting Titan – prominent in the bottom right-hand corner. Opposite them, of course, and smudged by countless generations of Wykehamical fingers, is our own part of the world.

Liam Dunne (Theology and Philosophy)

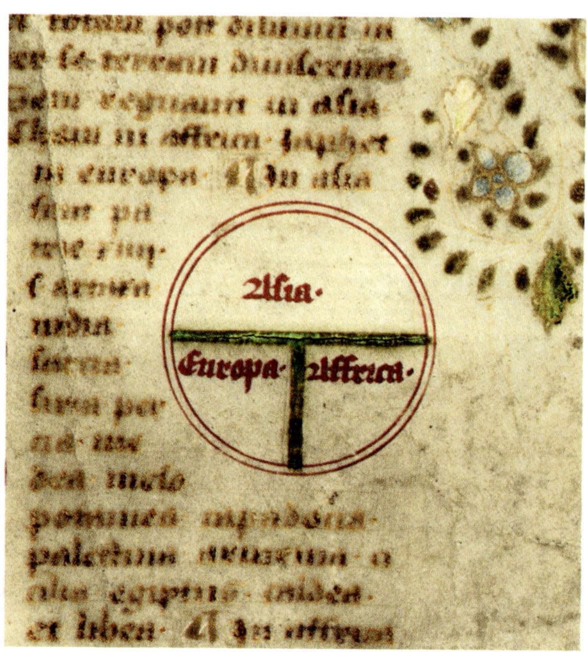

MS 13B: a diagrammatic representation of the world from a genealogical roll showing the descent of Henry VI, mid-15th century.

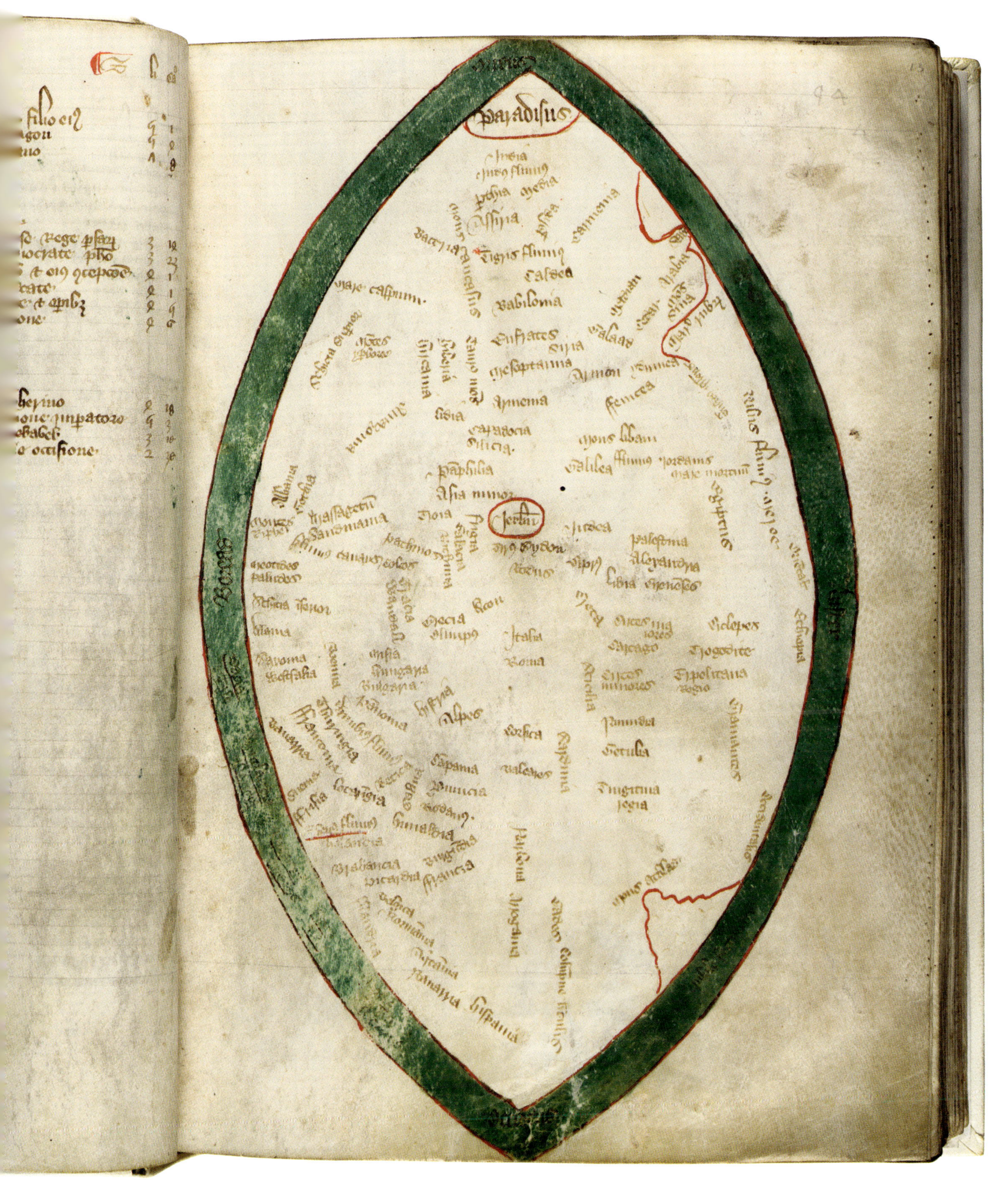
Oriens
Paradisus
India
Physon fluvius
Bactria Media
Assiria Persea
Caspiana
Mons Caucasus
Tigris fluvius
Caldea
Babilonia
Eufrates
Siria
Mesopotania
Armenia
Fenices
Capadocia
Cilicia
Mons Libani
Galilea
fluvius Jordanis
Mare mortuum
Egiptus
Paphilia
Asia minor
Jerlm
Judea
Palestina
Alexandria
Libia Cirenesca
Sidon
Tyri
Athene
Grecia
Olimpus
Leon
Italia
Roma
Ethiopia
Ciclopes
Trogodite
Affrica
Ellas minores
Tripolitana regio
Pannonia
Pamula
Westfalia
Ungaria
Bulgaria
Getulia
Bictania
Sclavonia
Hispania
Corsica
Valencia
Sardinia
Alpes
Aquilegia
Danubius flumen
Campania
Provincia
Saxonia
Francia
Frisia
Renus fluvius
Brabancia
Flandria
Francia
Scotia
Hibernia
Britannia Hispania
Occidens

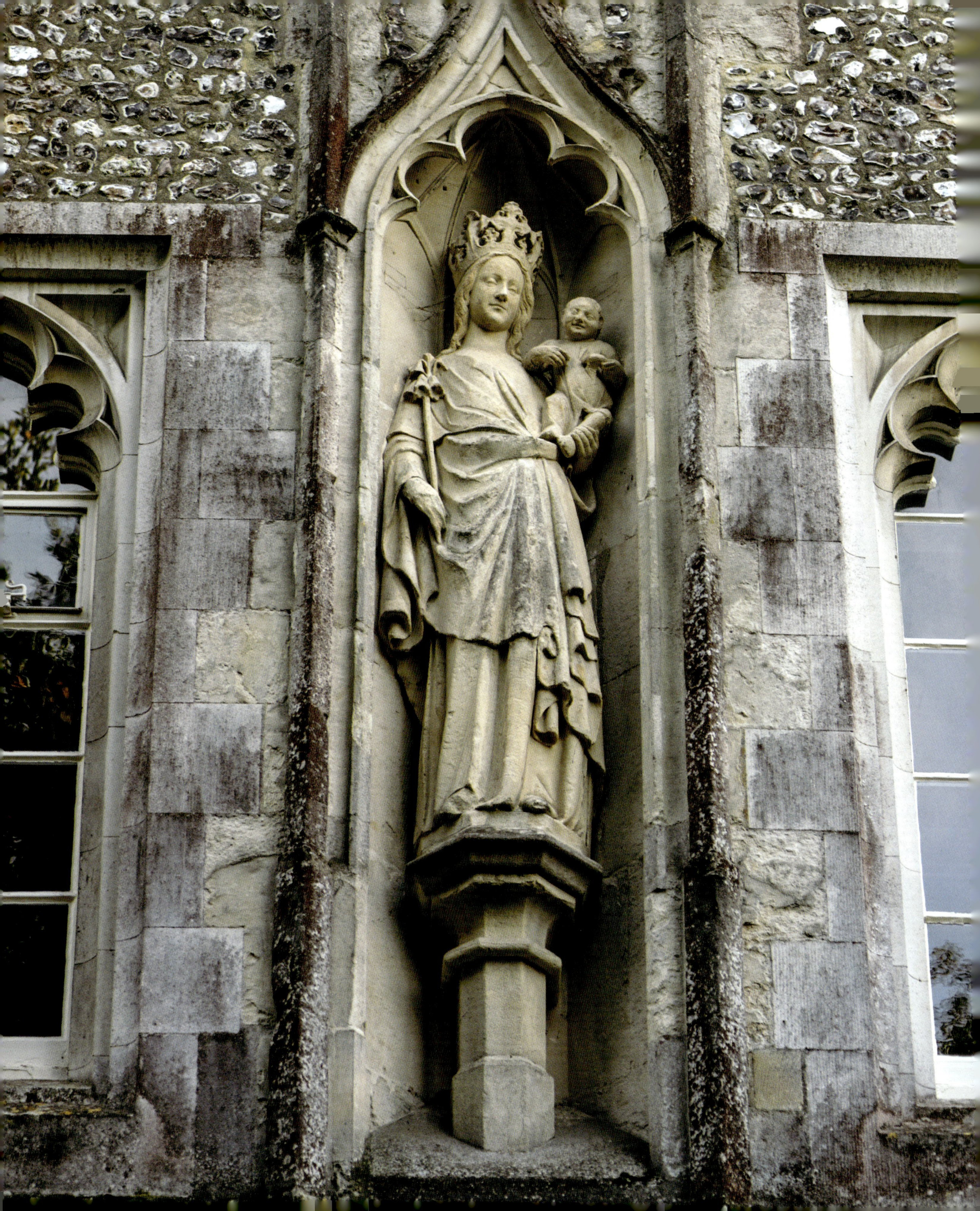

Virgin and Child, Outer Gate, 1393–94

Limestone with traces of pigment (H. 210 cm)

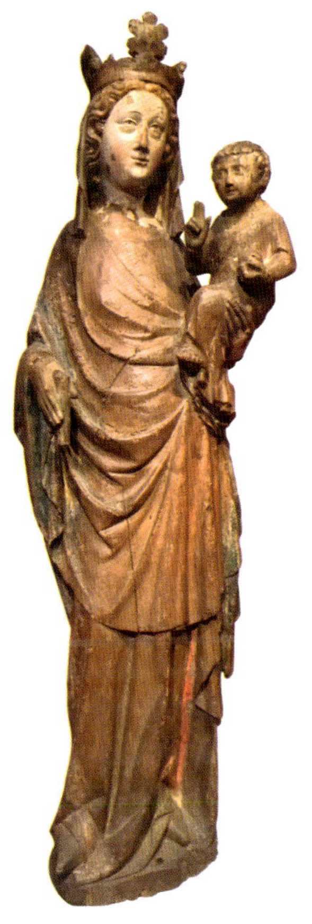

Virgin and Child, France, mid-14th century. In the collection of Nicholas Ferguson.

The Virgin and Child above Outer Gate is an exceptionally important example of late fourteenth-century sculpture. In 1951 Arthur Gardner, in his *English Medieval Sculpture*, described it as 'among the finest productions of this period'. Dating from 1393–94, it was perhaps made by John Sampson, a master mason known to have worked for Wykeham and referred to in documents as skilled in the art of stone carving. Mary stands holding Christ with her left arm. She wears a gown draped from her right shoulder, with ample folds down to her protruding right foot, and a crown, symbol of the Queen of Heaven. Her right hand holds a lily, indicating her virginity at the time of Christ's conception. She has a faint smile. Christ is also smiling, bubbling with life. He holds a bird, presumably a goldfinch, which likes thorns, alluding to his future crucifixion. The statue, of beer stone, is unquestionably original. Both statue and niche were once painted, and traces of colour were found during a restoration in 1956 when the statue was coated with a protective limewash.

Why did William of Wykeham choose Mary as patron of the College? He was not alone. The cult of Mary grew steadily after the Council of Ephesus (431) proclaimed her 'Theotokos', the Mother of God. By early in the second millennium she was by far the most popular saint. From 1066 to 1260, 44 per cent of all English parish churches were dedicated to her, and all twelfth-century Cistercian monasteries, far more than any other saint. As St Bernard explained: 'She is placed in the middle, between God and us, to facilitate our communion with God'. Thomas Aquinas acknowledged that as Mother of God she should be accorded a special degree of veneration. By 1250 she had prominence in the English liturgy. The catastrophic plagues of the fourteenth century further increased her attraction as chief intercessor. So Wykeham picked the top saint.

Early medieval statues of the Virgin and Child normally show a stern Mary, sitting four-square, holding a rather grown-up Christ on her knee. This form is known as the *Sedes Sapientiae*. Around 1170 the style changed, as the Virgin became more human and Christ more child-like. The statue at Winchester shows the influence of French sculpture, and it may be compared with a similar wooden Madonna and Child made in Paris in the mid-fourteenth century. By this time images of the Virgin were prolific throughout Europe. She had become, in Petrarch's words, 'the beautiful Virgin', the name given to Madonnas such as ours.

Nicholas Ferguson (C, 1961–66, Fellow)

Jesse Window, College Chapel, 1393–94

Stained glass with added paint (430 × 320 cm)

The windows of Chapel were the most important works of art William of Wykeham commissioned for the College. They were made by the workshop of Thomas of Oxford, and Wykeham's household accounts for the year 1393 show that 19 shillings and 3 pence was paid for two 'chariots' to carry the glass to Winchester. The painting of the glass probably followed the designs of a German artist referred to as Herebright of Cologne, one of the many craftsmen employed by Wykeham on his various projects. Most of the windows now in Chapel are nineteenth-century copies; they faithfully replicate the medieval designs, which include the Tree of Jesse in the east window. This depicts the recumbent figure of Jesse, father of King David, with a genealogical diagram of Christ's ancestors including David and Solomon above him. Below Jesse are the small figures of the craftsmen who built the College, among them the glazier.

The windows were replaced because over the centuries a thin film or incrustation had developed on the surface of the fourteenth-century glass. In the 1820s the College sent the east and side windows to the glaziers Betton and Evans in Shrewsbury for restoration. An eyewitness who saw them said they were 'so greatly decayed as to have [become] nearly opaque'. The idea of restoration seems to have been abandoned and copies were made instead. The colours of the nineteenth-century version are not authentic; Sir William Hayter, former Warden of New College, described how in the Jesse window 'the soft olive-green has become a harsh emerald, the rose-pink and aubergine have turned to puce and magenta'.

Betton and Evans disposed of the original glass and for many years its whereabouts was unknown, although about a third has now been located. The largest fragment was found in a private chapel in Ettington Park in Warwickshire, and in 1949 this was purchased for the College by the art historian and Old Wykehamist, Sir Kenneth Clark. After successful restoration it was installed in Chapel in the west window of Thurburn's Chantry, which had formerly featured some nineteenth-century memorial panels described in 1914 as 'work of a bad modern period, and not good examples of it'. Some of the most significant figures from the original east window are now here: William of Wykeham with the Virgin and Child, and King Richard II with John the Baptist. Seven more figures from the original Jesse window are nearby, in Fromond's Chantry.

Kenneth Clark presented the glass anonymously in memory of his former Headmaster, Monty Rendall, whose lectures on the art of Italy had ignited Clark's interest. He later wrote: 'I can never describe what those lectures meant to me. I had been brought up on the realistic art of a godless bourgeoisie … it was for me like a religious conversion'. The memory of Clark is very much alive in the school today, with a society in his name and an annual competition in which boys share their knowledge and enthusiasm for a work of art that has impressed them.

Suzanne Ceiriog-Hughes (Art History)

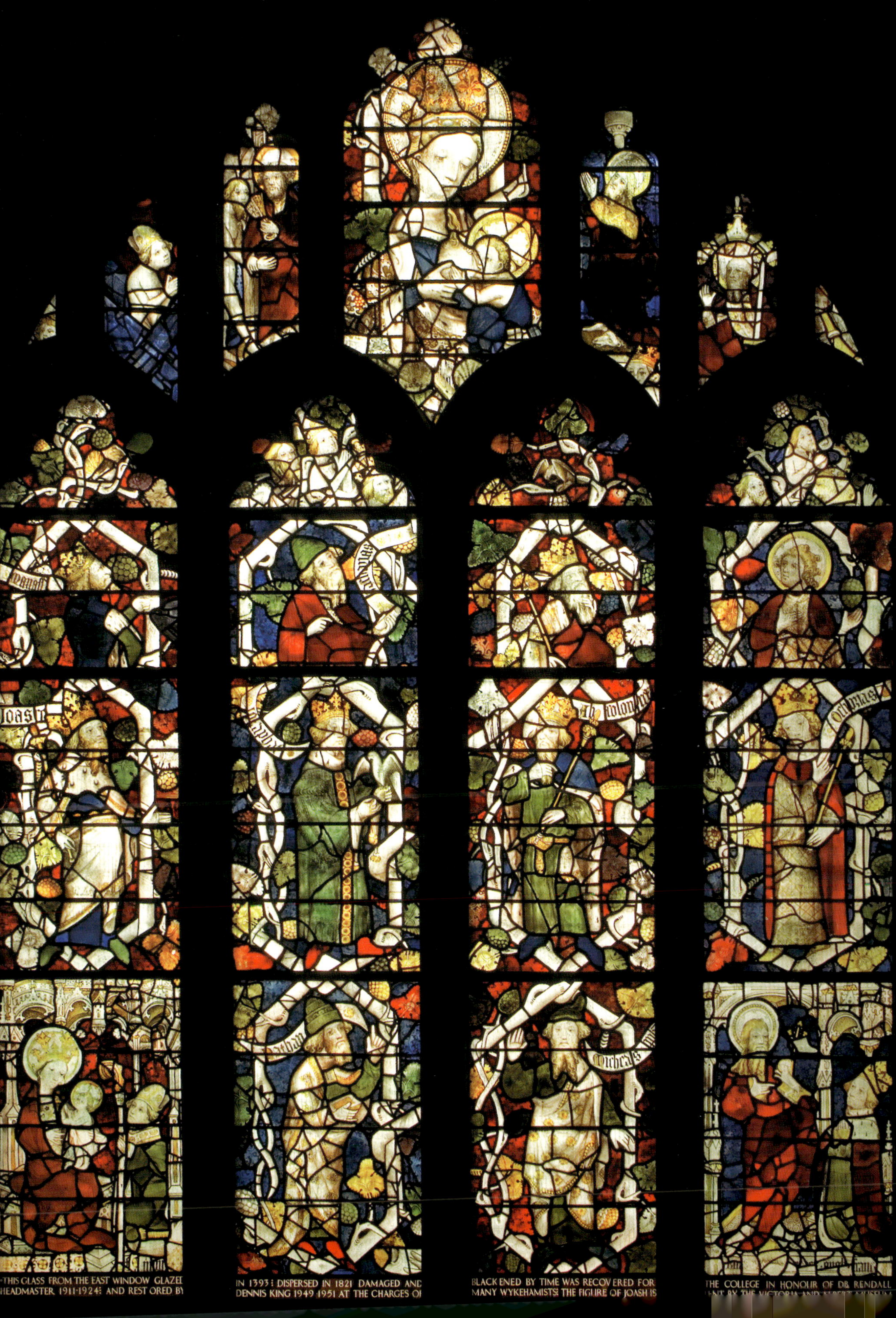
THIS GLASS FROM THE EAST WINDOW GLAZED IN 1393: DISPERSED IN 1821 DAMAGED AND BLACKENED BY TIME WAS RECOVERED FOR THE COLLEGE IN HONOUR OF DR RENDALL
HEADMASTER 1911-1924: AND RESTORED BY DENNIS KING 1949-1951 AT THE CHARGES OF MANY WYKEHAMISTS: THE FIGURE OF JOASH IS LENT BY THE VICTORIA AND ALBERT MUSEUM

In nomine sancte ac indiuidue trinitatis patris & filij & spiritus sancti necnon be-
atissime marie virginis gloriose omnium q[ue] sanctorum dei. Nos Willelmus de Wykeham
p[er]missione diuina Wyntonien[sis] Ep[iscopu]s de summa rerum opifi[c]is bonitate confisi in vo-
ta auictorum in eo fidencium cognosc[er]e dirigit & disponit de bonis fortune que nobis
in hac vita de sue plenitudinis gra[ci]a tribuit habundanter duo p[er]petua Collegia
ꝙ[uorum] videlicet Collegium p[er]petuum pauperum & indigenaum scolarium clericorum
in studio vniuersitatis Oxonie lincolnien[sis] dioc[esis] in diuersis sciencijs & facultatib[us] studere ac p[ro]ficere debencium Seinte marie College of Wynchestre in Oxenford vul-
gariter nuncupatum et quoddam aliud Collegium p[er]petuum aliorum pauperum & indigenaum scolarium clericorum gramaticam addissere debencium p[ro]pe Ciuitatem
Wyntonie Seinte marie College of Wynchestre similiter nuncupatum ad laudem
gloriam & honorem nominis crucifixi ac gloriosissime marie matris eius sustentacione
& exaltacionem fidei xpiane ecclie sancte p[re]fentam diuini cultus liberalium q[ue] arcium scienciarum & facultatum augmentum auctoritate [...] regia ordinac[i]o[n]um instituim[us]
fundauimus & stabiliuimus p[ro]ut in certis & literis n[ost]ris patentibus sup[er] ordinacionib[us]
institucionibus ac fundacionibus Collegiorum ip[s]orum confectis plenius continetur. Unde nos p[ro]uidere aliqua que in p[re]sen[tem] n[ost]re occurrunt memorie facere statuere ac eciam ordinare que dicto n[ost]ro Collegio p[ro]pe Ciuitatem Wyntonie scolaribus clericis p[res]-
biteris p[er]petuis & p[er]sonis alijs ac possessionibus & bonis eiusdem Collegij necnon cali-
bri regimini eorundem necessaria & vtilia reputamus et que doctrinam incrementum
et p[ro]fectum ip[s]orum respicere dinoscuntur xpi nomine primitus inuocato ad futuram & p[er]petuam
rei memoriam ad ea p[ro]uidimus in hunc modum In primis siquidem statu-
imus ordinamus & volumus dictum n[ost]rum Collegium p[ro]pe Ciuitatem Wyntonie in e[o] de numero
vnius Custodis qui omnibus eiusdem Collegij p[er]sonis possessionibus rebus & bonis ip[s]ius sc[un]d[u]m
ordinac[i]ones & statuta n[ost]ra n[is]i astripta p[re]mineat atq[ue] p[re]sit Septuaginta q[ue] pauperum & indi-
genarum scolarium gramaticali sciencie intendere debencium decem presbiterorum sociorum p[er]
p[er]petuorum trium q[ue] capellanorum & trium clericorum conducticiorum & remotiuorum ac sexdecim
puerorum choristarum capelle dicti Collegij in diuinis officijs seruire debencium vnius eciam
magistri informatoris in gramatica ac vnius alterius instructoris sub eo Hostiarij scolariu[m] vul-
gariter nuncupandi circa informacionem instruccionem & erudicionem dictorum scolarium assi-
due & diligenter vacare & intendere debencium conducticiorum & eciam remotiuorum semp[er]
subsistere debere & deo p[ro]pi[ci]o p[er]petuis futuris temporibus p[er]manere Item statuimus ordinamus & volum[us]
ꝙ[uod] in omni electione scolarium futuris temporibus in dictum n[ost]rum Collegium p[ro]pe Wyntoniam
facienda principaliter & ante alios quoscu[m]q[ue] omnes illi qui sunt & erunt de consanguinita-
te n[ost]ra & genere si qui tales sint s[c]ilicet fuerint oriundi seu moram traxerint p[er] vicaria
Spenale p[ro]gen[er]ue absq[ue] difficultate qualibet in dictum Collegium p[ro]pe Ciuitatem Wyntonie
p[ro] eorum sustentacione & doctrina iuxta effectum ordinacionum & statutorum n[ost]rorum in dicto Collegio habendis recipiantur & eciam admittantur ꝙ[uod] q[ue] omnes & singuli in idem Collegium n[ost]rum p[ro]pe Wyntoniam in scolares eligendi sint pauperes indigentes bonis moribus ac con-
dicionibus p[re]diti ad studium habiles & conuersacione honesti in lectura plano cantu & anti-
quo donatu competenter instructi. Vult[us] q[ue] in dictum n[ost]rum Collegium p[ro]pe Wyntoniam ad

The Statutes of Winchester College, 1400

Manuscript on parchment, ff. 26, bound in reversed pigskin over pasteboard with silk ties (40 × 31 cm)

At first sight the Founder's Statutes appear unprepossessing. The pigskin cover is plain and unadorned. But the eye is immediately caught by Wykeham's seal, stitched into the very fabric of the document, as if irrecoverably weaving his authority into what is, by any standards, an extraordinarily detailed set of instructions determining how the College must be run.

The cover is deceptive. Once open, it reveals a table of contents which is both exquisite and pragmatic. The text is beautifully justified, with the ruled margins visible on each page. There is red lettering for every statute, together with a number in red in the margin – a wholly practical way to make instant reference to any detail. Although the College was founded in 1382 and began to educate pupils from 1394, the earliest versions of the statutes have not survived. These final statutes of 1400 are fascinating because they incorporate additions which reflect the medieval realities of running a school, whether these concern the forbidding of wrestling in College Hall, urination in the upstairs chambers or the physical appearance of female servants. This copy is intended to be definitive, and what changes there are remain small and may be detected by the slight roughening of the texture of the parchment where a scribe has scratched out a section of text. The most significant of these comes early on, where the words '*apostolica est*', referring to the ultimate authority of the pope, have been removed, almost certainly under the direction of Henry VIII in 1535.

The England of 1400 was a theocracy in which religion was not merely woven into the civil government of the state, but was an extension and manifestation of it. But this was also a fragile, unpredictable world and the statutes make provision for the sudden deaths of boys, catastrophic harvests, economic downturns and conspiracies. While one cannot but be struck by the sheer strength of will stamped on every one of the statutes, the detailed safeguarding against false accounting, forged proclamations and the like vividly demonstrates Wykeham's administrative genius. They are set out in such a way as to leave no possible room for doubt, misconstruction or chance. Wykeham is careful to stress the College's autonomy, referring to it as 'Our College of Mary near Winchester', so lying outside the jurisdiction of the city. At times the statutes are so preoccupied with process that the charitable purpose appears momentarily lost. But if there is something almost suffocating about the degree of control, it is interesting to note how much is

left to the discretion of the Warden, and the admonition he makes to the older Scholars to exercise a sense of responsibility towards their younger peers is an extraordinarily far-sighted principle which is very much at the heart of our pastoral care of pupils today.

At times Wykeham's iron grip relaxes, albeit reluctantly. While the statutes close with an admonition to future Wardens that no details must ever be changed, Wykeham reveals that his hopes are greater than his expectations. He declares that he knows of no foundation which has not strayed from its founder's original intentions. This is partly a challenge to future generations not to follow the norm, but as a man of the world, Wykeham could not have expected that his foundation would be any different. And notwithstanding this, he recognises that he has a choice: to leave his wealth to those he terms 'improvident', or to make a leap of faith and establish his colleges for posterity. We can only be grateful that he chose the latter course.

Nicholas Wilks (Second Master)

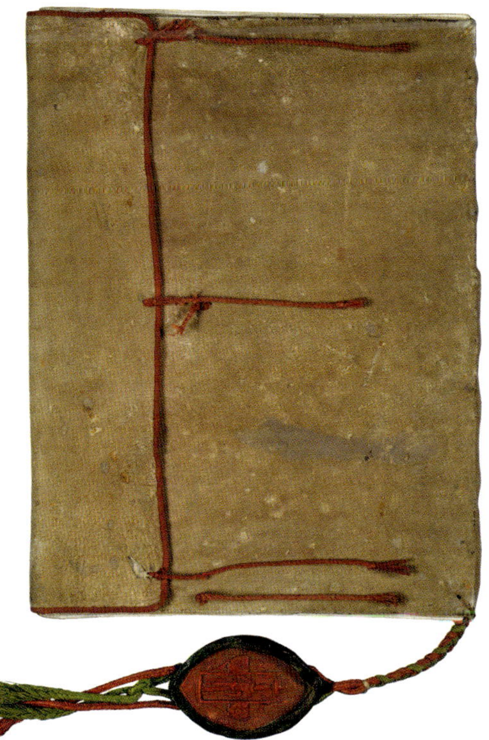

Agincourt Account Roll, 1416

Manuscript on parchment (4500 × 28 cm)

'Agincourt?' the company gathered in Hall exclaims, 'where on earth's that?' It is November 1415 and John Coudray, son of Edward Coudray, esquire of the Bishop of Winchester, has brought news to the College of the king's famous victory. A payment to him is recorded in the Bursars' annual accounts, and so one of the earliest known references to this famous battle appears in the College Archives.

The extraordinary detail of Winchester's medieval accounts is a consequence of the meticulous instructions for the financial management and reporting laid down by William of Wykeham in his statutes. Each Michaelmas two of the Fellows were appointed Bursar and at the end of their term, as today, they were required to present a formal record of the year's income and expenditure for inspection, in those days to Electors from New College. Account rolls survive for every year from 1394 to 1556, when they gave way to account books.

Made of individual parchment sheets stitched together, the rolls are densely packed with descriptions in Latin of every transaction in the year, each listed in chronological order under an appropriate heading. The same headings were used almost without exception from the 1390s to 1865 and reveal much about the life of the foundation and medieval preoccupations. The College's landed estates came first, then matters closer to home where Chapel and Library took first place, followed by kitchen, Hall and pantry; brewery; exchequer (or Bursars' expenses); porters; garden and meadow; Warden's Lodgings; expenses of the house; liveries and clothes; mill and water; legal costs; stipends and portions; foreign expenses; legacies; distributions to the poor; and finally the costs of educating the Founder's kin.

Until 1520 the Steward of Hall, one of the Fellows appointed on a weekly basis, also maintained 'Hall Books'. One long, thin page per week listed the names of those dining in Hall, allowing the Bursars to calculate the daily feeding allowance or 'commons' for those whom the statutes required the foundation to feed: 2 shillings a week for the Warden, 1 shilling a week for each Fellow and 8 pence a week for each Scholar. To this day pupils who are not Scholars are still known as 'Commoners', because they were once distinguished by the fact that they paid for their meals.

These records provide an intimate, although sometimes tantalisingly incomplete, snapshot of the life of the College. John Coudray's visit was recorded in the Account Roll for 1415–16. He was paid 6 shillings and 8 pence, 'for bringing news to the college from overseas of the dukes, counts, barons, knights and other men of France captured by our lord king of England in a certain battle made at Agyncourt on the feasts of St Crispin and St Crispinian in the third year of his reign and conveyed towards England with our said lord king'. It is not clear if Coudray was travelling up from Southampton on his return from France. Or was he perhaps on his way to Wolvesey Palace on an errand for his patron, the bishop, who as chancellor had been in charge in London during the king's absence? And was his father Edward the same man who served on naval expeditions in 1387 and 1388, had property near Basingstoke and was sheriff of Hampshire and Berkshire in the early fifteenth century? We may never know. But the Bursar was able to answer one of the company's questions. Next to the word 'Agyncourt', he added above the line, '*in Picardia*'.

Steven Little (Bursar)

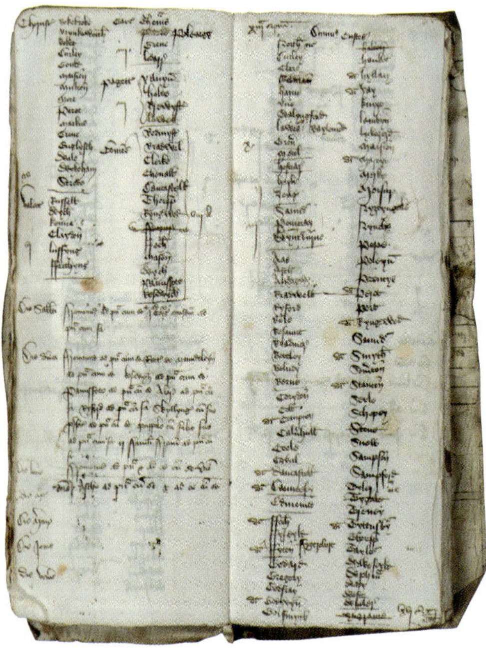

Hall Book for 1415–16, manuscript on paper.

[illegible] [illegible] collect[illegible] [illegible] [illegible] [illegible]
de Rippon q[uod] [illegible] conduc[tus] colleg[io] [illegible] cuj[us] [illegible] et [illegible] [illegible] et [illegible] [illegible]
+ [illegible] h[ab]e[t] d[e] xx d. ob[olum] [illegible] xij d. [illegible] [illegible] s[i] [illegible] [illegible] cuj[us] et [illegible] f[ec]o [illegible]

ix d. vij d.   Sm[a]   x d. vij d.

Rep[er]iss[e] [illegible] d[i]c[t]o [illegible] d[i]c[t]e [illegible] ord[i]n[ar]y filio Coll[egii] [illegible] [illegible] [illegible] d[i]c[t]e [illegible] d[i]g[nitat]e [illegible] nove [illegible] de colleg[io] de [illegible]
de d[i]uers[is] [illegible] [illegible] ant[iquit]a[tibus] et ad [illegible] de [illegible] [illegible] p[ro] [illegible] [illegible] in anno [Regn]i Anglie in quod[am] [illegible] f[ac]to apud
[illegible] in f[est]o [illegible] [illegible] et [illegible] d[e] [illegible] [illegible] [illegible] et [illegible] in Anglia [illegible] [illegible] [Reg]e d[i]c[t]o q[uod] d[e] [illegible]
f[illegible] [illegible] [illegible] [illegible] et [illegible] [illegible] [illegible] q[uod] bono [illegible] consilio [illegible] in [illegible] [illegible] [illegible] [illegible] de [illegible]
[illegible] [illegible] d[e] [illegible] d[i]c[t]o [illegible] [illegible] [illegible] de [illegible] q[uod] d[i]c[t]o [illegible] [illegible] in n[ov]o colleg[io] xx d. [illegible] [illegible] [illegible] [illegible]
[illegible] [illegible] et [illegible] eod[em] [illegible] [illegible] p[ro] [illegible] [illegible] x [illegible] [illegible] [illegible] [Reg]e [illegible] [illegible] [illegible]
[illegible] de [illegible] et alium [illegible] [illegible] de [illegible] [illegible] [illegible] et [illegible] [illegible]
[illegible] ad conduc[endum] [illegible] [illegible] xl d[e] [illegible] [illegible] [illegible] xxxv[iij] s. [illegible] [illegible] [illegible] [illegible] [illegible] [illegible] [illegible]
et [illegible] [illegible] de [illegible] [illegible] [illegible] [illegible] p[ro] [illegible] [illegible] [illegible] [illegible] [illegible] [illegible] [illegible] [illegible] [illegible] colleg[io]
de [illegible] [illegible] [illegible] [illegible] [illegible] conuen[tus] [illegible] h[ab]e[t] d[e] [illegible] [illegible] [illegible] et [illegible] [illegible] [illegible] [illegible] [illegible] [illegible]
de [illegible] in d[i]uer[sis] [illegible] [illegible] [illegible] d[i]uers[is] de [illegible] [illegible] et [illegible] in [illegible] [illegible] [illegible] [illegible] [illegible]
d[i]c[t]o [illegible] in [illegible] [illegible] de [illegible] [illegible] [illegible] [illegible] [illegible] d[i]c[t]o [illegible] [illegible] [illegible] [illegible] [illegible] [illegible]

[illegible] [illegible] [illegible] et [illegible] [illegible] [illegible] [illegible] [illegible] [illegible] [illegible] [illegible] [illegible] [illegible] [illegible] [illegible]
[illegible] [illegible] et [illegible] de [illegible] [illegible] [illegible] q[uod] [illegible] [illegible] [illegible] [illegible] [illegible] [illegible] [illegible] [illegible] [illegible]
xx d[e] [illegible] [illegible] [illegible] p[er]tit[illegible] [illegible] et [illegible] [illegible] et [illegible] [illegible] [illegible] [illegible] colleg[io] [illegible] in [illegible] p[ro] [illegible] vij d. [illegible]
[illegible] et [illegible] [illegible] [illegible] colleg[io] [illegible] ad [illegible] [illegible] [illegible] colleg[ii] [illegible] [illegible] nove [illegible] [illegible] [illegible] [illegible] [illegible] [illegible]
et [illegible] in alio [illegible] colleg[ii] f[ac]to [illegible] [illegible] [illegible] [illegible] vij d. [illegible] [illegible] [illegible] p[ro] [illegible] [illegible] [illegible] [illegible]
[illegible] d[e] [illegible] d[i]c[t]o [illegible] [illegible] et bona [illegible] [illegible] consilio de colleg[io] xxvij de [illegible] anno [illegible] [illegible] [illegible] [illegible] ad
colleg[io] [illegible] et de [illegible] et [illegible] [illegible] [illegible] [illegible] [illegible] [illegible] [illegible] [illegible] [illegible] et [illegible] d[e] [illegible] [illegible] [illegible] [illegible]
[illegible] [illegible] de [illegible] [illegible] d[e] vij d. [illegible] q[uod] d[i]c[t]o [illegible] [illegible] [illegible] [illegible] [illegible] et [illegible] [illegible] d[e] [illegible] q[uod] [illegible]
de [illegible] [illegible] et [illegible] [illegible] et [illegible] [illegible] et [illegible] q[uod] [illegible] [illegible] [illegible] [illegible] [illegible] [illegible] [illegible]
[illegible] [illegible] [illegible] [illegible] [illegible] [illegible] [illegible] [illegible] [illegible] [illegible] [illegible] [illegible]

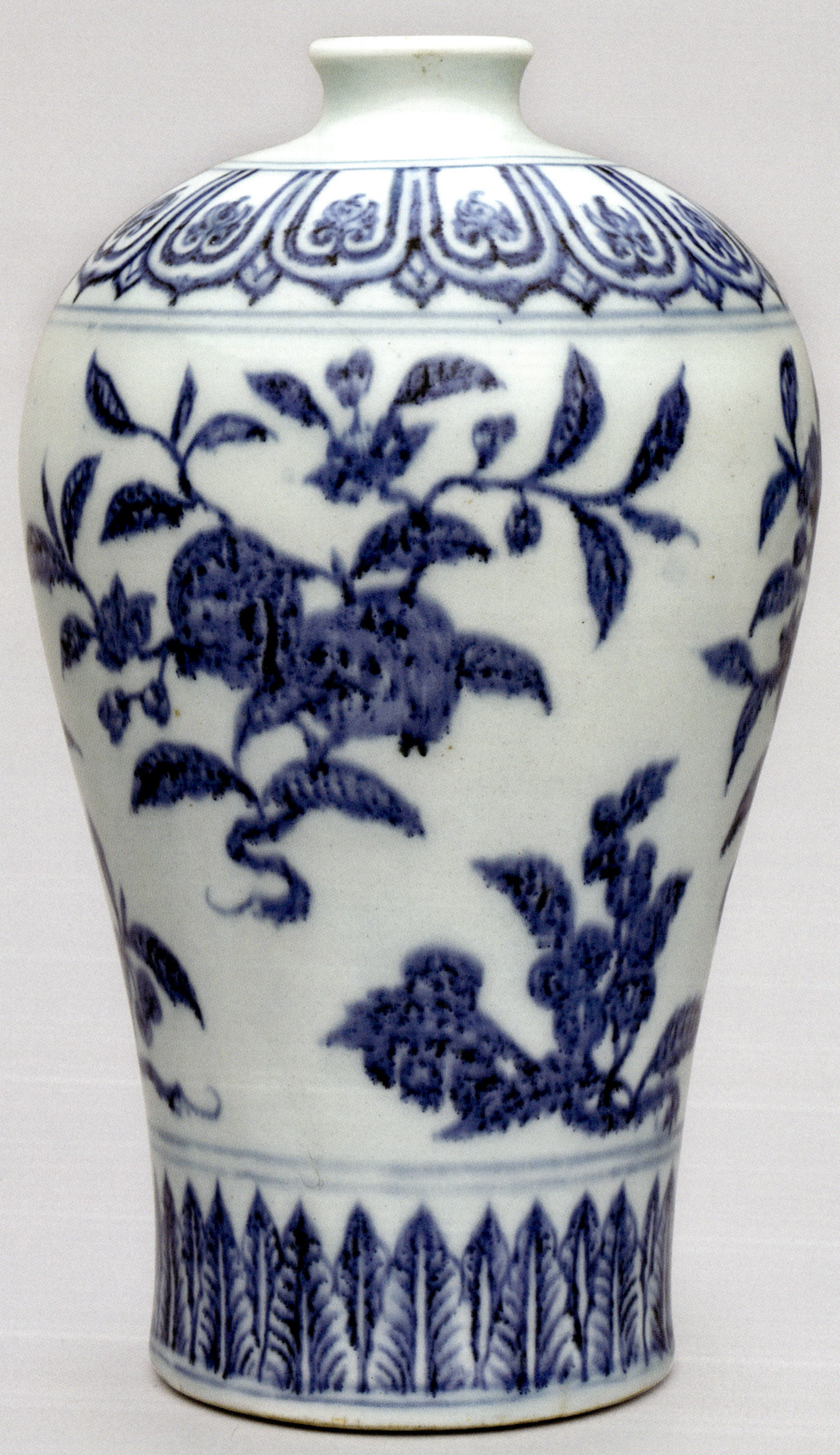

Ming Dynasty Meiping, early 15th century

Porcelain with underglaze blue decoration (H. 24.7 cm)

While 'blue and white' is the generic term used in the West, the Chinese refer to it as 'blue flowers' (青花瓷 *qing hua ci*). This family of ceramics exhibits a dazzling array of shapes and sizes, with blue floral and plant patterns painted on white backgrounds. The Winchester meiping is a definitive example of these objects of beauty. It was made during the reign of the Yongle Emperor (1403–24), early in the Ming Dynasty, when the process of preparing clay for making ceramics became thoroughly refined. The soft white hue of the porcelain is the result of a multi-ingredient clay recipe, strict and strenuous purification requirements, and a rigorous kneading technique. At this date the blue pigment would have been made with cobalt imported from Central Asia; only later in the Ming Dynasty did potters begin to use local sources of blue.

Vessels with this distinctive shape first appeared in the Tang Dynasty (618–907). The meiping is often said to have been inspired by the form of the female body. It was originally designed as a wine vessel, but in later periods its narrow neck, curvaceous silhouette and blue floral decoration made it ideal for arranging the slender and sophisticated cuts of plum blossoms. Meiping means 'plum vase'. The plum (*Prunus mume*) is a flowering tree native to southern China. It starts to flower in December, displaying elegant shades of white, pink and red. Much admired throughout history for flourishing in the depth of winter and as a harbinger of spring, it is a symbol of the unconquerable, self-assured and noble: all desirable qualities of a civilised person. The plum, pine tree and bamboo are affectionately known as the Three Friends of Winter.

Our meiping is decorated in four bands: the neck, shoulders, body and base, each separated from the other by two delicate framing lines of blue. Apart from the glaze the neck is left unadorned, giving it the warm and pure look of jade – simple yet effective in setting off the plum cuts. Under the jade-like neck is the shoulder panel, shawled with a repeating border of lotus lappets, emblematic of harmony, tranquillity and virtue. In Chinese the word for lotus is homophonic with the word for harmony, and this plant produces the most serenely beautiful flowers and leaves. Around the body are branches of peach, persimmon, pomegranate and lychee. Respectively, they are symbolic of life to be long lived, of wishes fulfilled, of families with lots of children as heirs, and of pursuit of academic excellence. This meiping demonstrates that nothing is accidental in classical Chinese art.

The jade-finish neck, lotus-covered shoulders and floral body rest on a round, unpretentious base surrounded by a band of continuous and repeating *Musa basjoo* leaves. The basjoo motif first appeared in the Shang Dynasty (1559–1046 BC) and has been passed down through the generations as a decorative pattern. However, its emblematic significance is uncertain. The leaves, particularly when raindrops are hanging on them, are often considered to be synonymous with melancholy, which is incompatible with the auspicious theme of this meiping. It is more likely that the large leaves of the basjoo are present in order to evoke the idea of very broad and continuous protection and blessing.

Let us hope that the meiping, with its hidden message of good wishes and overt celebration of beauty, will lend continuous joy and happiness to viewers and beholders for generations to come.

Chun Cai (Chinese)

Cast of Donatello's *David*, 1440s

Painted plaster cast, late 19th or early 20th century, of bronze original (H. 130 cm)

Donatello's *David* was the first free-standing life-size nude of the Renaissance, reviving the classical theme of the victorious athlete. Having defeated Goliath, David stands in the contrapposto pose, his weight on his right foot with the left resting forward on the severed head of the giant. In his left hand he holds his rock and sling, and in his right is Goliath's sword. Winchester's copy is a late nineteenth- or early twentieth-century plaster cast, painted to appear bronze. There are some differences in detail between the original and this version, notably the addition of a fig leaf, but it is a remarkable object in its own right.

Despite the subject-matter, this is a quiet, reflective work. David's head (which may have been modelled on portraits of Antinous, favourite companion of the emperor Hadrian) is slightly tilted, suggesting a point of momentary contemplation. The sculpture is a tender representation of the protagonist, youthful and fragile, at odds with the surrounding scene. Unlike other more athletic interpretations of David, there is here a subtle feeling of tension within the delicately defined muscles, resting beneath soft lifelike flesh. The fluid rendering of surface is balanced against the pronounced angles of the counterpoise: the twist of the hips, upper torso and limbs. These natural forms are framed within the harder lines of David's hat, moving down through Goliath's sword to the feathered helmet on Goliath's head.

Winchester's *David* was almost certainly purchased for the school by Monty Rendall around 1900. Rendall had joined the staff in 1887, becoming Second Master in 1899, and Headmaster from 1911 to 1924. He took a close interest in the development of the school's first museum, which opened in 1897, and was committed to promoting the arts throughout the community. He had been fascinated by the Italian Renaissance since his youth and regularly lectured to pupils on the subject. One notable beneficiary of Rendall's enthusiasm was Kenneth Clark, a pupil from 1917 to 1922. Clark was also encouraged by the art master, Alexander MacDonald, who set him to draw the casts in the school museum. In his autobiography Clark recalled drawing *David*, as well as copies of Luca della Robbia's *Cantoria* and the Dancing Faun from Pompeii, 'dozens of times from every angle'. The level of scrutiny and analysis required for this process developed a training that would become invaluable to Clark in his career as an art historian.

Today, Wykehamists are privileged to enjoy the same close access to this sculpture through the act of drawing that Clark found so important. For the student draughtsman the articulation of David's pose offers a way into the process, with reference points and angles to be measured. However, so subtle are the shifts and undulations of the form in places that one can easily become immersed in a response to the many gentle tonal transitions across the surface. Here we must remember that the whole is greater than the sum of its parts. Regardless of outcome, the process of studying such an accomplished work offers invaluable insights, and a glimpse of the world through the eyes of its creator.

Michael Bruzon (Head of Art)

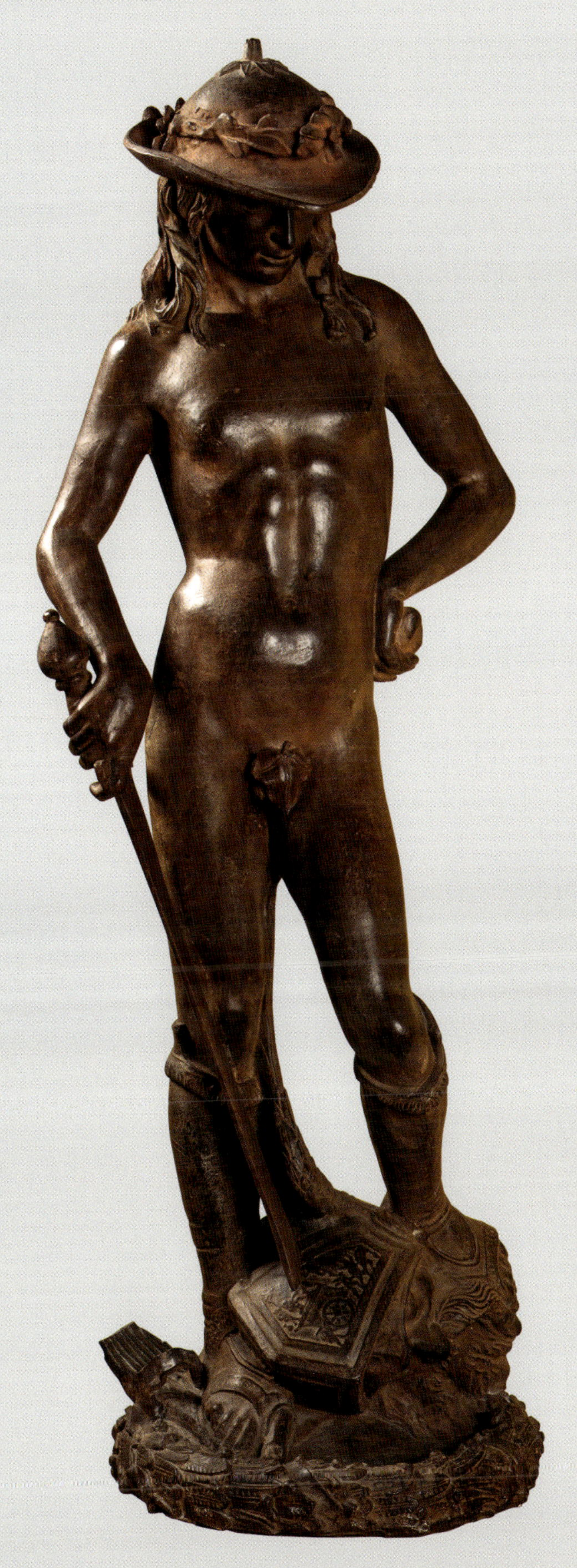

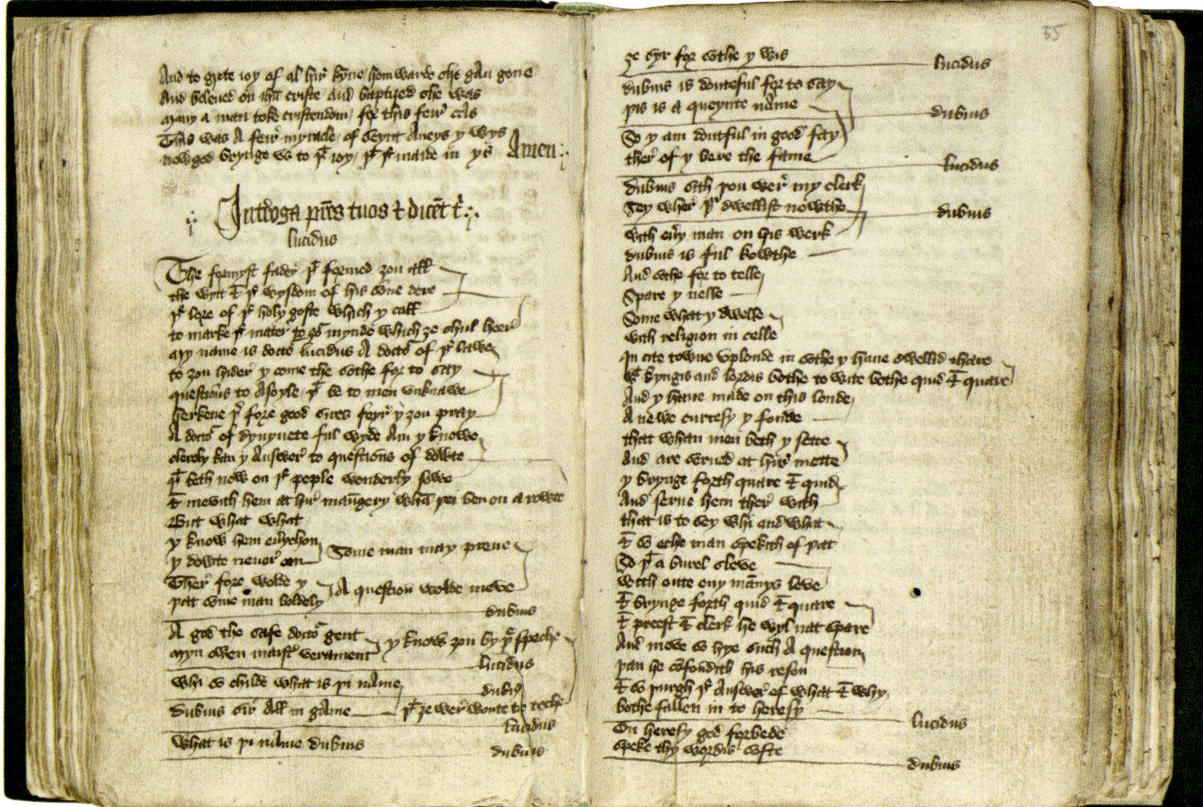

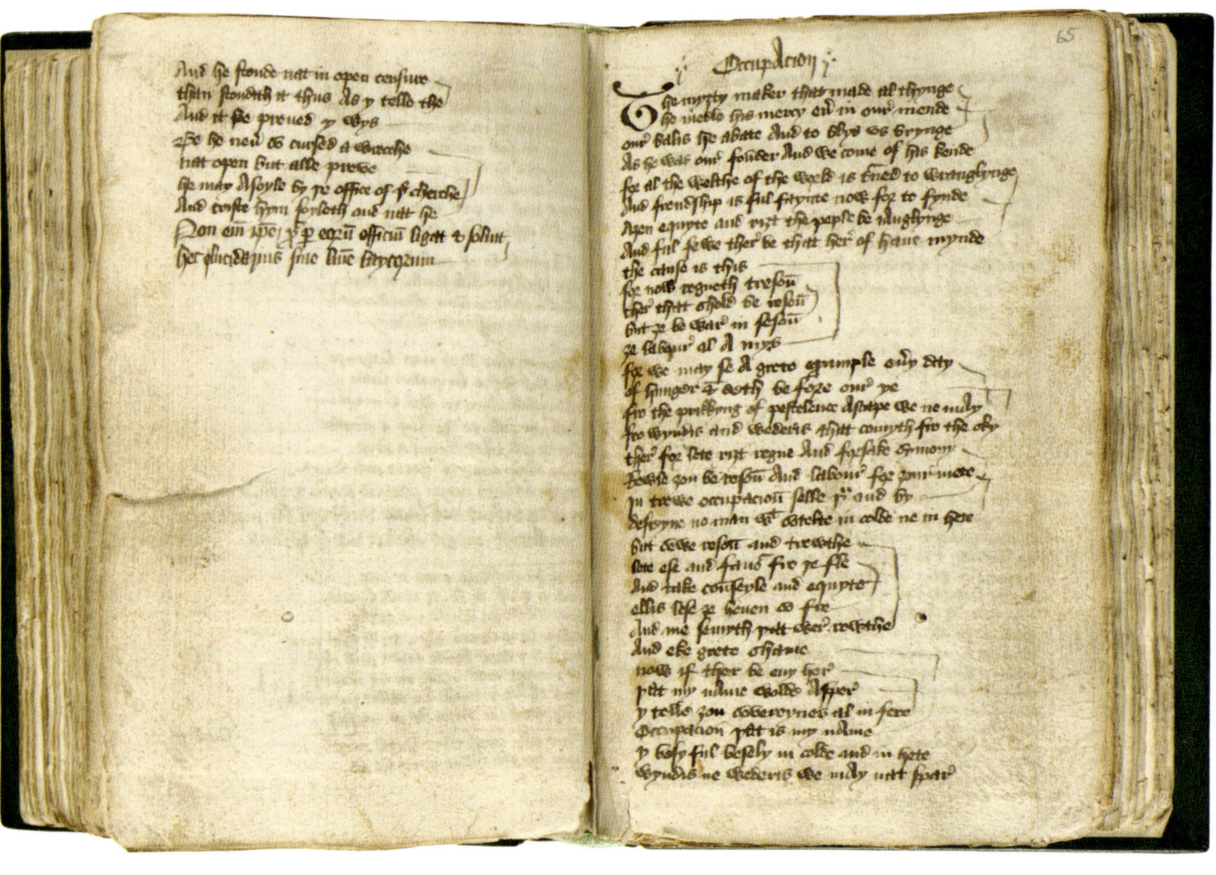

The Winchester Dialogues, 15th century

MS 33: Manuscript on paper with six works in Middle English, ff. 122, bound in 20th-century green morocco over pasteboard
by Richard Harsher (20.7 × 14.2 cm)

Drama has a long and distinguished history in England, in Winchester and indeed at Winchester College. The earliest medieval drama grew out of the liturgy of the major feasts of Christmas and Easter. It was initially performed (or perhaps chanted, in Latin) in the chancel by the clergy, but performances soon moved away from church buildings. By the end of the fifteenth century, many professional and amateur theatrical troupes (often connected with guilds) had been established. These troupes would perform in their own and neighbouring towns. A reference to such a performance at the College can be found in the Bursars' accounts of 1398–99 when payment was made *lusoribus civitatis Wynton* ('to players of the city of Winchester'). Another such group performed four interludes at Epiphany in 1466, for which they were paid 2 shillings. John Pontisbery and his companion were paid the same sum in 1467, *ludentibus in aula in die circumcisionis,* (for playing in the hall at the Feast of the Circumcision). This is presumably a reference to College Hall, the scene of a great many dramatic productions.

Traditional religious drama remained popular until its gradual suppression in the Elizabethan period. The term 'religious drama' covers a variety of different sorts of plays: some retold a biblical story or the life of a saint; others dealt with miracles or (through allegory) moral themes. Of those English morality plays written before 1500, nine remain. Two of these survive only in a mid-fifteenth-century manuscript in the school's collection.

The first text, *Lucidus and Dubius,* is more of a dramatic dialogue than a play. It reads like a sermon in question-and-answer form (with Dubius asking such questions as 'how longe was Lucifer in heven?' and 'was Crist leyde in his tombe al naked?') and contains very little of the sort of conflict that is the main ingredient of the dramatic genre in later centuries. This is unsurprising as it is in fact an adaptation of the *Elucidarium*, a late eleventh-century Latin theological dialogue between a pupil and his teacher. *Occupation and Idleness,* on the other hand, is recognisably a play; indeed, it seems to be a forerunner of the sort of didactic interlude common in the sixteenth century. It contains action, conflict and a dramatically satisfying conclusion: the witty (and rather fun) character of Idleness rejects the religious teaching of Occupation and Doctrine (whose arrival necessitates the only stage direction in the piece, *tunc venit Doctrina*). Idleness is punished (by being beaten with a birch), repents and converts.

We do not know who wrote these texts, although scholars have suggested an origin in the East Midlands. The manuscript is first recorded in a seventeenth-century catalogue of the Fellows' Library, but it may have been at the College much earlier than that. It is of course tempting to wonder whether the texts were performed for or by pupils at Winchester. Indeed, the subject-matter of *Occupation and Idleness* would seem particularly appropriate for a school setting – is Idleness a schoolboy, perhaps? Such idle speculation, just the sort of thing abhorred by the author of the second dialogue, is ultimately fruitless. We would do better to focus on the great importance of these pieces for our understanding of the all-pervading religiosity of the fifteenth century and of the history of the development of English drama.

Sam Baddeley (Classics, Head of Drama)

Election Cup, late 15th century

Silver-gilt with applied pastes (H. 44 cm)

Election Cup is among the finest examples of English Gothic plate, one of only a handful of late medieval cups comparable in size and richness of decoration. It was presented to Winchester in 1555 by Bishop John White of Lincoln, an Old Wykehamist and formerly Warden of the College. At the time of its presentation it was probably seventy or eighty years old, although there has been considerable disagreement about its date of manufacture. The cup has no hallmarks, and so can be dated only approximately, on the basis of style. The very absence of marks may suggest that it was made before 1478, when an ordinance of the Goldsmith's Company required all plate to be appropriately marked.

The silver-gilt cup stands on a tall stem with domed foot and has a gourd-like bowl and cupola-shaped cover with a hemispherical finial. The foot, bowl and cover are embossed and chased with naturalistic shell, petal or leaf motifs on a matted ground, and the edges are applied with an open cresting of foliage above stamped dentils. An inventory of College plate made in 1565 described it as '1 great standing cuppe with the cover all gylte with stones in the brym of the foote & of the cover commonly called the Election Cuppe'. The foot and cover are set at intervals with 'enamels of divers colours'. There are mounts for thirty-six of these colourful pastes (jewels) but it is clear that some have been pilfered and only seventeen now remain. The finial may originally have been surmounted by a decorative figure.

In presenting the cup to Winchester College, Bishop White wrote that he was 'sendynge thys pore counterfetyd cuppe, which I desire maye remayne as an ymplemente of The electyon herafter'. The exact meaning of this phrase has been debated by scholars of English silver. In the sixteenth century, 'counterfeit' was not always used in its modern sense of a forgery or imitation, but could be simply a synonym for 'wrought'; 'pore' probably referred to the cup being incomplete, damaged or outmoded. White's gift is named after Election, the examination by which new Scholars are selected for the College. The first Election of Scholars took place in 1393 and it continues to this day. How the bishop imagined the cup might be used 'as an implement' in the process is unclear. Should it be used as a chalice to refresh the examiners or as a container from which names could be drawn? These days it stands vigil over the decision-making discussions but retains its air of intrigue.

Ian Fraser (Master in College)

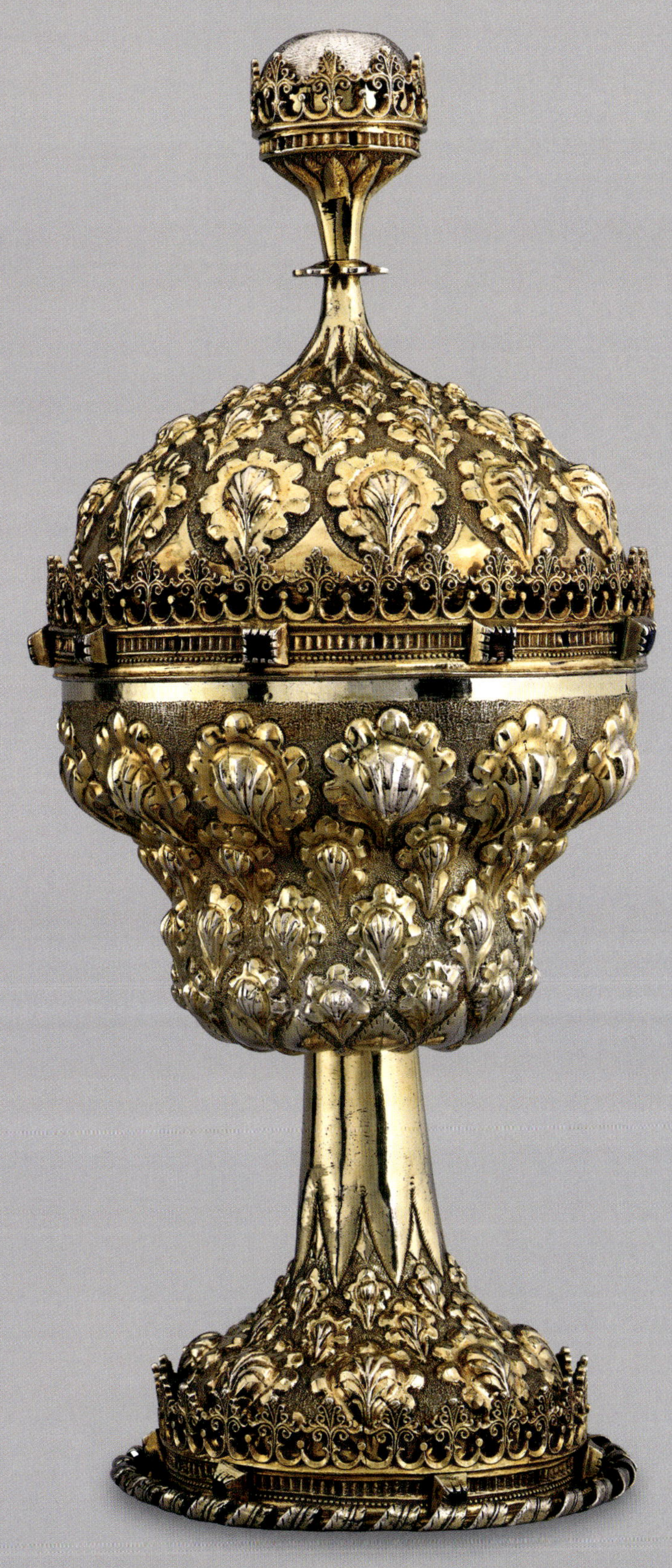

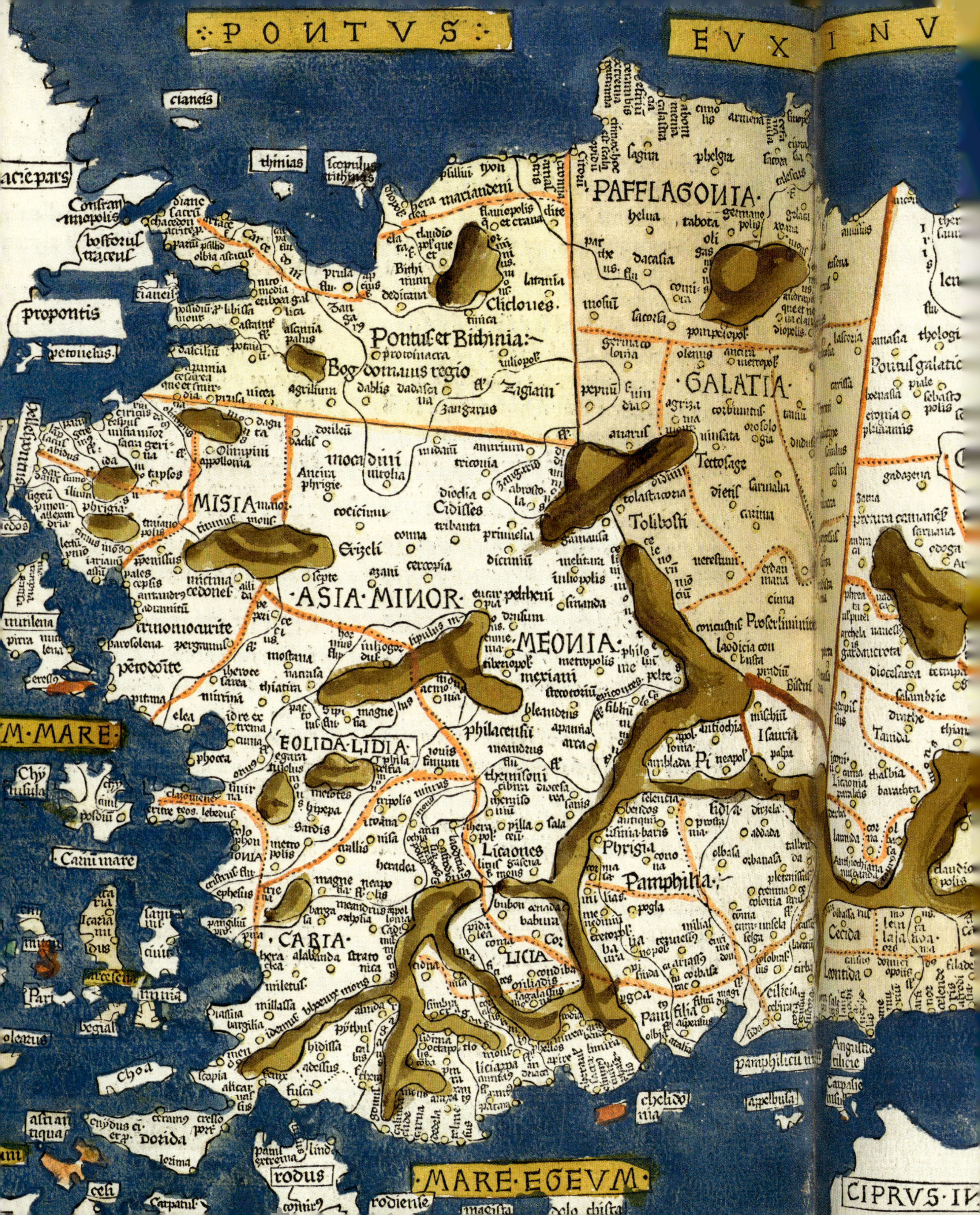

PONTVS EVXINV
MARE EGEVM
M MARE
PAFFLAGONIA
GALATIA
Pontus et Bithinia
Bog domanus regio
ASIA MINOR
MEONIA
MISIA maior
EOLIDA LIDIA
CABIA
LICIA
Phrigia
Pamphilia
Philacensi
Tolisbsi
Tectosage
Constantinopolis
bossorul traceul
propontis
thinias
cianeis
Chyu insula
Carru mare
Pari
Choa
rodus
Ciprvs i
Sardis
ephesus
miletus
phocea

The Ulm Ptolemy, 1482

Claudius Ptolemy, *Geographia* (Ulm, 1482), bound in 18th-century calfskin over pasteboard (42.5 × 28.5 cm)

The most important geographical treatise to survive from antiquity is Ptolemy's *Geography*, written in Greek in Alexandria in the second century AD. It was later translated into Arabic and Latin, but if it had originally been accompanied by maps, these did not survive transmission. One of the main tasks of Ptolemy's Renaissance editors, therefore, was to recreate the necessary maps. In so doing, these scholars used the coordinates provided by Ptolemy's text, but also supplied new projections and even new maps of lands Ptolemy had not known.

One of Winchester College's most splendid books is the 1482 Ulm edition of Ptolemy's *Geography*, a folio of exceptional craftsmanship and expense. Although it is not the *editio princeps* – that had appeared in Vicenza seven years earlier, without maps – the Ulm Ptolemy, printed by Lienhart Holle, was the first world atlas to appear north of the Alps, and included certain post-Ptolemaic maps, such as a map of the Holy Land, and the earliest printed depictions of Iceland and Greenland. Of the many surviving copies (around 120 out of an edition of perhaps just over twice that number), most are hand-coloured, but no two copies are exactly alike in either decoration or cartographic detail.

Like many early printed books, the Ulm Ptolemy was closely modelled on a specific manuscript. Fortunately the very manuscript survives, presenting the Latin translation of the humanist Jacobus Angelus accompanied by the maps of Donnus Nicolaus, a fifteenth-century Italian illuminator. So close are the handwriting of the manuscript and the printed typeface that the latter must have been commissioned to imitate the former. The thirty-two woodcut maps were all again prepared specially for this edition, and their cutter, one Johannes Schnitzer of Armsheim, was proud enough of his world map to sign it. He is also distinctive for the backwards 'N' he used in place-name inscriptions.

Holle was clearly taking a financial gamble and it failed. He overprinted his edition, could not sell sufficient copies and ended up defaulting on the bill for his expensive Milanese paper. He had misjudged his market and the very qualities that render Holle's Ptolemy a masterpiece of its kind also ruined its printer. Within a year or so, Holle's business had vanished.

Winchester College acquired its copy of the Ulm Ptolemy in the sixteenth century from the bequest of William Moryn (d. 1543), an otherwise unremarkable cleric who had been a Scholar of the College in the 1490s. When the College's holdings were catalogued in 1565, almost all its texts in medicine, astronomy and geography came from this one source. Moryn's books included the medical works of Avicenna, a unique philosophical manuscript of Roger Bacon, the astronomical Alfonsine Tables, and two editions of Ptolemy's *Geography*, being this Ulm imprint and the *princeps* of 1475 itself. If we are to seek the origins of the study of the sciences in Winchester College, we must start with Moryn and his books.

William Poole (Fellow)

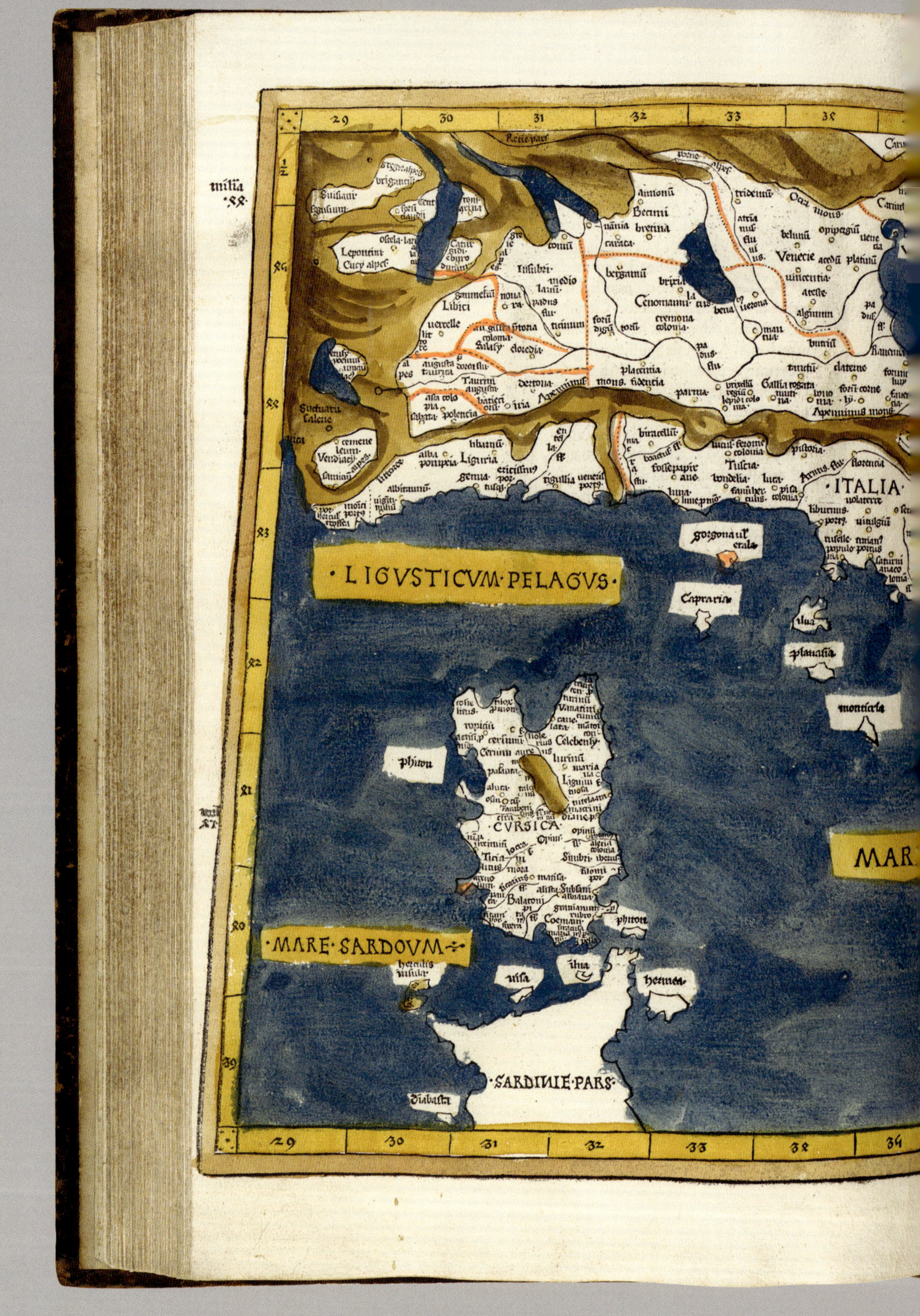

ITALIA
CVRSICA
LIGVSTICVM·PELAGVS
MARE·SARDOVM
SARDINIE·PARS
MAR
Veuecie
Cenomanni
Gallia togata
Apeninus mons
gorgona insula
Capraria
planasia
mouesarla
Phitou
Heraclis insula
uisa
ihia
hennes

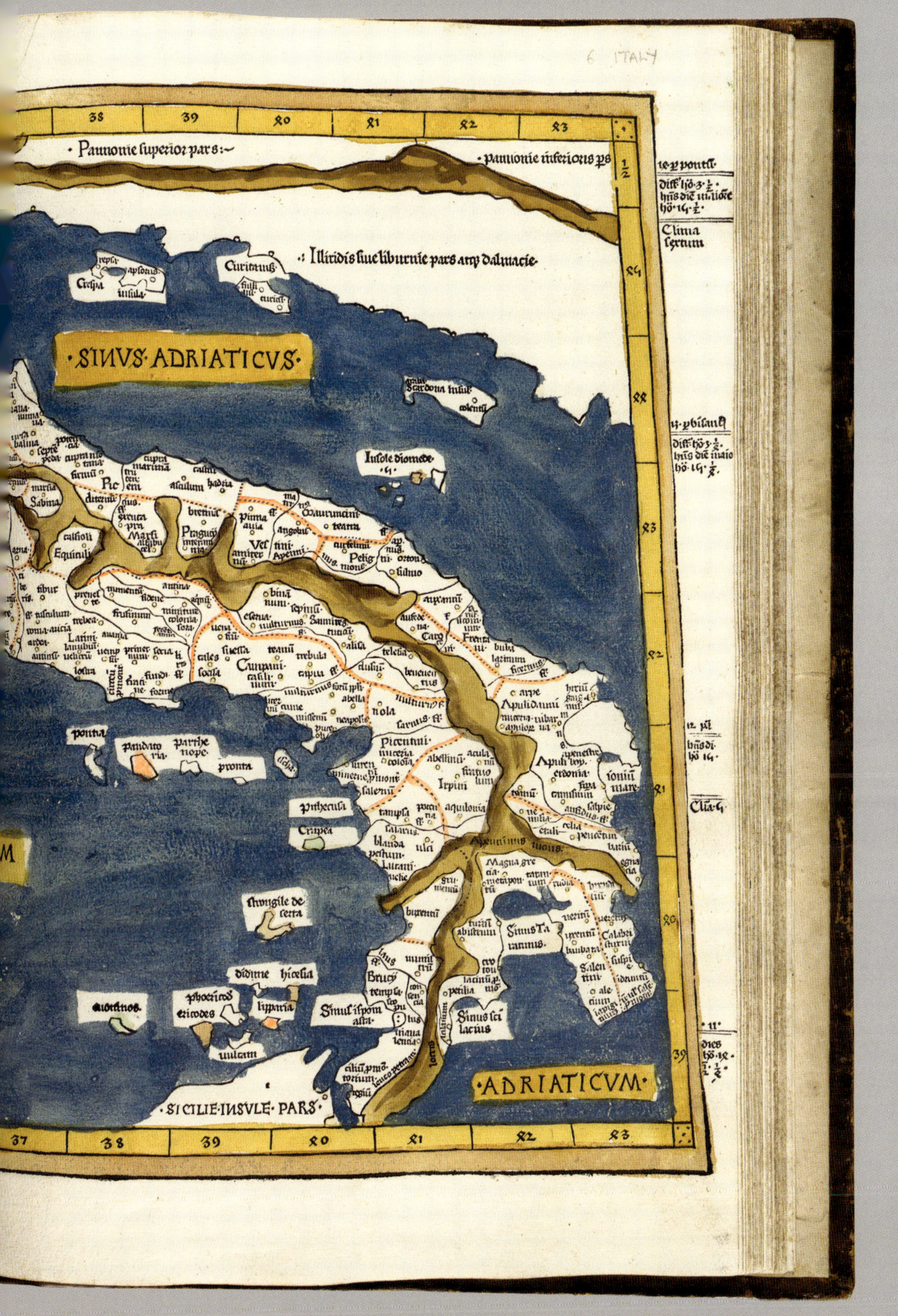
Pannonie superior pars
Pannonie inferioris ps
Illiridis siue liburnie pars atq͛ dalmacie
SINVS ADRIATICVS
Scardona insula
Insole diomede
Curitruis insula
Crexa insula
ADRIATICVM
SICILIE INSVLE PARS
Sinus Tarantinus
Sinus scilacius
Calabri
Brucÿ
Apuli
Campania
Picentini
Irpini
Samnites
Sabina
Picenum
Equiculi
Larini

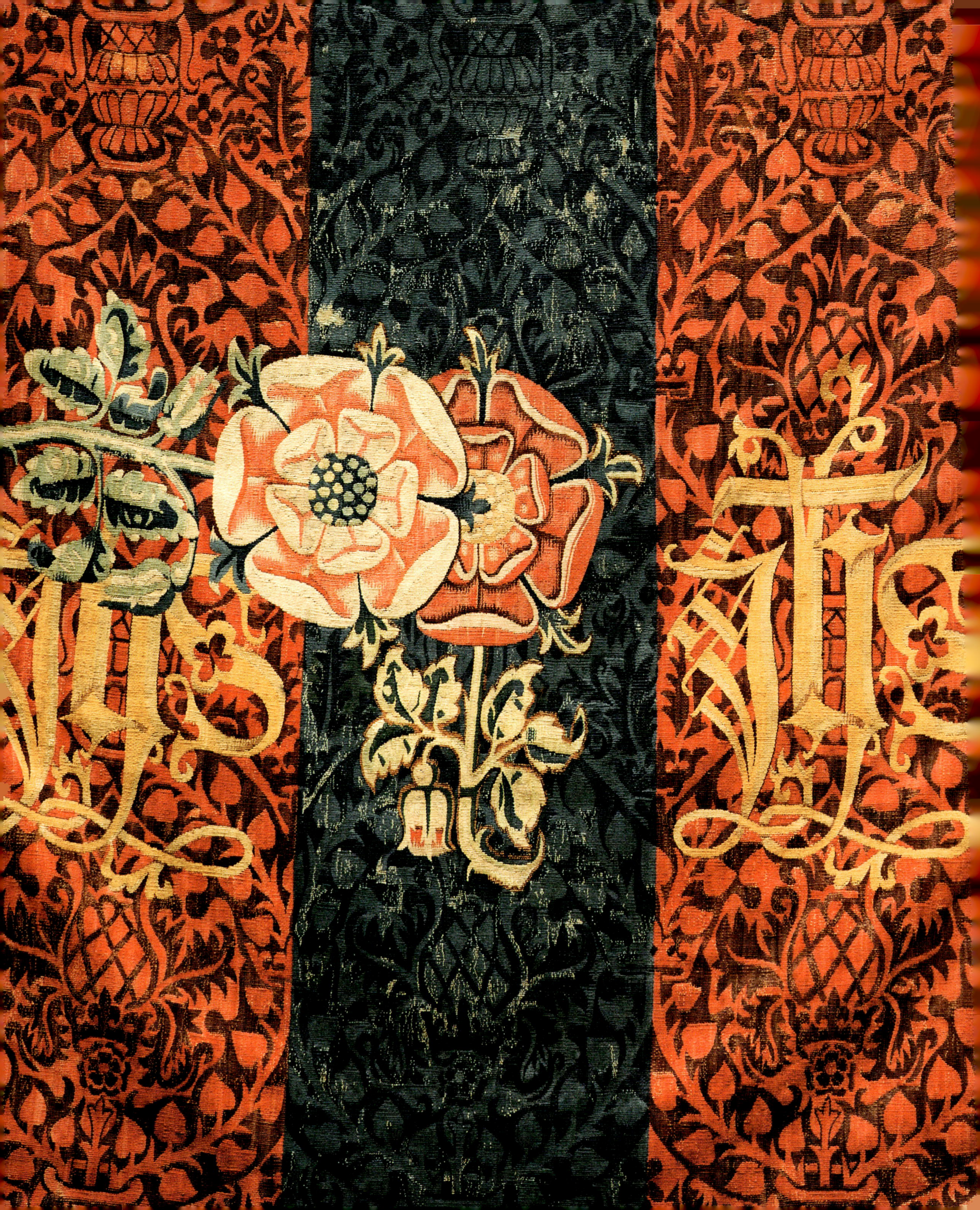

Rose Tapestries, 1480s

Wool and silk (largest 258 × 155 cm; smallest 50.5 × 48 cm)

In its 2017 exhibition, *Relative Values: The Cost of Art in the Northern Renaissance*, the Metropolitan Museum in New York focused upon the ever-interesting question of worth. Perhaps one of the most surprising revelations was how the values of objects had changed, sometimes dramatically, in the centuries since their production. Where a casual twenty-first-century visitor might well have ignored the tapestry of St Veronica in favour of the painting of the Virgin and Child resting on the flight to Egypt, a sixteenth-century connoisseur would have known that the former was far more valuable than the latter – ten times as valuable, according to the calculations of the exhibition's curator. Tapestries, not paintings, were where the really rich put their money in the Early Modern period.

The four Tudor Rose tapestries that have been in the College's possession since the reign of Elizabeth I are probably fragments of a single tapestry dating from the reign of her grandfather, Henry

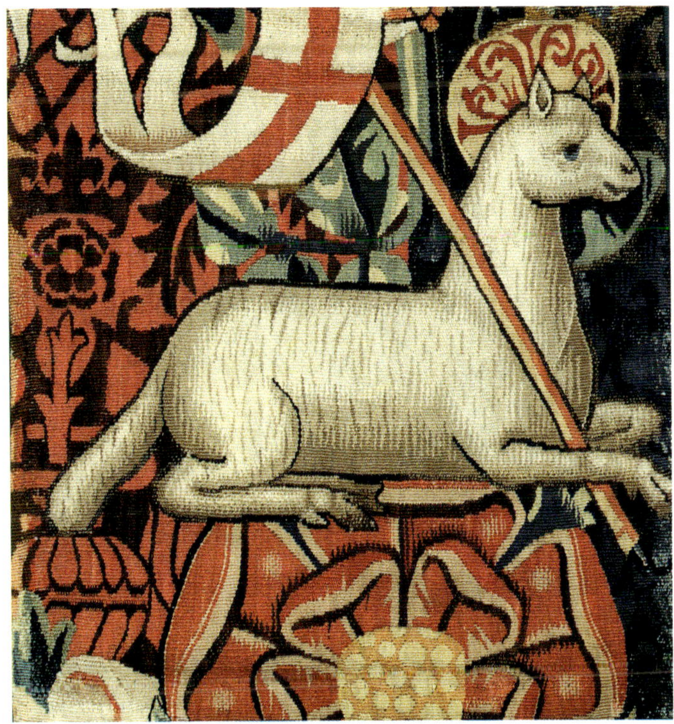

VII. The two large panels, currently on display on the east wall of New Hall, are woven with vertical stripes of blue and red, with a repeating pattern of pomegranates. At the top and bottom are horizontal bands of white roses and the IHS monogram. Overlaying the top devices in the centre stripes of each panel are shields azure with three crowns or in pale. The devices at the bottom of these stripes are superimposed with a red or white rose. The smaller fragments, probably originally forming part of the horizontal pattern, show respectively the Lamb and Flag seated on a red rose and the IHS monogram.

It is clear, from the proliferation of white and red roses that this tapestry was closely linked to Henry VII, the first Tudor king. With his shaky claim to the throne, Henry made much of the fact that his marriage to Elizabeth of York, Edward IV's daughter, brought the Lancastrians and Yorkists together in harmony. The shields with the devices of the three gold crowns were traditionally associated with the legendary King Arthur, namesake of Henry and Elizabeth's oldest son, Prince Arthur. These facts, together with the soteriological imagery of the Lamb and Flag and the IHS monogram, have led to the traditional association of the tapestry with Prince Arthur's baptism in 1486. That this happy event took place in Winchester Cathedral has also been suggested as a reason why the College has them in its possession. However, the art historian Thomas P. Campbell argues that the College's tapestry may be part of a set commissioned for Arthur in the late 1490s. This later dating, and the pomegranate background, suggest a possible link, not with the baptism, but with the betrothal of Arthur to Katherine of Aragon, whose badge the pomegranate was, in 1489.

James Webster (History)

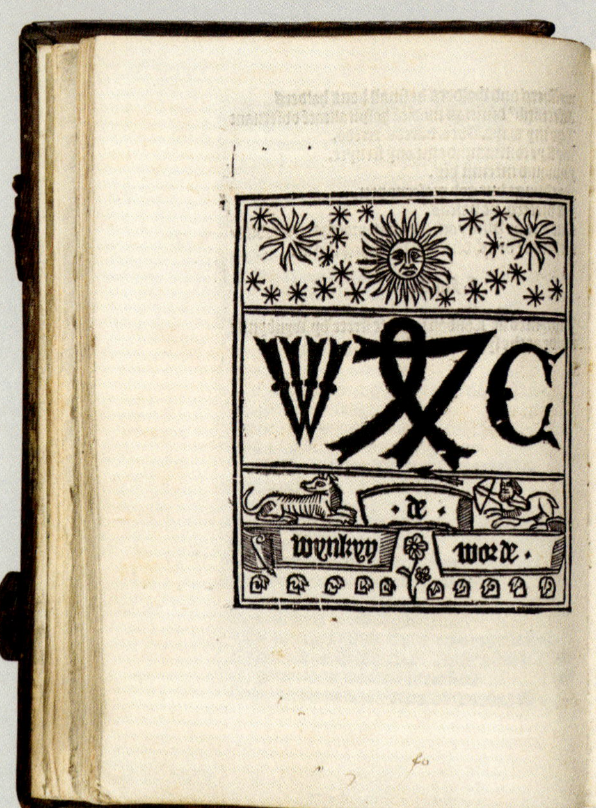

¶ Paruuloꝛum institutio ex sta[n]brigiana collectione.

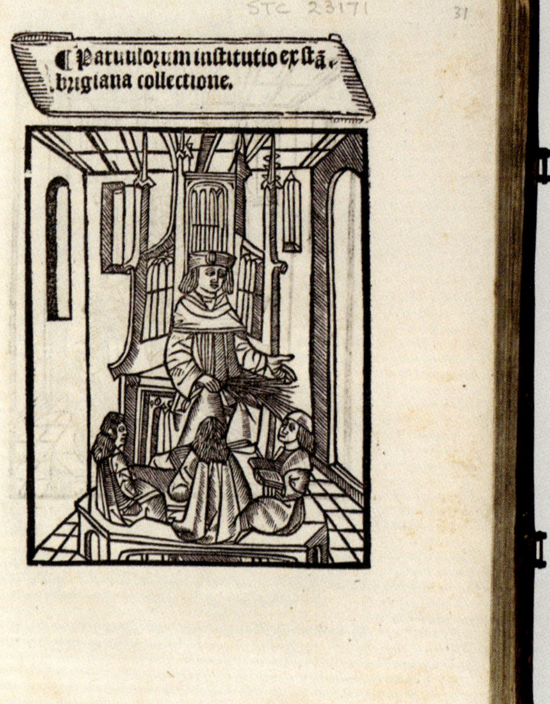

Pꝛeterito plusꝙper fecto rum | Amatus Doctus Lectus Auditus | ¶Whan I had be loued. esses vel fuissem/tus ees vel fuisses/tus eet vel fuisset. In plali cũ ti essem⁹ vl fuissem⁹ ti essetis vel fuissetis/ti essent vel fuissent.

Futuro rum. | Amatus Doctus Lectus Auditus | ¶Whan I shall be loued. ero vel fuero/tus eris vel fueris tus erit vt fuerit. In plalt cũ ti erimus vel fuerimus/ti eritis vel fueritis/ti erint vel fuerint.

Infiniti uo modo. | Amari Doceri Legi Audiri | ¶To be loued amatũ To haue oꝛ had belo / Pꝛeterito per doctum (ued. fecto & plusꝙ lectum esse/vel tum fuisse. perfecto auditum.

Duo ptici pia veni sit ab hoc verbo pas siuo: alte rũ pꝛeteri ti: vt | ¶Futuro amatũ iri vel amandum esse: to be loued.

Amatus Doctus Lectus Auditus | I loued. Alterũ posterioꝛis futuri: vt | Amãdus to be loued Docendus Legendus Iudiendus.

Foꝛmpni ge of ten ses. | Of the pꝛeterperfectẽs of ꝑ indicatyf mode be .viii. tenses fourmed. The pꝛeterpluperfectẽs of the same mode/by chaungynge i in to e shoꝛte & puttynge to rã/as amaui amauerã. ꝑ pꝛeterperfectẽs of ꝑ opta tyue mode/& ꝑ cõiunctyue mode/by chaɡigynge i in to e shoꝛte/& puttynge to rim/as amaui amauerim. the futurtẽs of ꝑ cõiunctyf mode/by chaungynge i in to e shoꝛte/& puttynge to ro/as amaui amauero. The pꝛe terpluperfectẽs of the optatyue mode: of the potẽcyall mode/and of the coniunctyue mode/by puttynge to s/ and sem: as amaui amauissem. The pꝛeterperfectens of the infynytyue mode by puttynge to s/& se as ama

ui/amauisse. ¶How many concoꝛdes of grammer be there iij. The fyrst bytwene ꝑ nomynatyue case & the vbe. The secõde bytwene the adiectyue and ꝑ substã tyue. The thyꝛde bytwene the relatyue & ꝑ antecedẽs [margin: Cõcoꝛdes of gram mer.]

¶The nomynatyue case & the verbe must accoꝛde in nombꝛe & persone. ¶The adiectyf must accoꝛde with his substantyue in case/gendꝛe/& nõbꝛe. But nownes partytiues/dystributyues/cõparatyues/oꝛ superla tyue degres/& other lyke put partytiuely shal accoꝛde in gendꝛe with ꝑ genytyue case/oꝛ the other case that foloweth/& is gouerned of them. ¶The relatiue shal accoꝛde with his antecedent in gẽdꝛe nõbꝛe & persone.

Now knowe you a pticyple Foꝛ he is a parte of reason declyned w̃ case:& taketh parte of nowne and parte of verbe. what taketh he of nowne case gẽ dꝛe and nombꝛe. what of verbe Tẽs/sygnyfycacyon/ & fygure. ¶How many thynges lõge to a participple vi. gendꝛe case tens sygnyfycacyon nombꝛe/ & fygure. [margin: A party cyple.]

¶How many gendꝛes of participples be there iiij.ꝑ masculyne/as amatus:ꝑ feimpnyne/as amata:ꝑ neu tre:as amatũ:ꝑ com ꝑ of thꝛe:as hic & her & hoc amãs [margin: Gendꝛe.]

¶How many cases of partycyples be there vi.as be of nownes. ¶How many tẽses of partycyple be there iiij.a partycyple of the pꝛesentẽs/ a partycyple of ꝑ pꝛe tertens/a partycyple of the fyꝛst future/another of the latter futur. ¶How knowe you a partycyple of ꝑ pꝛe sentẽs Foꝛ his englysshe endẽth in ynge/as louynge & his latyn endeth in ans/oꝛ in ens: as amãs docens. [margin: Cases. Tenses. Pꝛesen tens.]

¶Of whome is ꝑ partycyple of ꝑ pꝛesentẽs fourmed Of the fyꝛst persone synguler nõbꝛe of ꝑ pꝛeterpfectẽs of ꝑ indycatyf mode/by chaunginge the last syllabe in to n & s:as amabã amãs/loquebar loquẽs poterã po tẽs. out take pꝛesens obsens & iens of ibã/quiẽs of qui bã w̃ theyꝛ cõposides:ꝑ make theyꝛ gerũdyues i cũdi/

Acci.stã.   C.i.

Tudor Schoolbooks, 1512–20

John Stanbridge, *Accidentia* (London, 1520) together with eight other titles (various imprints, 1512–20),
bound in early 16th-century blind-tooled calfskin over wooden boards (19.5 × 13.5 cm)

In the Middle Ages schoolboys learnt their Latin from textbooks that were themselves written in Latin. But in the late fifteenth century schoolmasters began to produce new books that taught Latin through the vernacular. One of the first to do so in England was John Stanbridge (1463–1510). Educated at Winchester and New College, in 1487 he went to teach at the recently founded Magdalen College School. He became Headmaster there the following year.

Stanbridge wrote six short works which soon became popular textbooks. They were in use at Winchester as well as at Eton by the 1520s. Four early editions of Stanbridge's works are brought together in this volume. The first is his *Accidentia*, a grammar dealing with the parts of speech. The second is the *Vulgaria*, an English–Latin dictionary. Then there is *Parvulorum Institutio*, an exposition of syntax. And the fourth is a *Gradus*, a list of irregular comparatives and superlatives, and of irregular verbs. Bound with these are five other works: another English–Latin phrasebook; a summary in Latin of the grammatical treatise of Lorenzo Valla (1470–1457); the *Fables* of Aesop in Latin (used at Winchester and Eton as a class reader in the lower forms); a work entitled *De Vera Nobilitate*, consisting of quotations from classical authors and the Bible, all of which illustrate some quality required in a gentleman; and a Latin poem on the four cardinal virtues. The volume has an early sixteenth-century leather binding decorated with rolled bands depicting dancing peasants, including a bagpiper. There were originally two clasps, now lost. Within the volume are a number of illustrative woodcuts, and several examples of the printer's device of Wynkyn de Worde (d. 1534), the collaborator and successor of William Caxton. The image of the schoolmaster, switch in hand, is used more than once.

The book provides a snapshot of the Renaissance educational ideal: designed to produce a facility in Latin at a time when it was the language of the classical authors as well as the Church and much of the business of life, it aimed also to create a Christian gentleman. We do not know when or how the book came to Winchester. An inscription in Latin at the front, and in English at the end, shows that one of its early owners was named Libbe Orcherd. She paid 8 pence for it. Her handwriting dates her to the sixteenth century.

The modern Wykehamist does not study Latin all day every day, as his forebears did. Nor does his Classics don beat the grammar into him. He would not enjoy Stanbridge's method either – question and answer to be learnt by rote: 'How many parts of reason be there? [Ans:] VIII: nowne, pronowne, verbe [etc.] … How knowe you a nowne? [Ans.] For he is a part of reason declyned with case.' But every boy at Winchester still does study Latin to GCSE, and like the boys of long ago, he still has to memorise the endings of nouns and verbs, and learn the vocabulary.

Andrew Leigh (Classics)

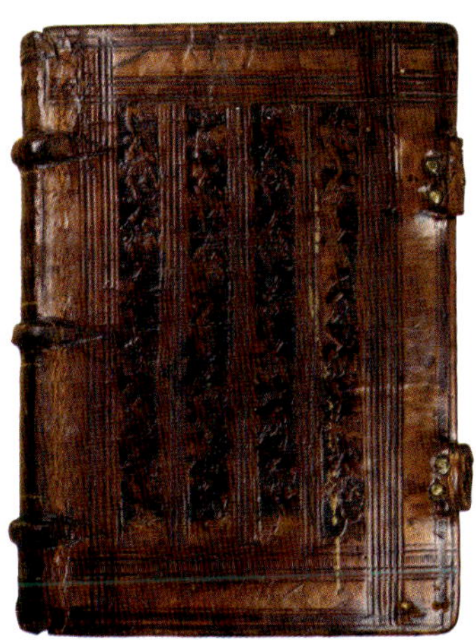

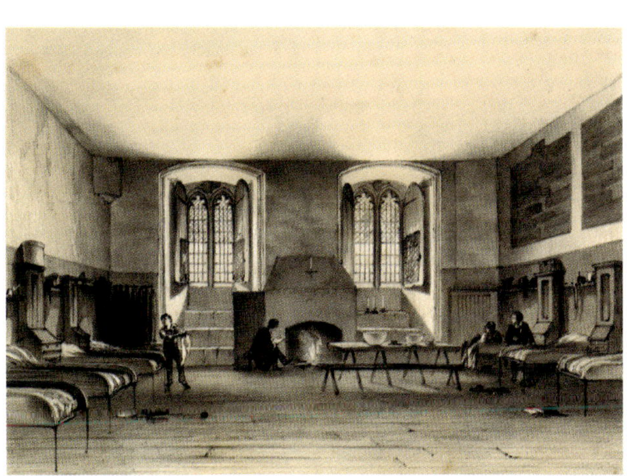

An early 19th-century view of VIIth Chamber. This was the original medieval schoolroom, later converted into a dormitory.

The Andwell Map, 1530s

Watercolour and ink on paper (24 × 63 cm)

Winchester College has owned land at Andwell, near Basingstoke, since the 1390s. William of Wykeham purchased the land from the priory of Andwell, a daughter house of the Abbey of Tiron. This area might seem to be a quiet rural backwater, but in the sixteenth century the residents of Andwell took part in a number of long-running disputes. This affected Winchester College because one of its tenants was involved.

The Hoke and Jakes families were neighbours in Hurstland, a part of the parish of Andwell. In 1520 John Hoke sold some timber from his land to a Mr Chapman of Greywell, but John Jakes questioned whether Hoke had cut the timber from his own freehold land or from the part of Hurst Wood that he, Jakes, rented from Winchester College. An inquiry was held and Hoke was found to be at fault, and Jakes's rights to the land confirmed. But the dispute rumbled on and was taken up by the sons of the two men. In April 1536 John Hoke junior and his friends had evidently had one too many in the local tavern and broke into a close of land belonging to Nicholas Jakes, armed with swords, cudgels and arrows, uttering insults and generally disturbing the king's peace.

Another inquiry was called to investigate and this met at Odiham in December 1536. It was unable to reach a decision and the matter dragged on yet again until March 1552, when arbitrators were appointed to settle the dispute once and for all. This plan of the land in question may have been drawn up in either 1536 or 1552, but 1536 seems the more likely as we have a reference dating to 1536 that states: 'Willyam Waterman … seyth he hath viewed and esteemed hurstlond'. If Waterman was the surveyor, he has done a great deal more than just draw the lie of the land. We have instead a beautifully decorative topographical drawing of the landscape, more a bird's-eye view or picture-plan. The surveyor clearly shows field boundaries, gates and paths. The wooded areas are demarked and there is evidence of pollarding of some of the trees. A barn, still standing, is shown in a design typical for Hampshire at the time: three bays divided by a central large door, half-hipped at both ends.

This is certainly the most unusual plan in the College Archives, and one of the earliest watercolour views of an English landscape. It may be compared with the contemporary plans of Dover Harbour made for Henry VIII and now in the British Library, although these lack the pictorial detail and atmospheric evocation of place that make the Andwell Map so remarkable. The surveyor, perhaps better described as the artist, has clearly enjoyed himself a little, drawing packhorses and a horse and cart on the main London to Basingstoke road, now the A30. These figures have great movement and character. The winter wood in the distance is painted with grey washes, giving the impression of a dense tangle of branches.

But what of the dispute between Jakes and Hoke? The arbitrators ordered them to cease their quarrel. Jakes, as tenant of the College, was permitted the use of Hurstland, but the neighbouring grove of land was to be equally divided between the two men: the difference in colouring on the plan would seem to reflect this division of the land.

Suzanne Foster (Archivist)

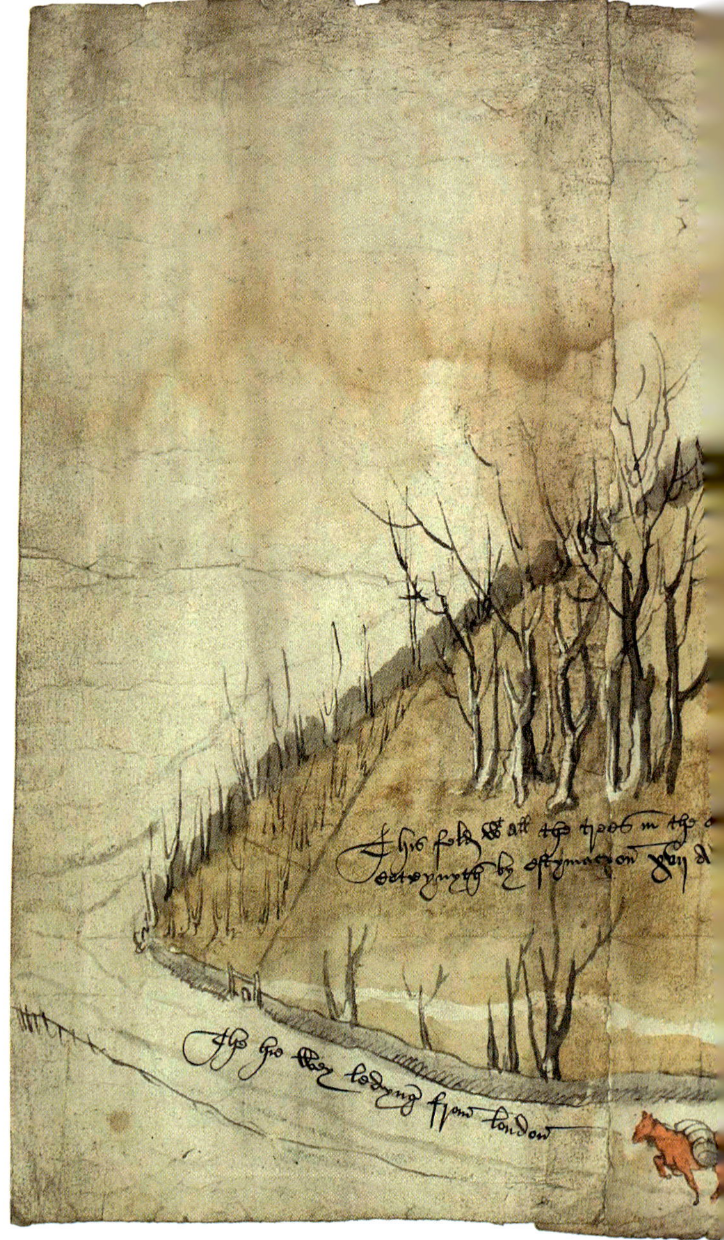

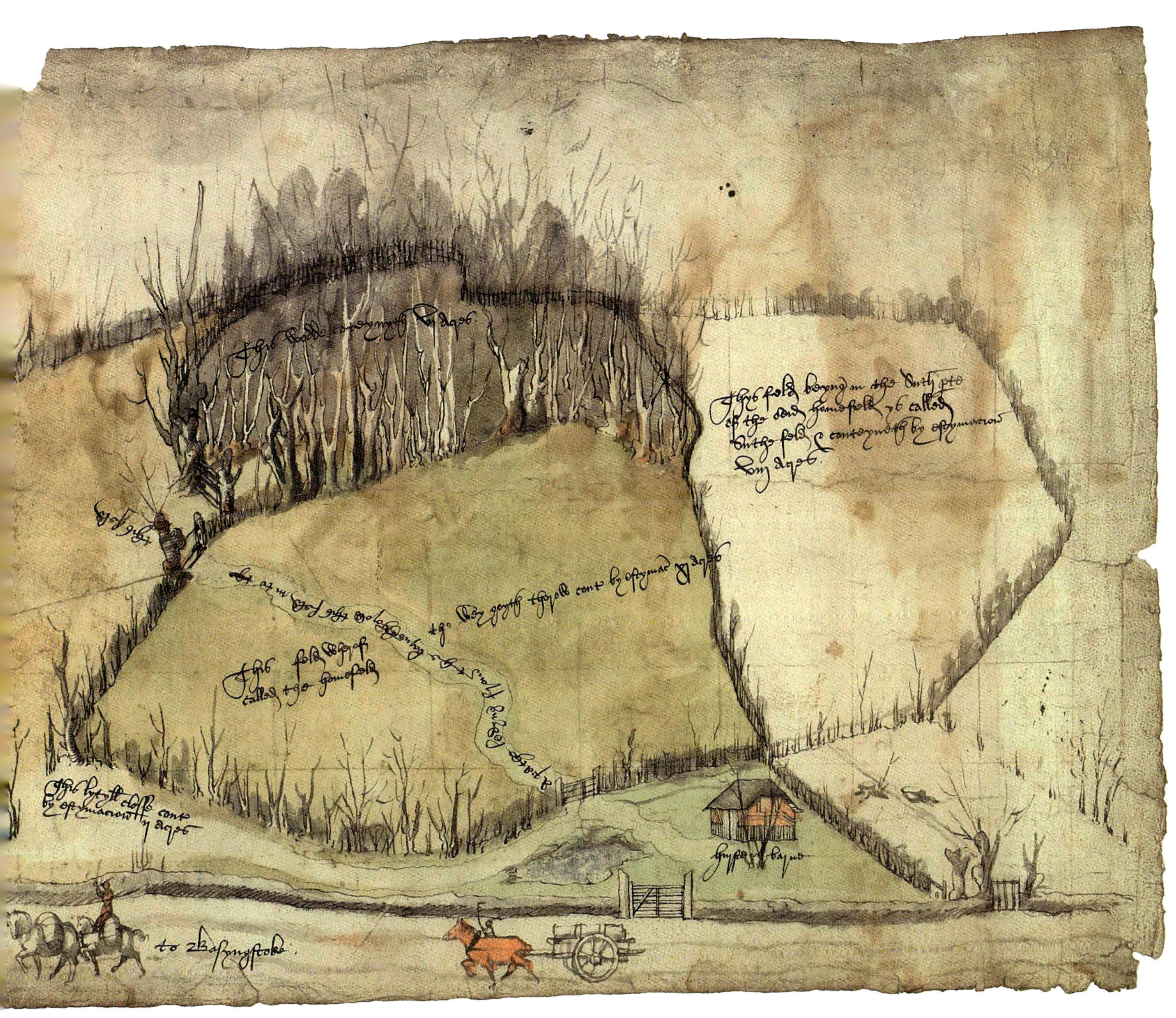
to Basyngstoke

Henslowe Ewer and Basin, 1563

Silver and parcel-gilt (basin D. 40.5 cm; ewer H. 22.8 cm)

The inventory of 'the stuffe and plate in Mr Warden's custodye', made in August 1569, included a 'basen and ewer, parcell gillte, with the founder's armes in the bottome, of Mr Rafe Henslowe's reparynge'. 'Repairing' is probably a considerable understatement. As well as the Founder's arms in the centre of the basin and ewer lid, the basin bears two inscriptions in elegant Lombardic script (the same as that used in the College's War Cloister). Around the centre run the words 'MANERS MAKET MAN QUOTHE WYLLYAM WYKEHAM', and on the rim 'HANC PELVIM CVM SVO GVTTVRNIO DE NOVO FECIT RADOLPHVS HENSLOWE A⁰ DNI 1563 CVI DEUS RETRIBVAT IN ILL[A] DIE' (Ralph Henslowe made anew this basin with its ewer in 1563 AD; may God reward him on that day [the Day of Judgement]).

The most probable interpretation of this is that Henslowe paid for the substantial remodelling, in accordance with contemporary Renaissance taste, of a ewer and basin already in the College's possession and which may until then have been decorated in the Gothic style. The 1562–63 London hallmark would then refer to the silversmith who redesigned the pieces rather than to their original maker. Ralph Henslowe was a Hampshire squire from Boarhunt near Portchester who had served as MP for Portsmouth in 1555. His second son, Henry, headed the list of Scholars elected to College in 1563, a fact which may set the gift in a clearer context.

Basins and ewers formed an essential part of dining-room equipment before the use of forks became widespread, and servants were expected to pour water, often scented with roses, over the guests' hands at intervals during their meals. Besides this practical use, these vessels also played an important role in enhancing the status of their owner, whether individual or corporate, by being displayed prominently on the sideboard among other pieces of silver. Henslowe's gift was still fulfilling this function at dinners in the Warden's Lodgings right up to the early years of this century.

Only six English sets of matching ewer and basin survive from before 1600 and the Henslowe set is an exceptionally fine example of Elizabethan silverware. The circle at the bottom of the basin, where the water would sit, has been left in plain silver, but the rim and central boss are gilded and elaborately decorated with engraving and repoussé. In the centre, trophies of armour alternate with baskets of fruits, suggesting perhaps the owner's successes in husbandry and in warfare. The weapons, which include tridents, swords, spears, scimitars and halberds together with a firebrand and spiked club, are of great variety and ferocity, while the fruits pouring out between the openings in the baskets seem to depict gourds as well as apples and pears. The ewer has similar motifs on its lid, but the sides show the heads of a man and a woman in the manner of Renaissance portrait medallions. Set within a band of scrolling foliage, and with confident and engaging expressions, these add a welcome human touch to the rich decorative scheme.

John Falconer (Curator of Treasury, 2001–14)

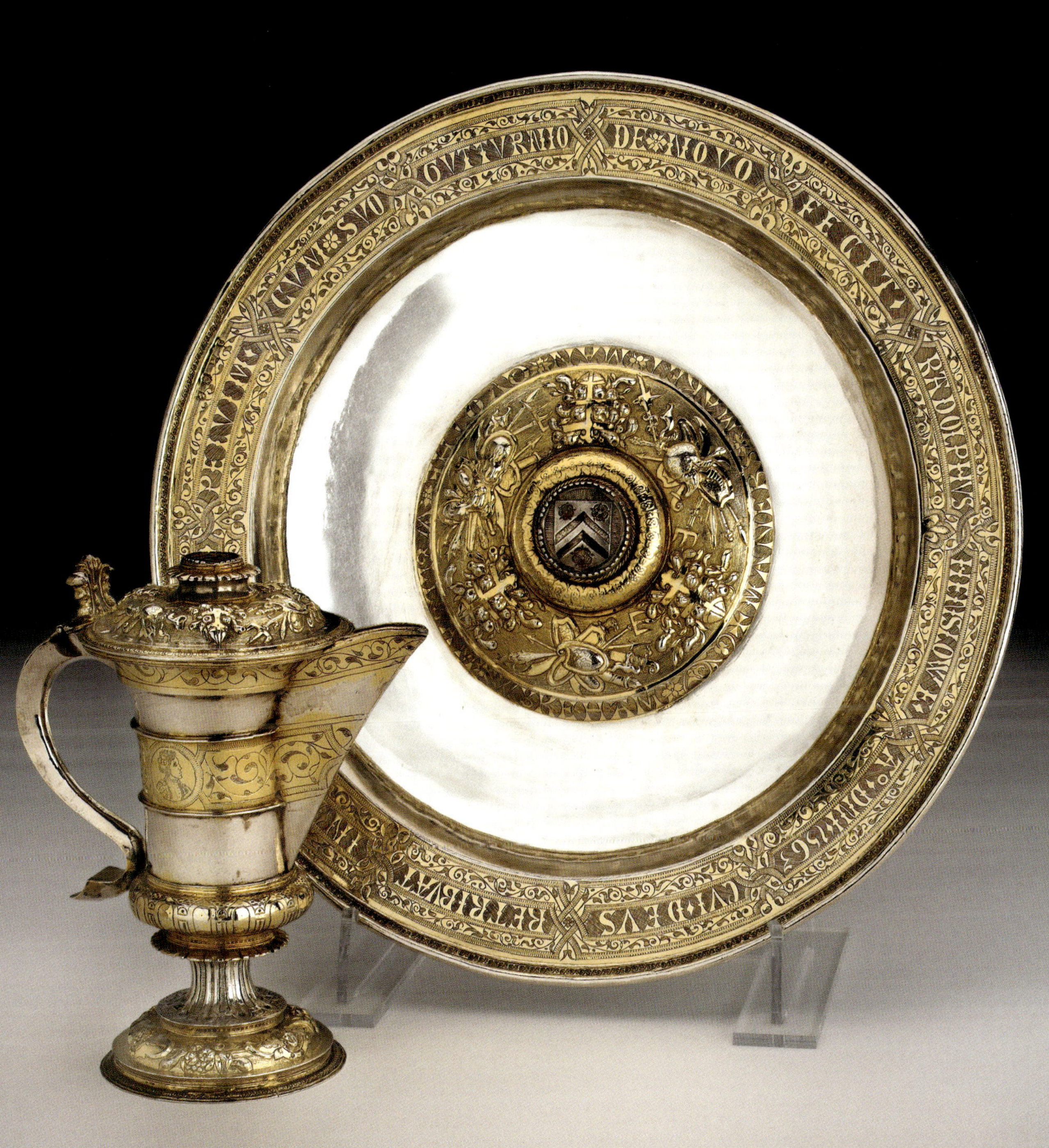

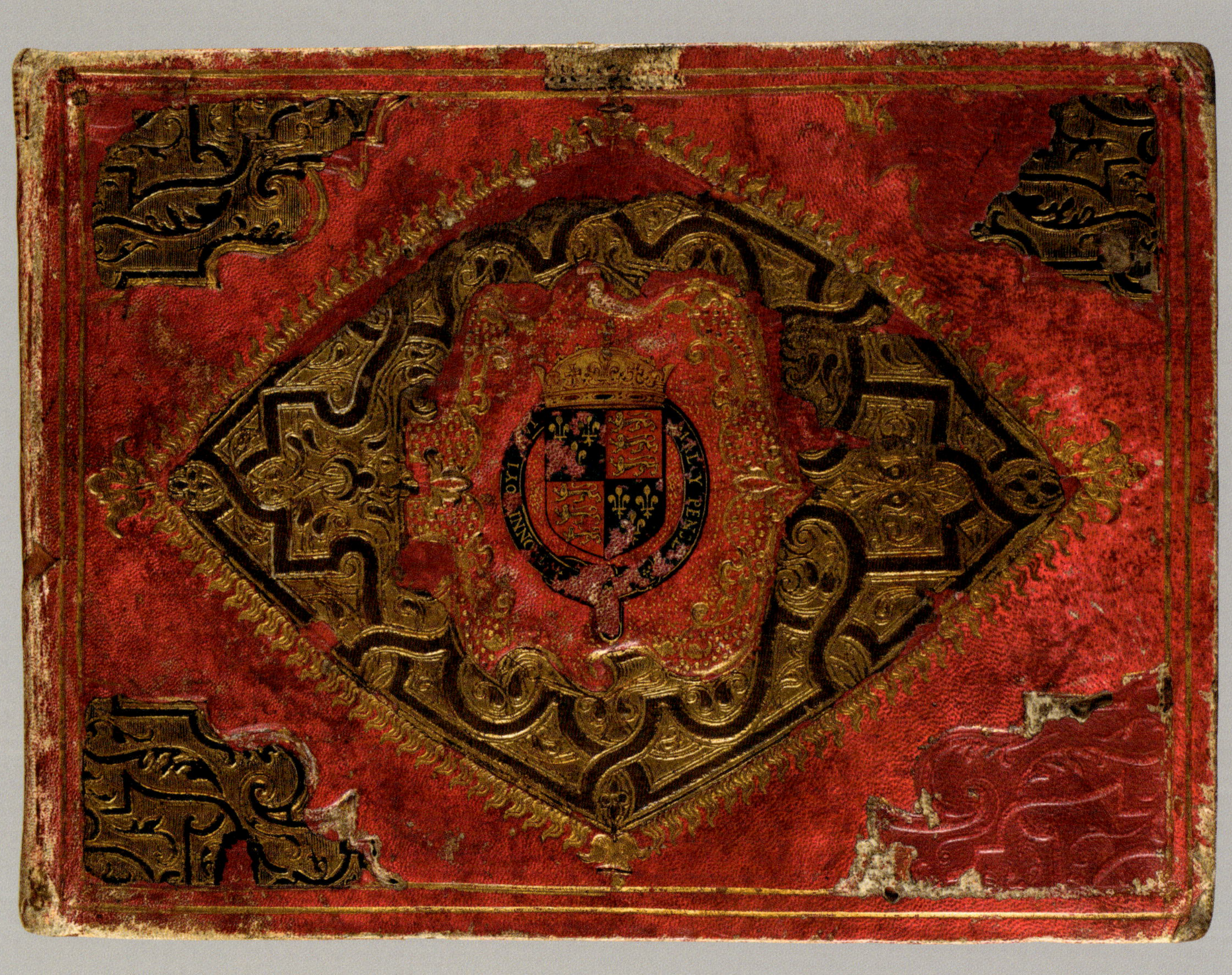

The Winchester Partbooks, 1564–66

MS 153: Manuscripts on parchment, each ff. 121 or ff. 122, bound in 16th-century red sheepskin over pasteboard,
tooled and painted in blue, red and gold, with the arms of Elizabeth I within a stamped border (each 17 × 23.5 cm)

This set of musical manuscripts, which has been in the possession of Winchester College since at least the early years of the nineteenth century, has been described as 'one of England's musical treasures'. The four books, one for each voice part, contain a selection of Italian and English madrigals and French chansons composed during the sixteenth century. The books are handsomely bound and tooled with the arms of Elizabeth I, and are a rare example of handwritten (rather than printed) music from the period. Many pieces are unique to these partbooks, which are exceptional for the quality of their bindings and decoration, and their fine state of preservation.

Recent research has shown that the books were almost certainly commissioned by King Erik XIV of Sweden from Jan Franchois, a well-known copyist in Antwerp, between 1564 and 1566, at a cost of £126 (the equivalent of ten years' wages for an ordinary labourer). The bindings were probably made in the workshop of Christopher Plantin, also based in Antwerp. According to the music historian Kristine Forney, there is no doubt that these were sumptuous presentation volumes: 'the presence of silken ties, different coloured leather for corners and the centrepieces, hand-painted coats of arms, and the lavish use of gold leaf all suggest that no expense was spared in the binding of the manuscript.'

Erik XIV ascended the Swedish throne in 1560. He was a keen musician, employed numerous singers and instrumentalists at his court and owned a substantial library of music. He was keen to extend Sweden's political influence in Europe through marriage with Elizabeth of England. Although never considered a serious contender by the queen, who described him as 'barbaric', Erik was perhaps her most tenacious suitor, devoting ten years to his unsuccessful attempt to secure her hand. These beautiful books appear to have formed part of this suit; they were certainly present at Elizabeth's court by the 1570s, when Sir Philip Sidney supplied new words for some of the tunes.

Of the 107 works in the partbooks, eighty-one are in Italian, sixteen are in French and ten (added later) are in English. The composers chosen are among the finest from across northern Europe and include Orlande de Lassus, Adrian Willaert, Jacques Arcadelt, Claude de Sermisy and Philippe Verdelot. Of particular importance are the thirty-five works ascribed to Hubert Waelrant, a Flemish composer largely forgotten today, for whom these manuscripts constitute the largest surviving collection of his music.

Little is known of the history of these manuscripts after the sixteenth century. They are first recorded at Winchester College in 1802, but may have belonged to the library long before that. It seems unlikely that they were ever used in performance, but three works from the books were performed by the specialist early music ensemble Stile Antico at a concert in Winchester College in April 2018.

David Thomas (Master of Music)

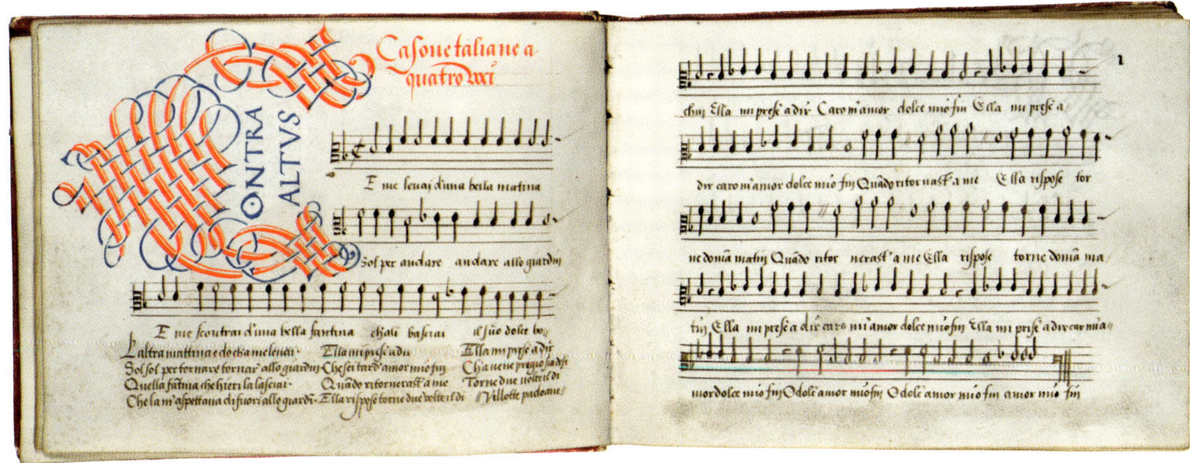

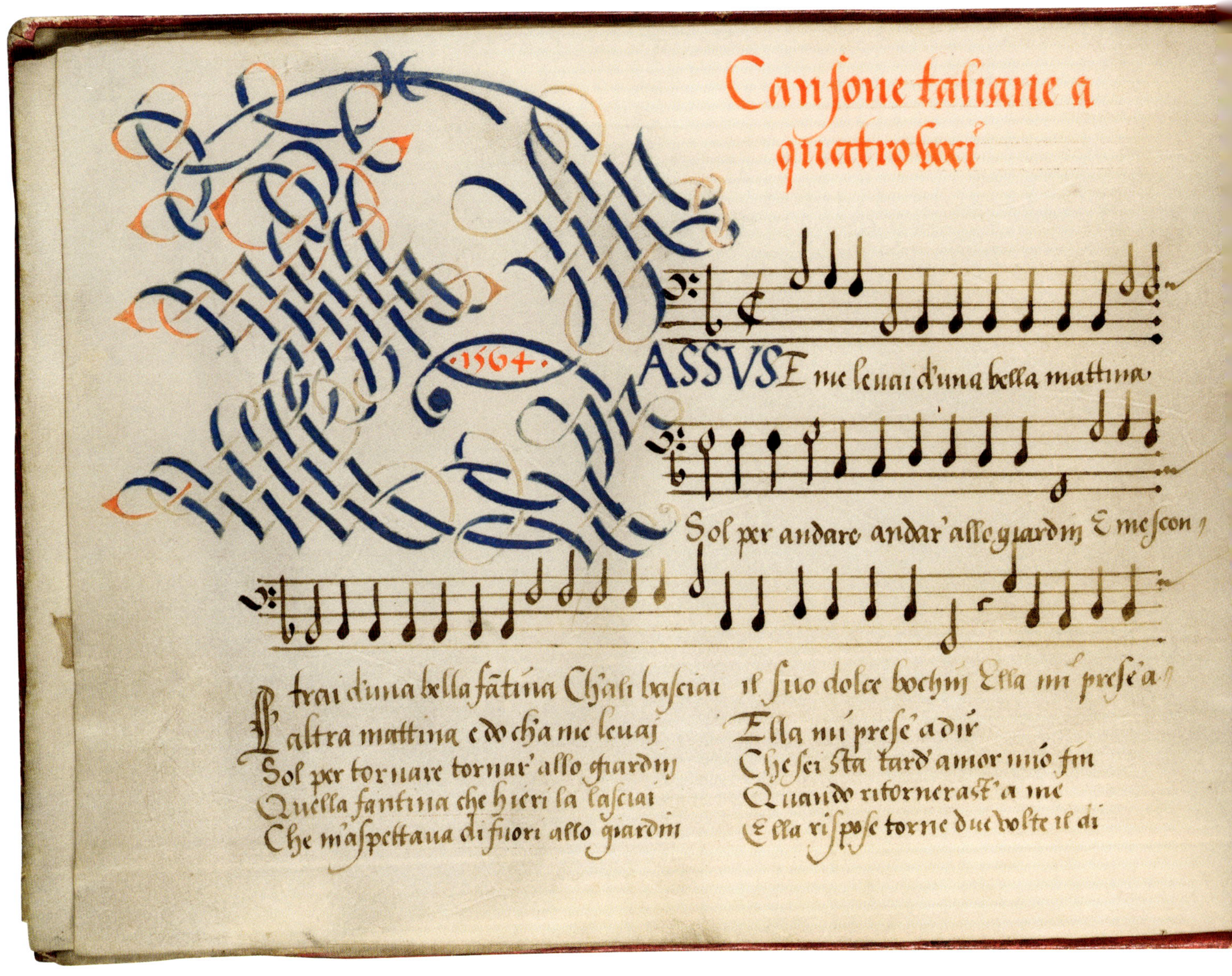
Cansone taliane a
quatro voci
1564
ASSVSE me leuai d'una bella mattina
Sol per andare andar' allo giardin E me scon
trai d'una bella fatina Ch'ali basciai il suo dolce bochin Ella mi prese a
L'altra mattina e do ch'ia me leuai
Sol per tornare tornar' allo giardin
Quella fantina che hieri la lasciai
Che m'aspettaua di fuori allo giardin
Ella mi prese' a dir
Che sei sta tard' amor mio fin
Quando ritornerast' a me
Ella rispose torne due volte il di

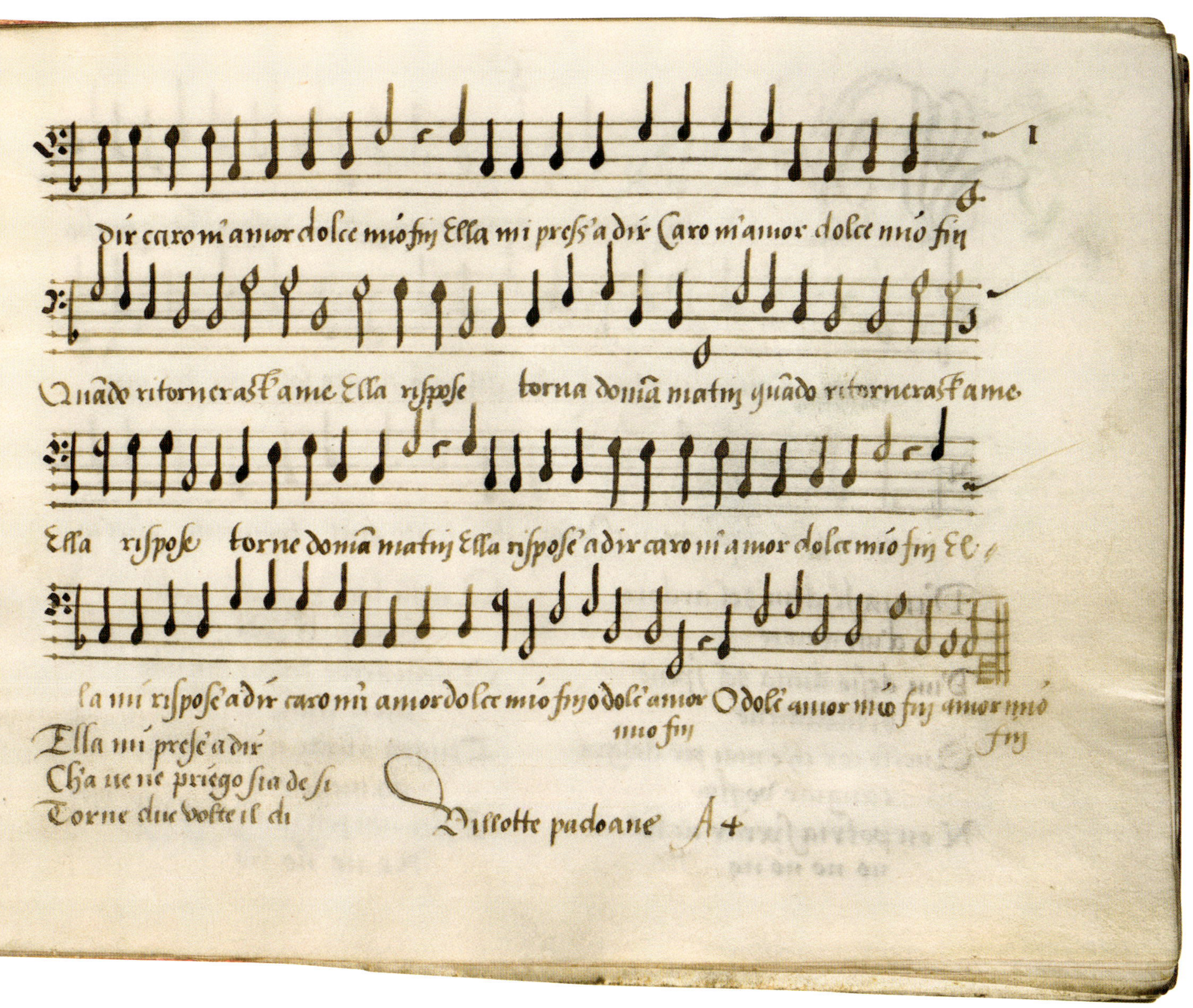
dir caro m'amor dolce mio fin Ella mi prese'a dir Caro m'amor dolce mio fin
Quado ritorneras a me Ella rispose torna donna matris quado ritorneras a me
Ella rispose torne donna matris Ella rispose'a dir caro mi amor dolce mio fin El
la mi rispose'a dir caro mi amor dolce mio fn o dolc'amor O dolc amor mio fn amor mio
mio fin
Ella mi prese'a dir
Cha ue ne priego sia de si
Torne due volte il di
Villotte padoane

King James Bible, 1611

The Holy Bible (London, 1611), bound in 17th-century panelled calfskin over oak boards (40.2 × 25.8 cm)

No other text has had a greater influence on the English-speaking world than the King James Bible. The earliest versions of the Bible in English were the illicit translations of John Wycliffe (*c.* 1380) and William Tyndale (1535). After the Reformation authorised versions were approved by the Crown, beginning with the Great Bible (1539) and then the Bishops' Bible (1568). But none of these achieved the definitive status of the translation 'to be read in the whole Church', commissioned by King James soon after his accession to the throne.

The new translation had its origins in the Hampton Court Conference of 1604, which was convened partly in response to a Puritan delegation that had met James on his journey from Scotland, presenting him with a petition, signed by over a thousand clergy, demanding further Protestant reform of the English Church. Although there was no actual request for a new translation of the Bible in the petition, this project was an important outcome of the conference. James disliked the Geneva Bible (1560) favoured by Puritans, and decreed that special pains be taken 'for a uniform translation, which should be done by the best learned men in both Universities, then reviewed by the Bishops, presented to the Privy Council, lastly ratified by the Royal authority'. Fifty-four scholars were therefore appointed and strict rules for the translation drawn up. It was to use old familiar terms and names, and to be readable in the idiom of the day. Rule 8 sets out the strategy: 'Every particular Man of each Company, to take the same Chapter or Chapters, and having translated or amended them severally by himself, where he thinketh good, all to meet together, confer what they have done, and agree for their Parts what shall stand.'

That a new complete translation of the Bible from its original Hebrew and Greek texts took only seven years might be considered miraculous. The six teams of translators – convened in Oxford, Cambridge and Westminster – were not, however, working entirely from scratch. Rather, they refined the existing Bishops' Bible, consulting other European-language translations as well as their own reading of the Hebrew and Greek. At least five Wykehamists were involved: George Ryves, William Thorne, Arthur Lake, Thomas Bilson and, foremost of all, John Harmar, who was at the time Warden of Winchester College, having also been Regius Professor of Greek at Oxford. He led the Oxford-based team responsible for the Gospels, Acts and Revelation, and was one of three revisers who took nine painstaking months to review the whole translation, finally

published in 1611. The earliest copies have a number of errors that were corrected in later printings, for example in Ruth 3.15 where 'she went' is mis-set as 'he went'. The College's copy, purchased in 2009, has 'she'.

When Harmar was appointed Warden of Winchester he extended his lodgings to provide a well-proportioned study, comfortably placed above the bakehouse. There can be no doubt that much of his scholarly work would have taken place in this room, which is now part of the Fellows' Library and still houses his collection of Bible commentaries and foreign-language translations. It is fitting that a 1611 edition of the pinnacle of his scholarship and industry should take its place alongside the very books he treasured and pored over in its production.

Simon Thorn (D, 1979–84, Foundation Chaplain)

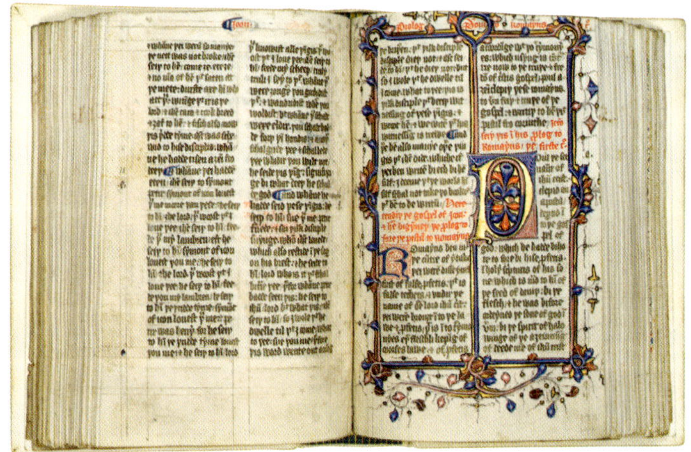

MS 42: The New Testament, manuscript on parchment, early 15th century. This copy of Wycliffe's translation was given to the College by one of the Fellows in 1609.

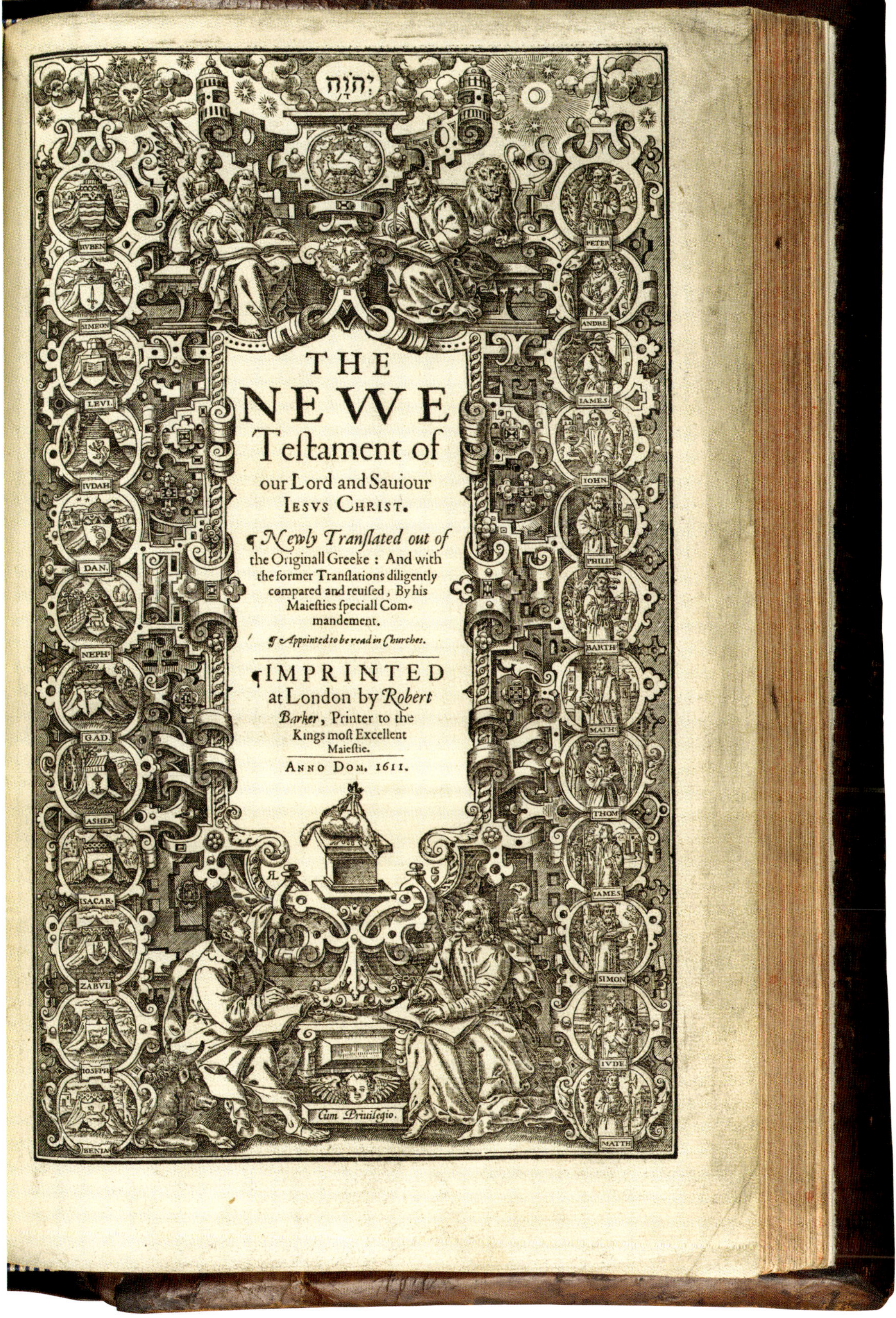
יְהֹוָה
THE
NEWE
Testament of
our Lord and Sauiour
Iesvs Christ.

Newly Translated out of
the Originall Greeke : And with
the former Translations diligently
compared and reuised, By his
Maiesties speciall Com-
mandement.
Appointed to be read in Churches.

IMPRINTED
at London by Robert
Barker, Printer to the
Kings most Excellent
Maiestie.
Anno Dom. 1611.

Cum Priuilegio.

THE TRAGEDIE OF
Anthonie, and Cleopatra.

Actus Primus. Scœna Prima.

Enter Demetrius and Philo.

Philo.

Ay, but this dotage of our Generals
Ore-flowes the measure : those his goodly eyes
That o're the Files and Musters of the Warre,
Haue glow'd like plated Mars :
Now bend, now turne
The Office and Deuotion of their view
Vpon a Tawny Front. His Captaines heart,
Which in the scuffles of great Fights hath burst
The Buckles on his brest, reneages all temper,
And is become the Bellowes and the Fan
To coole a Gypsies Lust.

*Flourish. Enter Anthony, Cleopatra her Ladies, the
Traine, with Eunuchs fanning her.*

Looke where they come :
Take but good note, and you shall see in him
(The triple Pillar of the world) transform'd
Into a Strumpets Foole. Behold and see.

Cleo. If it be Loue indeed, tell me how much.

Ant. There's beggery in the loue that can be reckon'd

Cleo. Ile set a bourne how farre to be belou'd.

Ant. Then must thou needes finde out new Heauen,
new Earth.

Enter a Messenger.

Mef. Newes(my good Lord)from Rome.

Ant. Grates me, the summe.

Cleo. Nay heare them Anthony.
Fuluia perchance is angry : Or who knowes,
If the scarse-bearded Cæsar haue not sent
His powrefull Mandate to you. Do this, or this ;
Take in that Kingdome, and Infranchise that :
Perform't, or else we damne thee.

Ant. How, my Loue?

Cleo. Perchance? Nay, and most like :
You must not stay heere longer, your dismission
Is come from Cæsar, therefore heare it Anthony.
Where's Fuluias Processe? (Cæsars I would say) both ?
Call in the Messengers : As I am Egypts Queene,
Thou blushest Anthony, and that blood of thine
Is Cæsars homager : else so thy cheeke payes shame,
When shrill-tongu'd Fuluia scolds. The Messengers.
Let Rome in Tyber melt, and the wide Arch
Of the raing'd Empire fall : Heere is my space,
Kingdomes are clay : Our dungie earth alike

Feeds Beast as Man ; the Noblenesse of life
Is to do thus : when such a mutuall paire,
And such a twaine can doo't, in which I binde
One paine of punishment, the world to weet :
We stand vp Peerelesse.

Cleo. Excellent falshood :
Why did he marry Fuluia, and not loue her?
Ile seeme the Foole I am not. Anthony will be himselfe.

Ant. But stirr'd by Cleopatra.
Now for the loue of Loue, and her soft houres,
Let's not confound the time with Conference harsh ;
There's not a minute of our liues should stretch
Without some pleasure now. What sport tonight ?

Cleo. Heare the Ambassadors.

Ant. Fye wrangling Queene :
Whom euery thing becomes, to chide, to laugh,
To weepe : who euery passion fully striues
To make it selfe (in Thee) faire, and admir'd.
No Messenger but thine, and all alone, to night
Wee'l wander through the streets, and note
The qualities of people. Come my Queene,
Last night you did desire it. Speake not to vs.

Exeunt with the Traine.

Dem. Is Cæsar with Anthonius priz'd so slight ?

Philo. Sir sometimes when he is not Anthony,
He comes too short of that great Property
Which still should go with Anthony.

Dem. I am full sorry, that hee approues the common
Lyar, who thus speakes of him at Rome ; but I will hope
of better deeds to morrow. Rest you happy. *Exeunt*

*Enter Enobarbus, Lamprius, a Southsayer, Rannius, Lucil-
lius, Charmian, Iras, Mardian the Eunuch,
and Alexas.*

Char. L. Alexas, sweet Alexas, most any thing Alexas,
almost most absolute Alexas, where's the Soothsayer
that you prais'd so to th'Queene ? Oh that I knew this
Husband, which you say, must change his Hornes with
Garlands.

Alex. Soothsayer.

Sooth. Your will ?

Char. Is this the Man ? Is't you sir that know things ?

Sooth. In Natures infinite booke of Secrecie, a little I
can read.

Alex. Shew him your hand.

Enob. Bring in the Banket quickly : Wine enough

Cleopa.

Shakespeare First Folio, 1623

Mr. William Shakespeares Comedies, Histories, & Tragedies (London, 1623), bound in modern 17th-century-style calfskin over pasteboard (29.6 × 19.7 cm)

On 4 November 1622 a Hampshire youth called John Leason became an apprentice in the London printing house of William and Isaac Jaggard. He would quickly have found himself involved in the printing of what has become an iconic book, for earlier that year the Jaggards had embarked upon the production of a 900-page volume containing thirty-six plays by William Shakespeare. We call the collection the First Folio (F) to distinguish it from the subsequent Shakespeare folios of 1632, 1664 and 1685. A folio is formed of printed sheets of paper, each of which is folded only once to produce two leaves (giving four printed sides). Eighteen of the plays in F had not been published before: without it, there would be no *Twelfth Night*, *Macbeth* or *Julius Caesar*, for example; but the texts of all the plays it contains are of great importance and authority.

The Folio was the brainchild of Shakespeare's fellow actors and business associates John Heminge (or Hemmings) and Henry Condell. During the years after Shakespeare's death in 1616, they and their allies gradually secured the rights to the thirty-six plays in F. They acquired *Troilus and Cressida* too late to include it in the first issue of the book; *Pericles* and *The Two Noble Kinsmen* were omitted from all three issues. Working either from earlier editions of single plays (quartos) or from manuscript copy, the Jaggards' compositors began to set type early in 1622. In October that year the book was advertised as forthcoming – in time for the Frankfurt Book Fair and just before John Leason began his apprenticeship. The first copies (of a run of perhaps 750) were sold in November 1623: 15 shillings unbound, £1 bound in calfskin.

A perfect copy of F contains 454 original folio leaves, including a title page with the portrait of Shakespeare by Martin Droeshout, preliminary material and the texts of the plays. Most of the 235 known copies are defective: of the eighty-two in the Folger Shakespeare Library in Washington, for example, only thirteen are properly complete. A fifth of the Winchester copy (of the third issue) is missing: title page, preliminaries, the first five Comedies, all but the first page of *Anthonie, and Cleopatra*, the whole of *Cymbeline* and seven other leaves. What survives is still a unique treasure.

The book's early history is unknown. By 1889 Thomas Kerslake owned it. At some point it passed to the Reverend C.H. Hawkins (1838–1900), the first Housemaster of Chawker's. In 1862 Hawkins helped establish the strong Winchester tradition of reading and performing Shakespeare with the founding of the Shakespeare

Society (oldest of the school's societies), precursor of SROGUS (Shakespeare Reading and Orpheus Glee United Society). SROGUS stopped operating for a brief period after about 1960 but now meets regularly to read a play aloud. Hawkins presented his First Folio to Winchester College Library. His generosity means that members of the school and visitors to it can still enjoy this direct physical link with Shakespeare and his age.

Robert Wyke (Second Master, 2001–15)

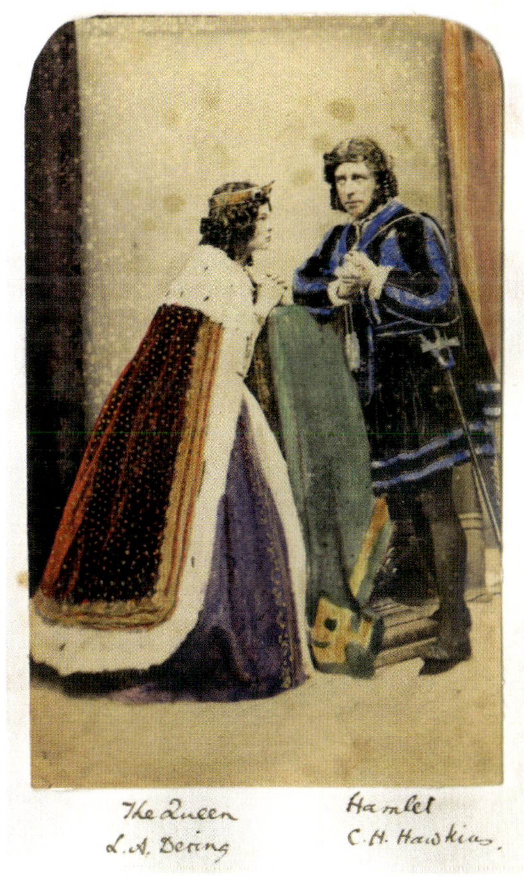

C.H. Hawkins as Hamlet, with L.A. Dering as the Queen, in a school production in 1866.

De Collegio Wintoniensi, 1640s

Manuscript on paper, ff. 7, bound in late 17th-century calfskin over pasteboard (19 × 12.2 cm)

This Latin poem, written by the Scholar Robert Mathew in the 1640s, describes Winchester College and offers a valuable insight into the pupils' daily lives. Despite the dramatic contemporary political backdrop (both Charles I and Oliver Cromwell came to Winchester while Mathew was at the school), the work is insulated from the outside world; its focus is entirely within the College walls.

Much of the poem is dedicated to the practicalities and traditions of the school. Mathew gives detailed descriptions of the boys' living chambers, the prefects' duties and the jobs of those

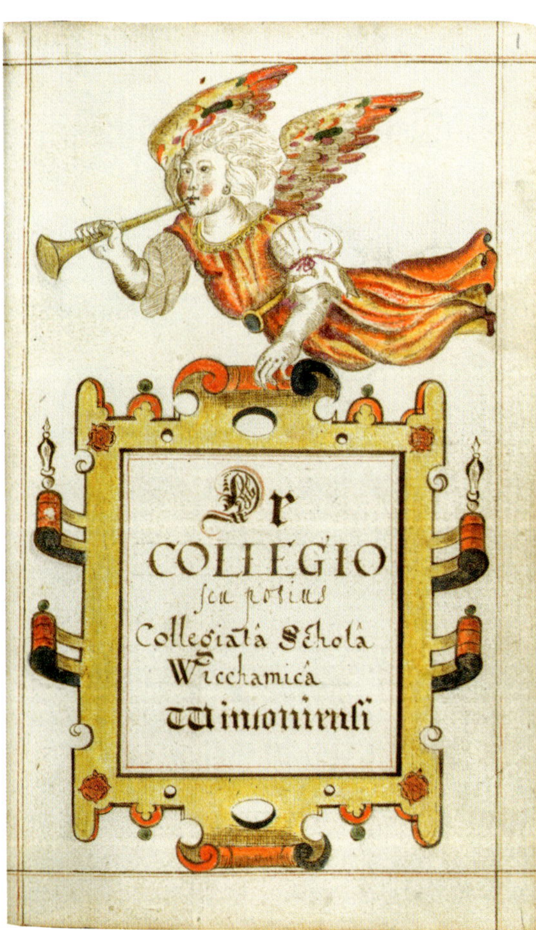

working around the College. Perhaps most shocking to a current pupil is Mathew's account of the daily timetable. Every boy was woken at 5 o'clock in the morning for prayers in Chapel, followed by three hours of work in the schoolroom until breakfast was served at 9 o'clock. The call to rise was done by a prefect, shouting '*Surgite … num stertitis? ohe! / Iam campana sonat; vos surgite, surgite, pigri!*' (Get up … surely you aren't snoring? Ho! The bell is already sounding; get up, get up you lazy things!). This brief passage gives a good idea of Mathew's honest and cheerful voice. Throughout the poem, his candid and enthusiastic tone is infectious. This is far more than an account of the College's inner workings; it is a personal response to life there. The section on boys' pastimes has lent the poem some small fame: a mention of 'bat-and-ball' on St Catherine's Hill has been interpreted as the first reference to cricket in Hampshire.

Mathew himself was elected to the school in 1643 and was admitted in September 1644. Even now, in Third Chamber (the boys' laundry room today), there remains an inscription to 'Robert Mathew 1647'. From Winchester he went up to New College, Oxford, and later entered the Church. However, as A.K. Cook noted in *About Winchester College* (1917), his authorship of *De Collegio Wintoniensi* has not always been recognised. In 1848 the poem was attributed by Charles Wordsworth to Christopher Johnson, Headmaster from 1561 to 1572. In 1899 J.S. Cotton made the discovery that the poem must date from a later period, for it contained a hidden reference to John Pottinger, Headmaster between 1642 and 1653. His name is spelled out by rubricated letters in the phrase 'POTENtiam eundi qui GERit'. Finally, in 1913, the identity of the author was discovered when another copy of the poem came to light in Magdalen College Library. This version is perhaps in Mathew's own hand and has his name written at the end.

While the Magdalen manuscript (now also in the possession of Winchester College) has a more accurate text of the poem, it lacks the charming pictures found in this volume. These include a portrait of William of Wykeham, an angel (which, according to Cook, possesses 'no great personal attractions') and the Trusty Servant. This strange creature has been a mascot of the College for centuries. He combines the attributes of various animals and represents the ideal servant, with a stag's feet for swiftness, the ears of an ass to hear his master calling and a padlock on his mouth to keep his secrets.

Joseph Scull (College, 2014–19)

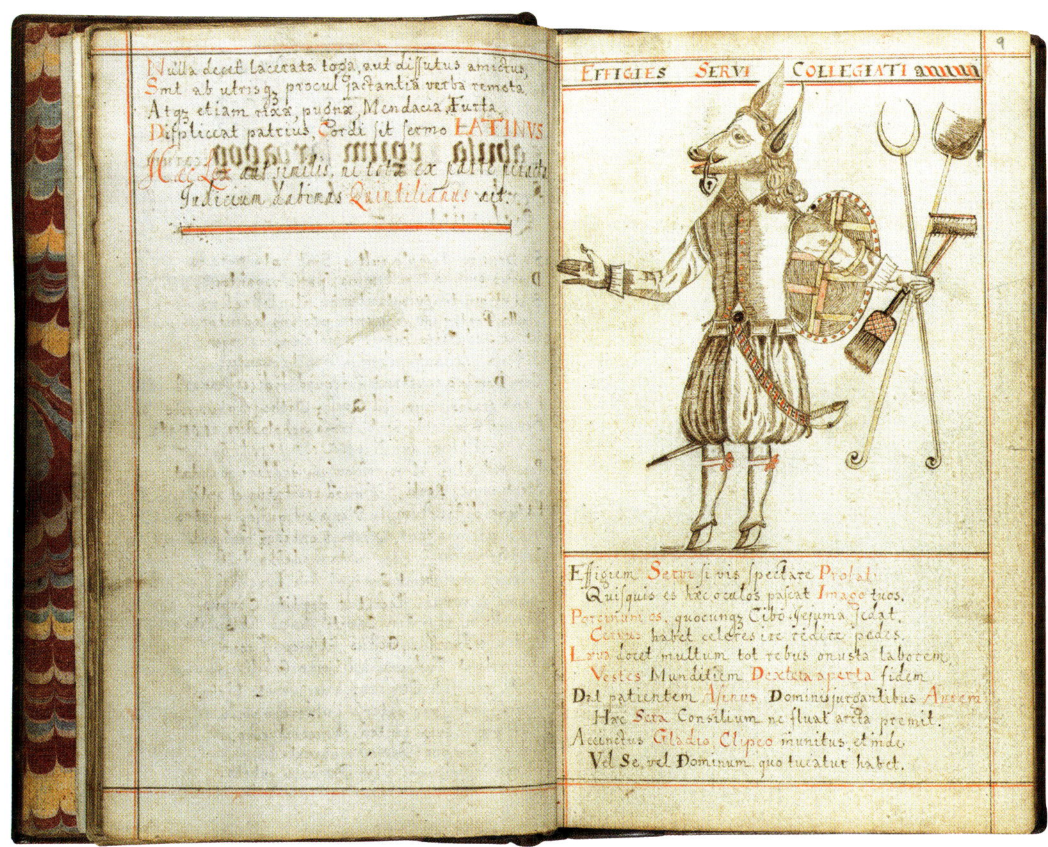

Nulla decet lacerata toga, aut dissutus amictus,
Sint ab utrisq; procul jactantia verba remota,
Atq; etiam rixæ, pugnæ, Mendacia, Furta,
Displiceat patrius, Cordi sit sermo LATINVS
Hæc Lex aut similis, ut totæ ex parte penuit
Judicium habendis Quintilianus ait.

EFFIGIES SERVI COLLEGIATI

Effigiem Servi si vis spectare Probati
Quisquis es hæc oculos pascat Imago tuos.
Porcinum es, quocunque Cibo jejunia sedat.
Cervus habet celeres ire redire pedes.
Læva docet multum tot rebus onusta laborem,
Vestes Munditiem Dextera aperta fidem
Dat patientem Asinus Dominis jurgantibus Aurem
Hæc Sera Consilium ne fluat arcta premit.
Accinctus Gladio, Clypeo munitus, et inde
Vel Se, vel Dominum quo tueatur habet.

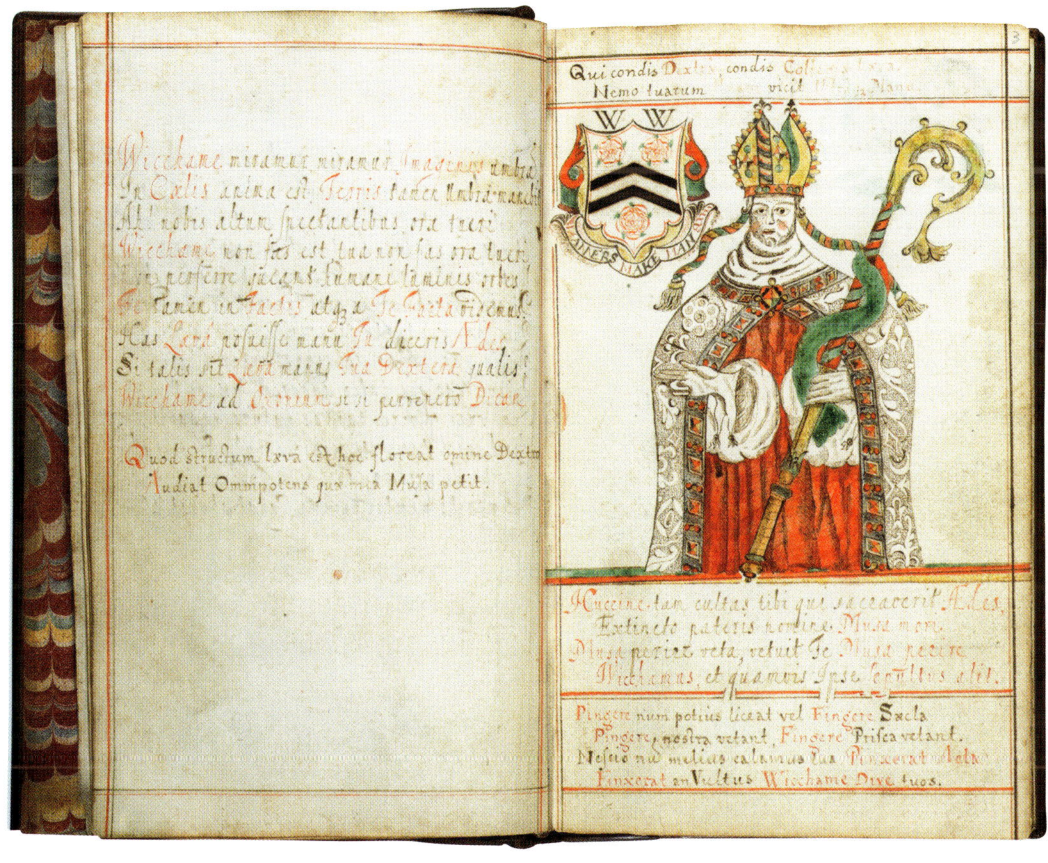

Wicchame miramur miramur Imaginis umbra
In Cælis anima est, Terris tamen Umbra manebit
At! nobis altum spectantibus, ora tueri
Wicchame non fas est, tua non fas ora tueri
ita perferre valeant lumini luminis ortes
... in factis atq; a Te facta videmus
Has Læta posuisse manu Te diceris N dei
Si talis sit Læta manu tua Dextera malis
Wicchame ad Ornum si si perverso Dicar

Quod structum lævâ et hoc floreat omine Dextra
Audiat Omnipotens quæ mea Musa petit.

Qui condis Dextra, condis Colleg[...]
Nemo tuarum ... vicit ... Manu

MANERS MAKE MAN

Huccine tam cultas tibi qui sacraverit Ædes,
Extincto pateris nomine Musa mori.
Musa periæ reta, retuit Te Musa perire
Wicchamus, et quamvis Ipse sepultus alit.

Pingere num potius liceat vel Fingere Sæcla
Pingere, nostra vetant, Fingere Prisca vetant.
Nescio num melius calamus tua Pinxerat, alter
Finxerat an Vultus Wicchame Dive tuos.

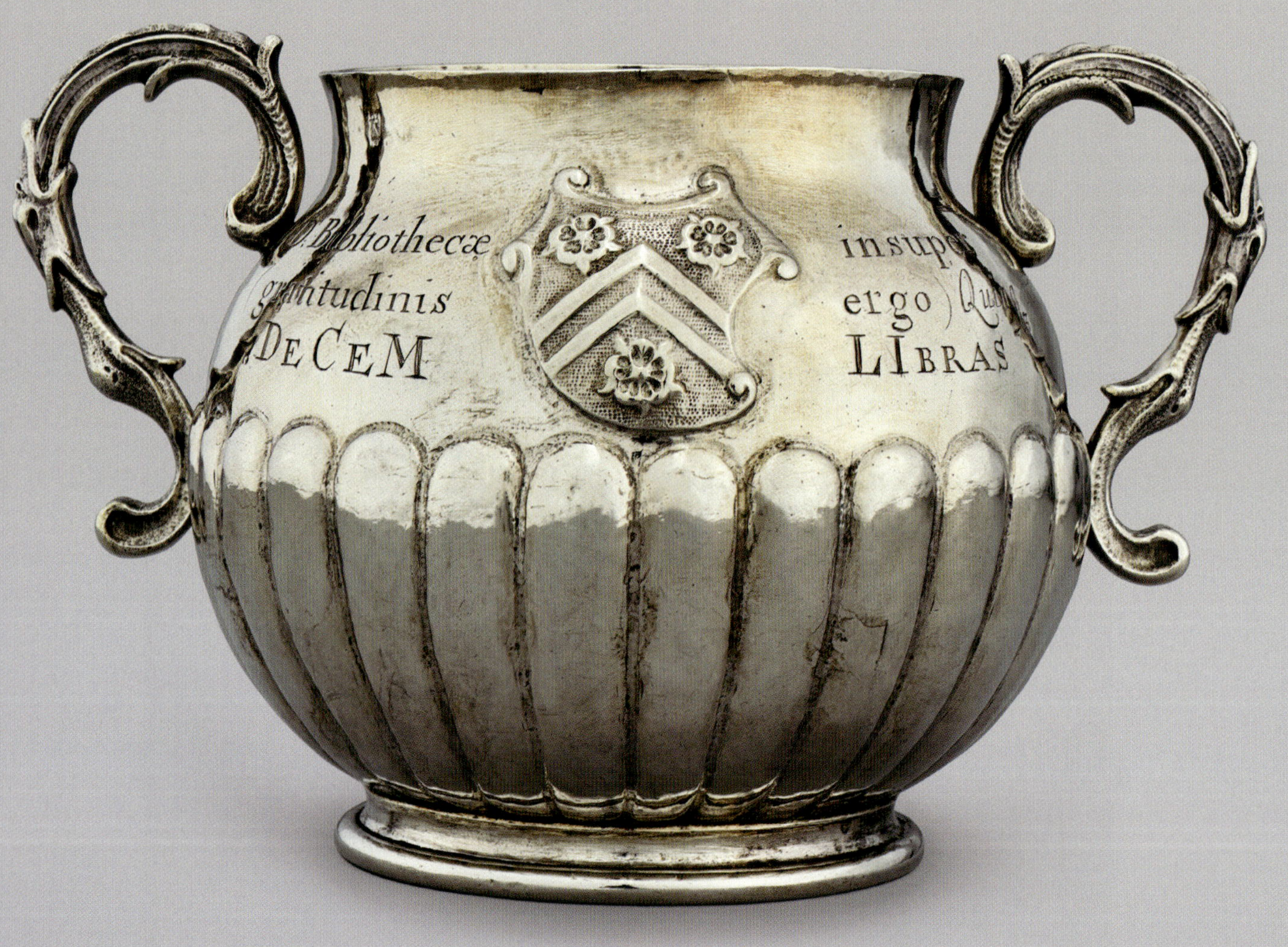
Bibliothecæ
gratitudinis
DECEM
insuper
ergo Quinq
LIBRAS

The Capel Cup, 1652

Silver (H. 10.5 cm, W. 20 cm)

Charles and Henry Capel must surely be the youngest donors to the collections of Winchester College. They entered the school as Commoners in 1651, aged fourteen and thirteen, and left the following year. On their departure from Winchester the Capel brothers made a gift of £20 (more than a skilled workman might earn in a year). The Bursars' accounts show that £15 from this was used to buy the works of Albertus Magnus in twenty-one volumes. These books are still in the Fellows' Library, handsomely bound with the Capel arms in gilt on each board. The remaining £5 was spent on this cup, which bears on one side the Capel lion rampant and on the other the College arms. An engraved inscription commemorates the generosity of the Capel brothers and records their gratitude for the education they had received.

The Capels came to Winchester at a difficult time for the family. Their father, Lord Capel of Hadham (1608–1649), had been one of the leading Royalist commanders in the English Civil Wars. He accompanied Queen Henrietta Maria on her flight to France in 1646 and helped Charles I in his escape to the Isle of Wight. After surrendering to Lord Fairfax at Colchester in August 1648, he was imprisoned in the Tower of London. Capel escaped from captivity, only to be betrayed by a Thames waterman engaged to row him from one hiding place to another, and was executed on the orders of Parliament in March 1649. He left a wife and seven children, five of whom are shown in a well-known portrait of the Capel family by Cornelius Johnson, now in the National Portrait Gallery. Arthur, the eldest son, succeeded to the barony and was made Earl of Essex at the Restoration. Charles died soon after leaving Winchester.

Henry became MP for Tewkesbury for 1661, served as First Lord of the Admiralty, and was ennobled in 1692. He established an exotic garden at Kew, the nucleus of the Royal Botanic Gardens.

When commissioning this cup, the College turned to Richard Blackwell, one of the leading silversmiths of the day. His career began around 1646 and he often worked for Royalist clients, specialising in sets of communion plate for their private chapels. Blackwell also made several of the earliest examples of a new form of drinking cup, with a broad bowl and two handles. Some of these are richly decorated, but others, like the Capel Cup, are quite plain. Despite the restrained decoration, the exceptional quality of this piece is clear. Although the bowl is only six inches wide it weighs more than twenty-four ounces. A series of raised panels subtly emphasises the convex profile of the cup, and shows off the lustrous quality of the metal. Within the bowl, thousands of hammer marks catch the light when it is turned. The handles are of serpentine form and were cast in a mould.

This object serves as a reminder of the human cost of the English Civil Wars, but also of the College's good fortunes during this period. While other institutions lost substantial quantities of silver to Royalists and Parliamentarians, Winchester kept its collections intact and commissioned several fine pieces. Unlike the Capels, who suffered for their loyalty to the Crown, the College conformed to the new regime. All of the Fellows and employees remained in their posts and there are many indications of the school's continuing prosperity.

Richard Foster (History, Fellows' Librarian and Keeper of Collections)

Diary of William Emes, 1661–1702

MS 16: Manuscript on paper, ff. 345, bound in 17th-century reversed calfskin over pasteboard with two clasps (10.1 × 6.2 cm)

MS 16, one of the smallest items in the Fellows' Library, was presented in 1956 by W.E. Philip (College, 1920–25) as the 'Diary' of William Emes. This is a misnomer. Although the writer records some occasions of national importance and other local or family events, much of the material appears to be aides-memoires, and there are years with only two or three entries.

Elected a Scholar in 1656 aged thirteen, Emes later proceeded to New College, becoming a Fellow from 1663 to 1672. On 7 August 1670 he was also elected Fellow of Winchester. In 1674 he was made Rector of Weeke and in 1677, the year he married, additionally collated to the College living of Ash in Surrey. To his two rectorships he added the Wykehamical prebendal stall of Exceit in the Chichester diocese in 1680.

There is surprisingly little about Winchester in the manuscript, and that often terse: 'By ye Warden, & majority of Fellows it was voted that a New-School should be built for ye College at Winchester' (21 April 1680). It would have been interesting to know who dissented. A slightly longer entry records that a Commoner, William Oldisworth, published a poem, *Cupid*, in 1698 and queries 'whethr this were not the first that ever putt out anything in print whist hee was actually a scholar of ye School'.

Meteorological records form the major part: a great wind damaged Oxford steeples in 1661; in December 1686 in Emes's church a 'Flash of Lightning rent ye Eastern wall, & passed through the Body of ye Church leaving behind a great smoake, & Smell of Brimstone'; and a July night in 1696 was so cold that 17 partridges were found dead 'with their heads lying together'. As today, the College swallows were of interest, appearing as early as 30 March in 1683, and in 1690 still flying about the river on 28 October, '7 weeks after their usuall time of going away'. He observed the Great Comet (1665) and Newton's Comet (1680), and drew what he saw.

Of national events Emes noted that Parliament met in Oxford in 1665 because of the Plague in London, the Lords sitting in the Geometry School, the Commons in the Convocation House. He described the Spanish ambassador lodging in New College when visiting Charles II and recounted the celebration of a High Mass on Christmas Eve 1665 in the Warden's dining room, attended by the ambassador, with an 'abundance of very large wax tapers'. This entry reveals Emes was aware that this little book might be read by others, adding: 'I did not goe into ye Chappell but lookt through

the door'. It would not have been appropriate for an Anglican cleric to have been in the room where Mass was being celebrated. The most dramatic entry is a description of the Great Fire of London. It may be read in Emes's very legible handwriting in the below illustration.

Geoffrey Day (Fellows' Librarian, 2005–14)

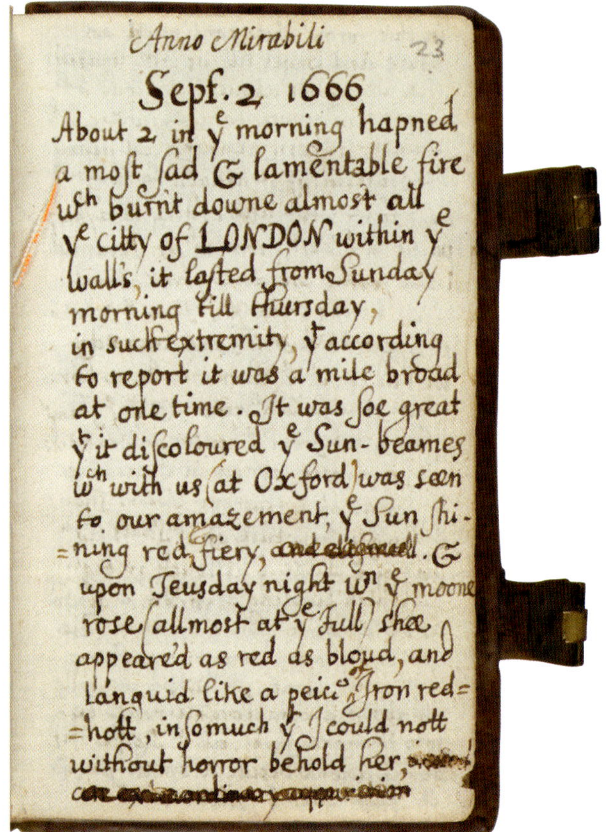

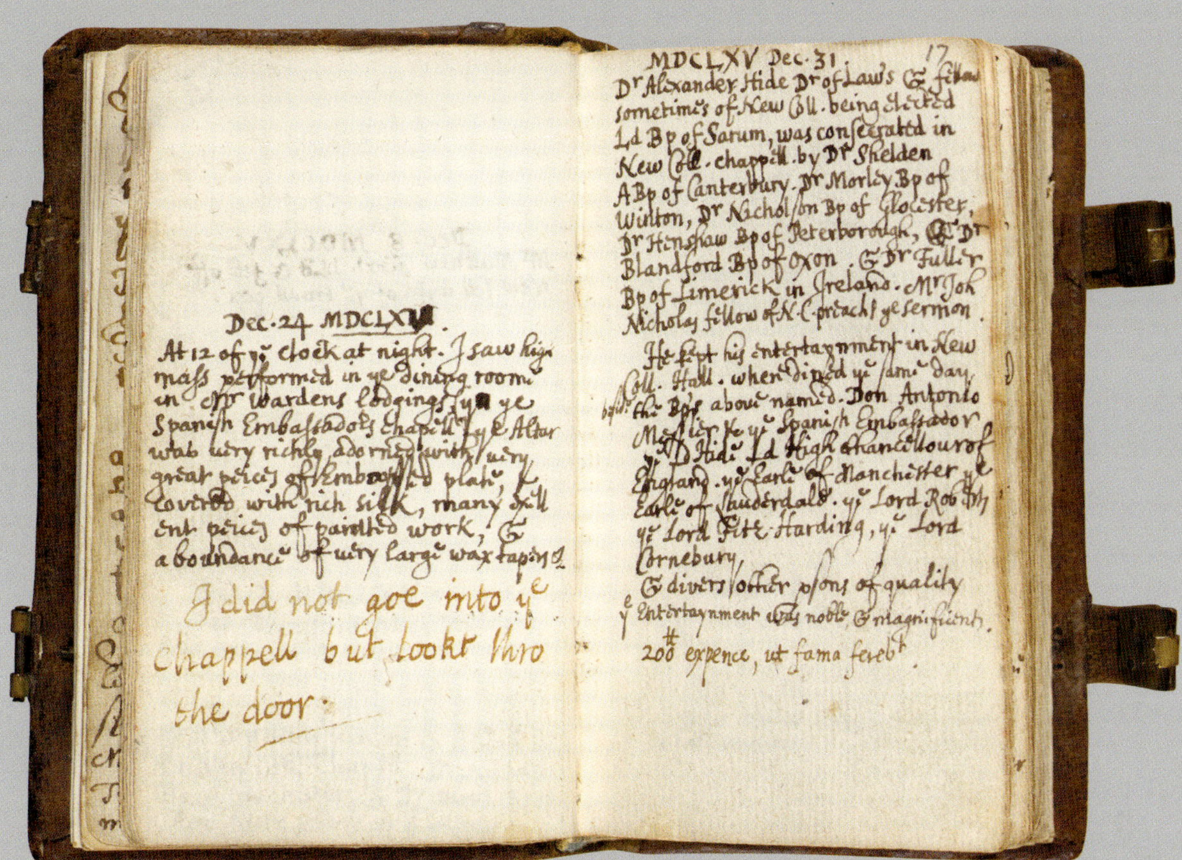

Dec. 24 MDCLXV.
At 12 of ye clock at night. I saw high
mass performed in ye dining roome
in cr wardens lodeings wth ye
Spanish Embassadors Chapell ye Altar
was very richly adorned with very
great peices of embossed plate,
covered with rich silk, many severall
ent peices of painted work, &
abundance of very large wax tapers.

I did not goe into ye
chappell but lookt thro
the door.

MDCLXV Dec. 31.   17
Dr Alexander Hide Dr of Laws & fellow
sometimes of New Coll. being elected
Ld Bp of Sarum, was consecrated in
New Coll. chappell. by Dr Shelden
A Bp of Canterbury. Dr Morley Bp of
Winton, Dr Nicholson Bp of Glocester,
Dr Henshaw Bp of Peterborough, & Dr
Blandford Bp of Oxon. & Dr Fuller
Bp of Limerick in Ireland. Mr Joh
Nicholas fellow of N. C. preacht ye sermon.

He kept his entertaynment in New
Coll. Hall. where dined ye same day,
the Bps above named. Don Antonio
Meslier. the ye Spanish Embassador
Dr Hid: Ld High Chancellour of
England. ye Earle of Manchester ye
Earle of Lauderdale. ye Lord Robrth
ye Lord Fitz Harding, ye Lord
Cornebury

& divers other psons of quality
ye Entertaynment was noble & magnifficent.
200li expence, ut fama ferebt.

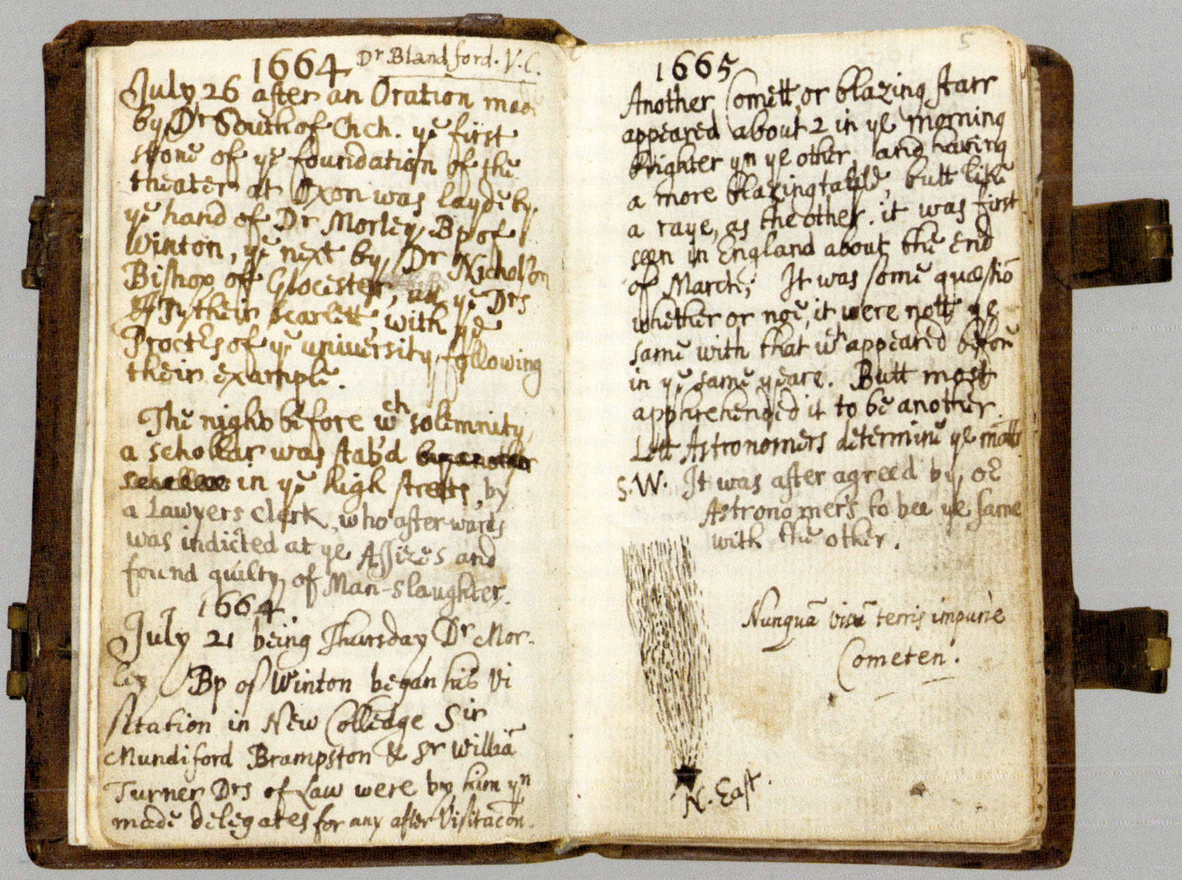

1664   Dr Blandford. V.C.
July 26 after an Oration made
by Dr South of Chch. ye first
stone of ye foundation of the
theater at Oxon was layd by
ye hand of Dr Morley Bp of
Winton, ye next by Dr Nicholson
Bishop of Glocester, ye both in scarlett, with ye
Proctrs of ye university, following
their example.

The night before wch solemnity
a scholar was stab'd
in ye High Streete, by
a Lawyers clerk, who afterwards
was indicted at ye Assizes and
found guilty of Man-slaughter.
1664.
July 21 being Thursday Dr Mor.
ley Bp of Winton began his Vi
sitation in New Colledge Sir
Mundiford Brampston & Sr William
Turner Drs of Law were by him yn
made delegates for any after Visitacon

1665
Another Comett or blazing starr
appeared about 2 in ye morning
brighter yn ye other. and having
a more blazing talle, butt like
a raye, as the other. it was first
seen in England about the End
of March; It was some questio
whither or noe, it were nott ye
same with that wch appeard before
in ye same yeare. Butt most
apprehended it to be another.
Lett Astronomers determine ye motio
S.W. It was after agreed by or
Astronomers to bee ye same
with the other.

Nunqua visa terris impune
Cometen.

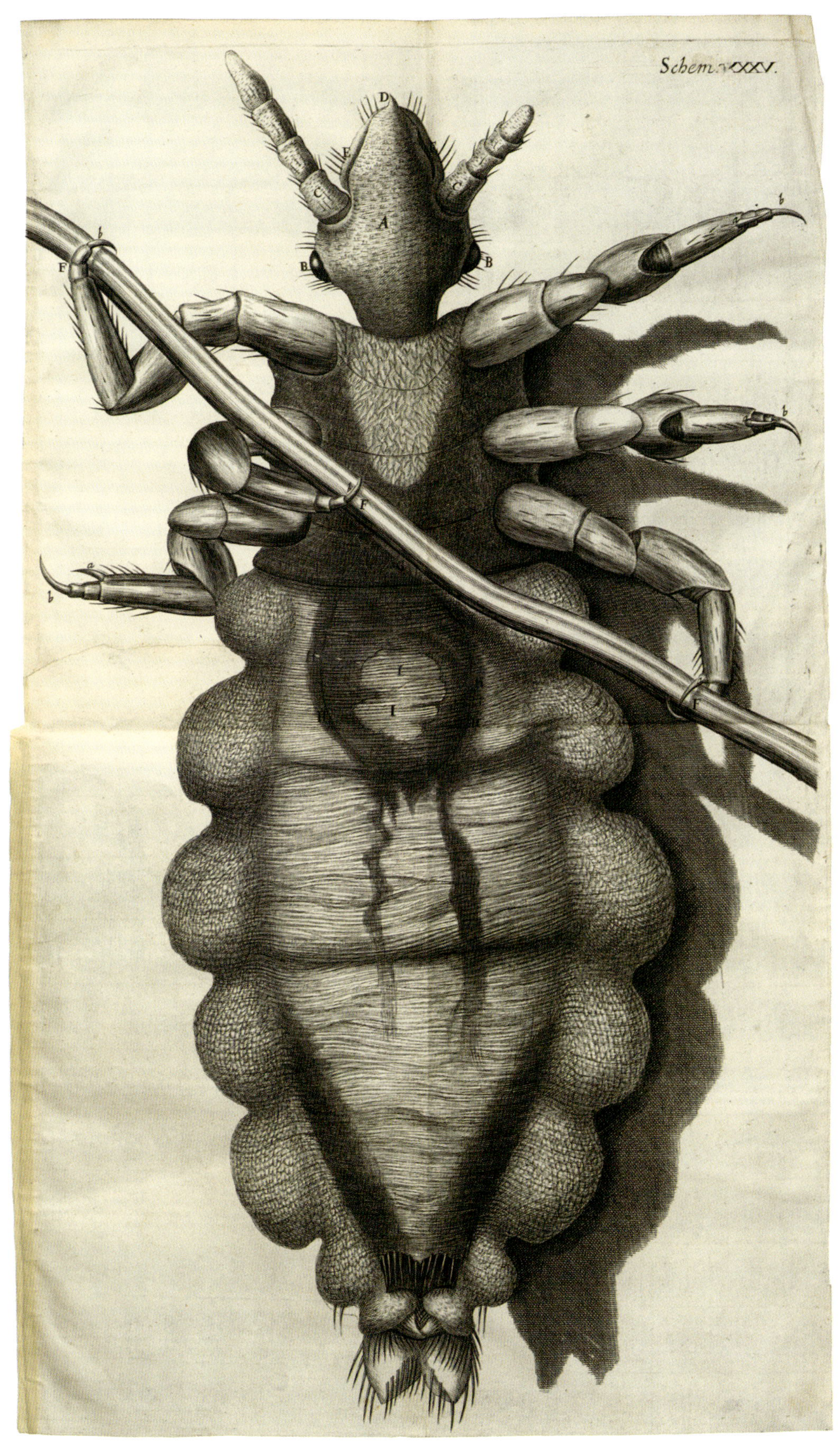

Hooke's *Micrographia*

Robert Hooke, *Micrographia: or Some Physiological Descriptions of Minute Bodies Made by Magnifying Glasses. With Observations and Inquiries Thereupon* (London, 1665), bound in 20th-century calfskin over pasteboard (29.4 × 19.3 cm)

Micrographia was the first book to show in detail the new world revealed by microscopes. Interested in how the limits of our perception influenced our understanding of the world, Robert Hooke set about close examination of a comprehensive array of objects, never before seen at such magnification. *Micrographia* brilliantly showcases the scientific method; Hooke made careful and detailed observations, recorded them meticulously and then mused on their possible significance. Upon examining a louse (illustrated here), and seeing it suck blood from his hand, he inferred that the blood must run close to the surface of the skin, as the mouthparts were neither particularly large, nor did they seem to be inserted very far. Of particular importance was Hooke's observation of a slice of cork; he noticed that it was made up of pores, surrounded by what he referred to as 'walls' (in fact, he was seeing the cell walls of the plant's conductive tissues). Later he refers to these pores as 'cells', from the Latin *cella,* meaning 'small room'. It was not until 1839 that scientists first recognised cells as the common unit from which living things are made, but the term was coined by Hooke 174 years earlier.

While there is much for scientists to admire in Hooke's thorough approach and the conclusions he draws, the broad appeal of the book is secured by the eye-catching images, allowing the reader to see what Hooke saw through his microscope. The most celebrated of the book's illustrations is an engraving of a flea, which must have seemed extraordinary when viewed for the first time. Hooke writes: 'The Microscope manifests it to be all over adorn'd with a curiously polish'd suit of sable armour, neatly jointed, and beset with multitudes of sharp pinns'. As well as eloquent descriptions of objects, the pages of *Micrographia* are packed with fascinating insights into Hooke's methods: 'I gave [the ant] a Gill of Brandy … which after a while, e'en knocked him down dead drunk, so that he became moveless'.

Micrographia was a groundbreaking work and it remains one of the most immediately engaging books in the history of science. The meticulous copperplate engravings found throughout give new life to familiar objects, captivating to science enthusiasts and casual observers alike. Hooke's desire to use his microscope to observe such a wide array of items is mirrored in the curiosity of schoolchildren who, when given a microscope, will enthusiastically set about observing the edge of the glass slide, a stray hair or a fingerprint. Light microscopy has been vital to the study of biology for centuries. It was in this way, through carefully crafted lenses, that microscopic organisms were first observed by Antonie van Leeuwenhoek in 1676 and, in the present day, advanced techniques are used to observe cells at a level of detail that Hooke could not have imagined possible.

Rachel Poole (Biology)

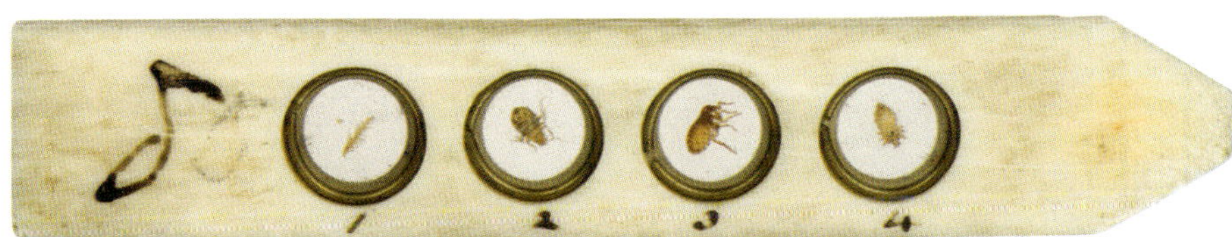

Slide from a microscope set purchased by the College in 1785, including a flea (no. 3) and a head louse (no. 4).

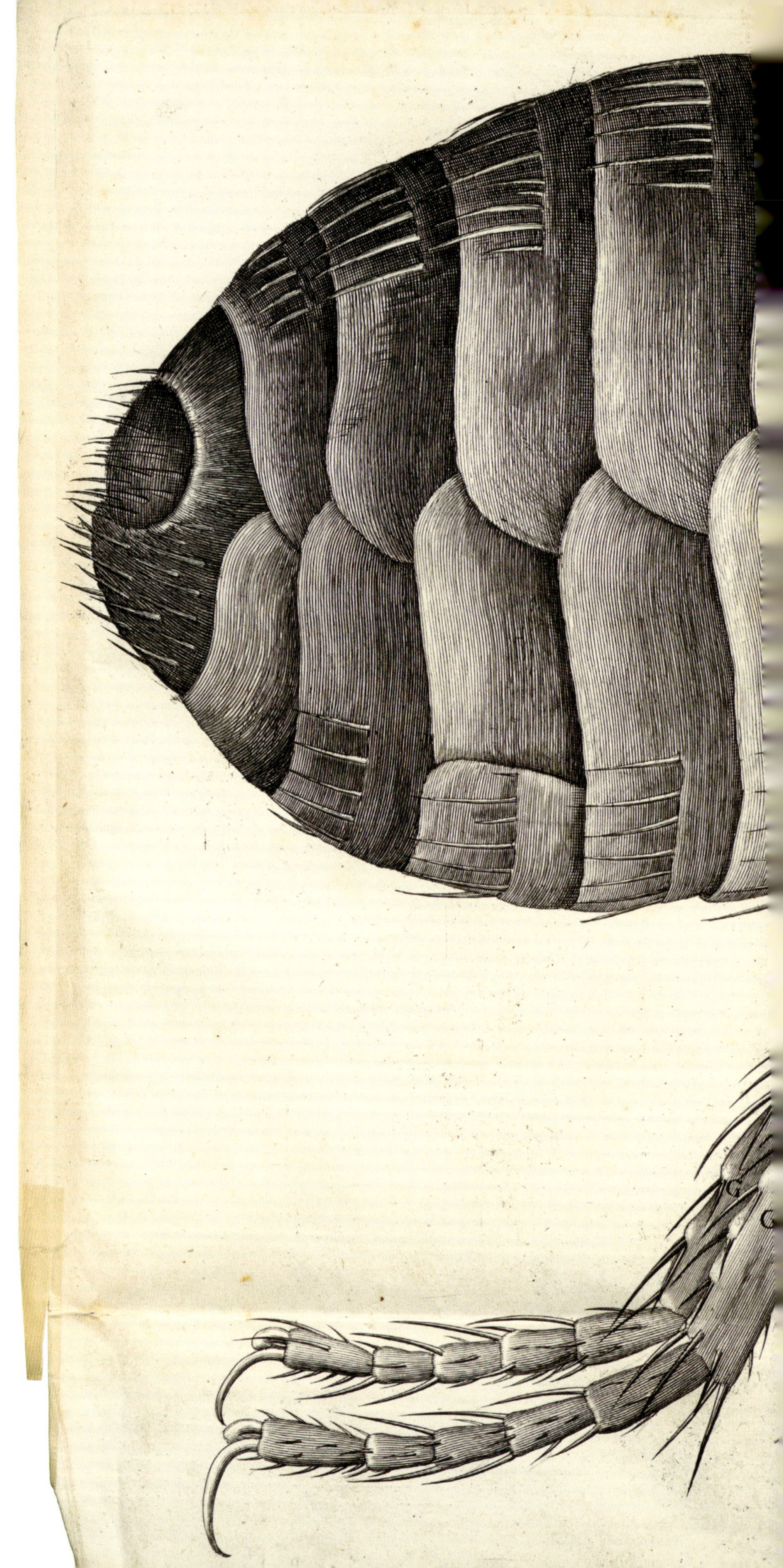

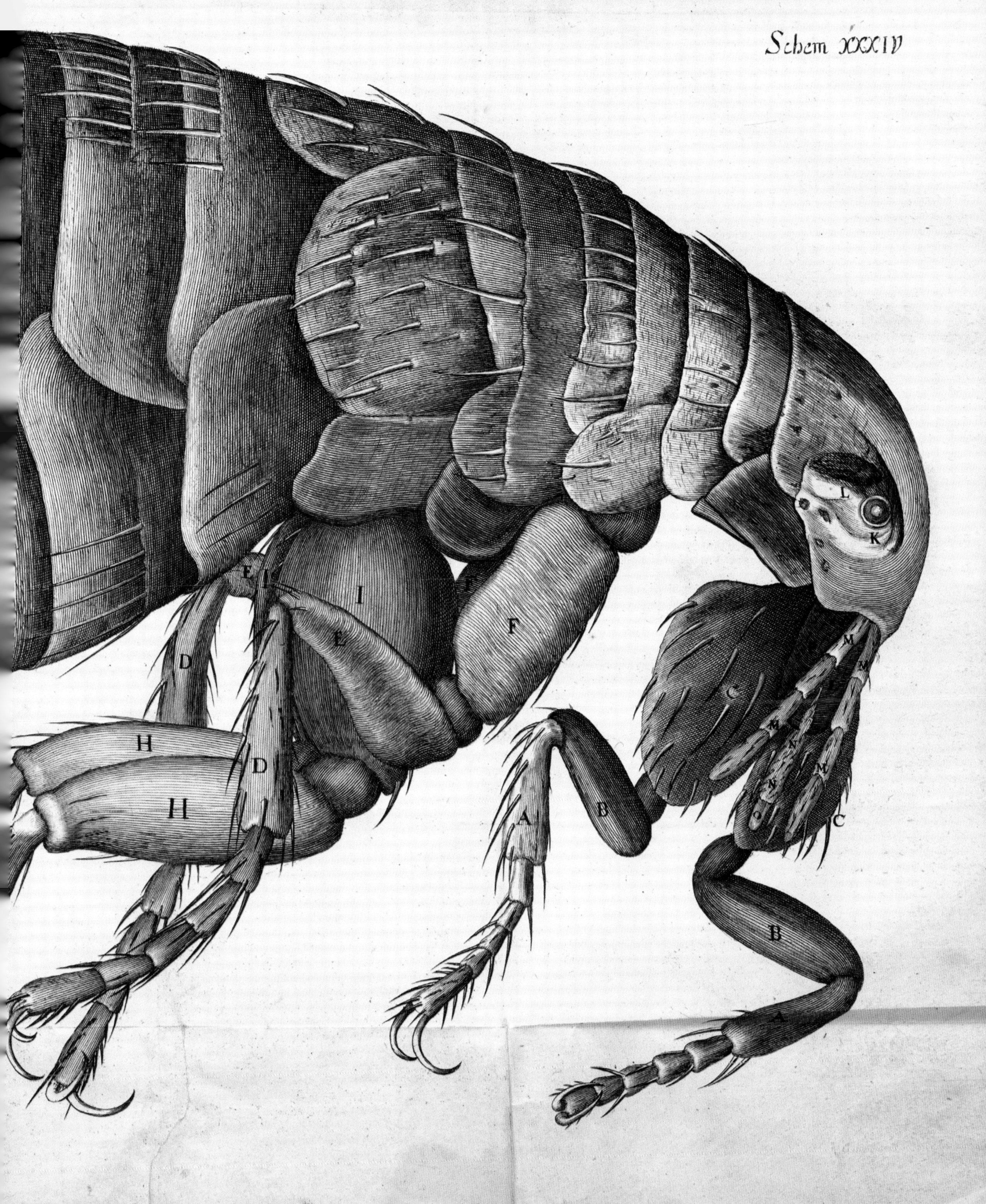

Schem XXXIV
L
K
M
M
M
N
M
N
C
C
A
B
B
A
I
E
F
D
H
II
D

Eliot's Indian Bible, 1685

Mamusse Wunneetupanatamwe Up-Biblum God (Cambridge, Massachusetts, 1685),
bound in 17th-century calfskin with gilt spine (18.5 × 15 cm)

Even the most talented linguist would be unable to read this remarkable book: it was published in the seventeenth century in a language that has since become extinct. However, it is a translation of the Bible with titles and chapter headings in English, so the contents are readily apparent. It was the product of the missionary vocation of a Puritan colonist in New England, John Eliot (1604–1690), traditionally known as 'the Apostle to the Indians'.

Like many Puritans, Eliot was convinced that the way to create a godly society was to make the Word of God accessible to all people, and from the 1640s he focused his proselytising zeal on the local Algonquian Indians. He gathered his converts into settled, segregated 'praying towns', where he encouraged them to adopt the Puritan faith and culture. With the help of English-speaking natives, he studied their unwritten language and devised a way to present it phonetically in writing. Eliot produced some twenty religious books in the Natick dialect of the Algonquian language, the most significant of which was the 'Indian Bible'. This was published in 1663 and gave no credit to his Indian colleagues: Job Nesutan, Cochenoe, John Sassamon and James Printer. It was the first Bible published in North America and was printed by the fledgling press at Harvard. The Winchester College volume is a copy of the second edition of 1685, which was commissioned after many of the earlier Bibles were destroyed in Metacomet's War of 1675–76. The printing of both editions was paid for by the Company for the Propagation of the Gospel in New England, and our volume includes a dedication to the Company's Governor, the great scientist Robert Boyle. The final pages contain a set of metrical Psalms and Eliot's 'Rules for Christian Living', also in phonetic Algonquian.

The 'Indian Bible' came to Winchester College in 1689, the gift of Samuel Sewall (1652–1730), an influential Boston merchant and magistrate, who was a close friend of John Eliot. It was Sewall's personal copy, inscribed on the title page with his name and date: 2 January 1685/6 (using both the old and new styles of the calendar). Sewall was born in Hampshire and was visiting friends and family in England at the time. In his diary he describes the visit, which evidently followed a similar route to modern guided tours: 'View'd Winchester Colledge, the Chapel, Library, built in the midst of the Green within the Cloisters. Left my Indian Bible and Mr Mather's Letter there. Was shew'd also the Hall, which is above

Stairs.' After his return to Boston, Sewall was one of the judges in the Salem witchcraft trials of 1692 and the only one to express any regrets subsequently.

The 'Indian Bible' is an extraordinary book. Not only does it provide a valuable insight into the world of colonial New England, but in recent years its text has also been used as a prime resource in attempts to recover and revive the lost language of the Algonquians.

Andrea Thomas (College Tour Guide)

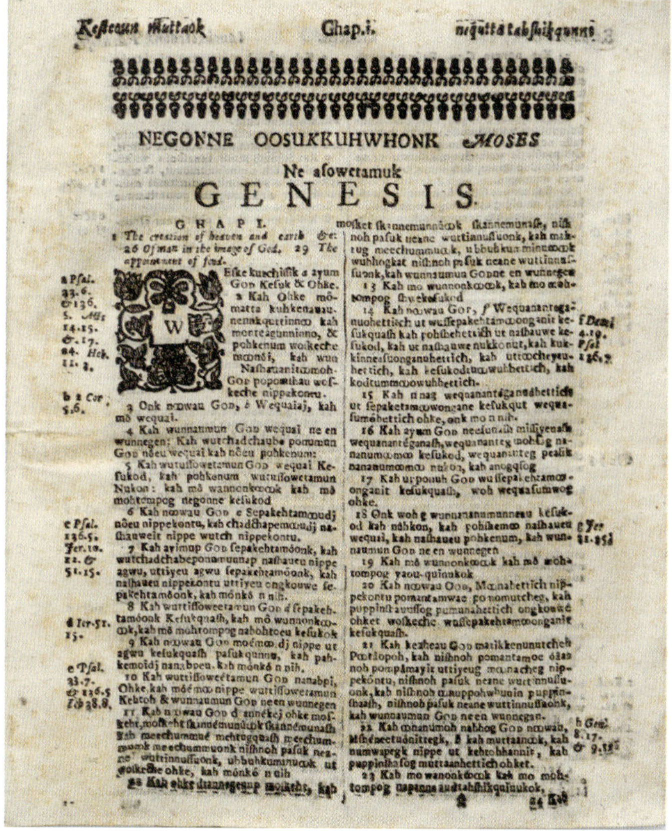

MAMUSSE
WUNNEETUPANATAMWE
UP-BIBLUM GOD
NANEESWE
NUKKONE TESTAMENT
KAH WONK
WUSKU TESTAMENT·

Ne quoſhkinnumuk naſhpe Wuttinneumoh *CHRIST*
noh aſoowefit

JOHN ELIOT.

Nahohtŏeu ontchetŏe Printeuŏŏmuk.

CAMBRIDGE.
Printeuŏŏp naſhpe *Samuel Green.*   MDCLXXXV.

Nam producantur AB, AD, AR ad *b*, *d* & *r*. Ipsi R*D*
agatur parallela *r b d*, & arcui AB similis ducatur arcus A*b*.
Coeuntibus punctis A, B, angulus *b* A *d*
evanescet, & propterea triangula tria
r A*b*, *r* A*b*, *r* A*d* coincident, suntq; eo
nomine similia & æqualia. Unde &
hisce semper similia & proportionalia
R*AB*, R*AB*, R*AD* fient ultimo sibi
invicem similia & æqualia. *Q. E. D.*

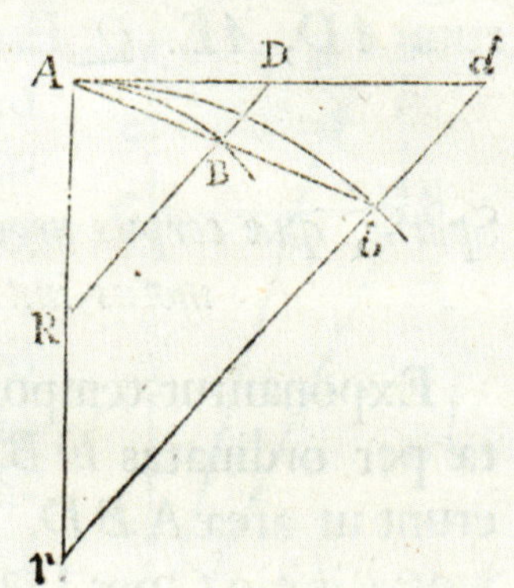

   Corol. Et hinc triangula illa in omni de
rationibus ultimis argumentatione pro se
invicem usurpari possunt.

Lemma IX.

Si recta A E & *Curva* A C *positione datæ se mutuo secent in angulo
dato* A, & *ad rectam illam in
alio dato angulo ordinatim ap-
plicentur* B D, E C, *curvæ oc-
currentes in* B, C; *dein puncta*
B, C *accedant ad punctum* A:
dico quod areæ triangulorum
A D B, A E C *erunt ultimo ad
invicem in duplicata ratione la-
terum.*

Etenim in *AD* producta ca-
piantur A*d*, A*e* ipsis *AD*, *AE*
proportionales, & erigantur or-
dinatæ *d b*, *e c* ordinatis D*B*, E*C* parallelæ & proportionales.
Producatur AC ad *c*, ducatur curva A*b c* ipsi A*BC* similis, &
recta A*g* tangatur curva utraq; in A; & secantur ordinatim appli-
catæ in *F*, *G*, *f*, *g*. Tum coeant puncta B, C cum puncto A, &
angulo *c* A*g* evanescente, coincident areæ curvilineæ A*b d*, A*c e*
cum rectilineis A*f d*, A*g e*, adeoq; per Lemma V, erunt in duplicata

Newton's *Principia*, 1687

Isaac Newton, *Philosophiae Naturalis Principia Mathematica* (London, 1687), bound in late 17th-
or early 18th-century calfskin over pasteboard (23.8 × 19 cm)

To physicists Sir Isaac Newton is 'the gaffer', the greatest ever, even better than Albert Einstein, the man whose theory of gravity finally superseded his after two and a half centuries. Newton is so special because not only did he (like Einstein) make major, fundamental advances across multiple fields of physics, he was also (unlike Einstein) one of the greatest mathematicians of the age and invented many of the tools necessary to describe and apply the physical laws which he discovered. The full title of his great work – *Philosophiae Naturalis Principia Mathematica* – draws attention to this fundamentally mathematical approach.

Embedded in the work are both Newton's celebrated inverse-square law of gravity and his three laws of motion. The crown jewels of physics, they are *universal* and *unifying*: the force that makes the apple fall from the tree is the same as that which keeps the celestial bodies in orbit. (Newton himself, incidentally, told the apple story to his biographer.) The discoveries of his great predecessors Kepler and Galileo are confirmed and explained by Newton's overarching scheme, along with a range of other astronomical phenomena known (but unexplained) since ancient times, such as the precession of the equinoxes.

Winchester College's copy of the first edition of Newton's most important work was donated by Robert Shipman, an Old Wykehamist and Fellow of All Souls, in 1762. One of its most striking illustrations is a large fold-out showing the path of the comet of 1680–81. Astronomers of the mid-1600s had suggested that comets might orbit the sun, but Newton put this on a firm footing, showing that they obey the laws of gravity just as planets do. Edmond Halley used these ideas to predict the regular return of the comet that now bears his name – a just reward, since it was Halley's encouragement that brought about the book's publication and Halley's money that paid for it.

Newton famously wrote '*Hypotheses non fingo*' – the empirical approach starts from experiment rather than from a speculative hypothesis. The patterns in the observations then reveal the laws that govern them. In line with this, he did not attempt to explain how gravity was transmitted; the data said nothing about that, only about its effects. This brought him under fire for endorsing the idea of 'action at a distance', an absurdity according to Cartesian orthodoxy – although Newton's point is that the mechanism ought to be left an open question.

In the decades following Newton's death, the stock of the *Principia* rose further as the theory's loose ends were resolved by his successors. Enlightenment luminaries such as Laplace developed the idea of the mechanistic 'clockwork universe', predictable and comprehensible. But there is also a Romantic view of Newton perhaps best expressed by Wordsworth's lines concerning his statue in Trinity College, Cambridge: 'The marble index of a mind for ever/ Voyaging through strange seas of Thought, alone'.

Jeremy Douglas (College, 1988–92, Head of Physics)

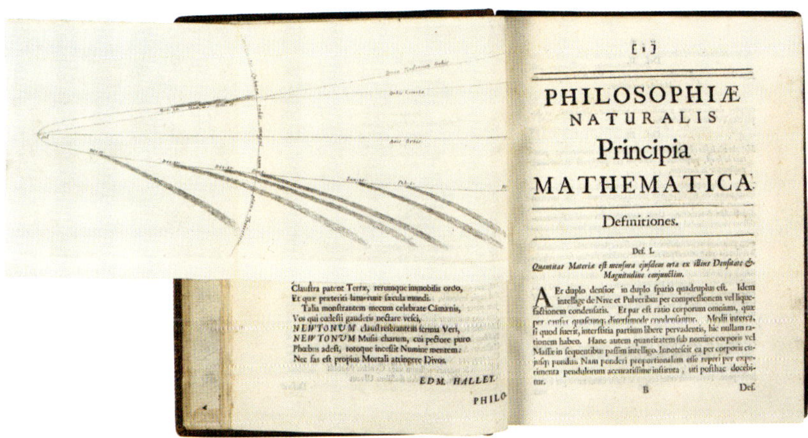

François Lemoyne, *The Annunciation*, 1727

Oil on canvas (208 × 127 cm)

François Lemoyne's beautiful altarpiece, signed and dated 1727, was presented to the College by Dr John Burton, DD (1690–1774), one of Winchester's most distinguished but least-known Headmasters. The Winchester College 'Book of Benefactions' reveals that in 1729 Burton 'Gave a beautiful Salutation-Piece painted by Le Moine, placed over the Altar in the Chapel which cost 80 guineas'. The Angel Gabriel salutes Mary at the Annunciation (Luke 1.28). The College's full name is 'St Mary College of Winchester by Winchester'. Two prominent eighteenth-century French commentators, the comte de Caylus and Pierre-Jean Mariette, recorded that Lemoyne's *Annunciation* was intended for England. This strengthens the likelihood of a special commission from Burton and may explain the prominent signature.

The Winchester *Annunciation* has been on loan to the National Gallery since 2013, which indicates its quality and rarity, as well as filling a lacuna in the national collection. It is in mint condition, revealing the fluency of Lemoyne's brushwork, the beauty of his drawing and colouring, together with the harmony, grace and invention of the composition. Several pentimenti are visible to the naked eye, indicating adjustments in the act of painting. Lemoyne exhibits his debt to Italian art. During his sojourn in Italy in 1723–24, according to Caylus, Lemoyne studied '*des grands Maîtres & des grandes machines*', paying particular attention in Rome to the frescos by Michelangelo in the Sistine Chapel and by Pietro da Cortona in the Barberini Palace.

The Chapel panelling, installed in 1680–82, had made provision for an altarpiece, but the space seems previously to have remained empty. The *Annunciation* has a painted rounded top, suggesting that an arched frame was originally intended, but the rectangular carved and gilded English frame is presumably the original, corresponding to the border mouldings in the surrounding woodwork. Painting and frame were first depicted *in situ* in John Cave's 1802 watercolour of College Chapel. This elegant scheme was dismantled in 1864–74 when the Chapel interior was reordered in the Gothic style. The panelling is now in New Hall. The *Annunciation* was moved to the Warden's Lodgings. It returned to Chapel in 1998, when it was hung over the altar in Thurbern's Chantry at the suggestion of Arthur Morgan, then Director of Art.

Until recently scholars of eighteenth-century French painting were unaware of the Winchester *Annunciation*, and it was presumed 'lost' in Jean-Luc Bordeaux's 1984 catalogue raisonné of Lemoyne's work. The rediscovery of the painting was published by the present author in the *Burlington Magazine* in March 2012. Its significance had become apparent during research for an article in the *British Art Journal* (Spring/Summer 2013) on Isaac Whood (1689–1752) and his portraits of 'Dr Burton's Commoners', described elsewhere in this volume.

There is a preparatory study for Lemoyne's *Annunciation* in the Courtauld Gallery, London, in black chalk with white highlights, on Lemoyne's characteristic blue paper. The engraving in reverse of 1727–28 by Laurent Cars (1699–1771), his former pupil, is dedicated to Lemoyne's protector, the duc d'Antin, '*Directeur général des Bâtimens et Jardins du Roy*'. Lemoyne later became Louis XV's *premier peintre du roi* and considerably influenced the subsequent generation of French painters, including François Boucher. The fact that Lemoyne's Winchester altarpiece was probably commissioned, and certainly acquired, by Dr Burton is indicative of his sophisticated good taste, evident in other aspects of his headmastership.

Christopher Rowell (K, 1965–70)

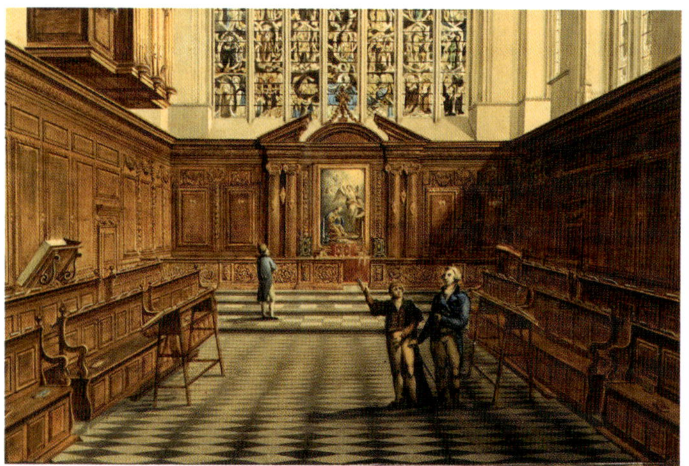

Detail from a watercolour of the Chapel interior by John Cave, 1802.

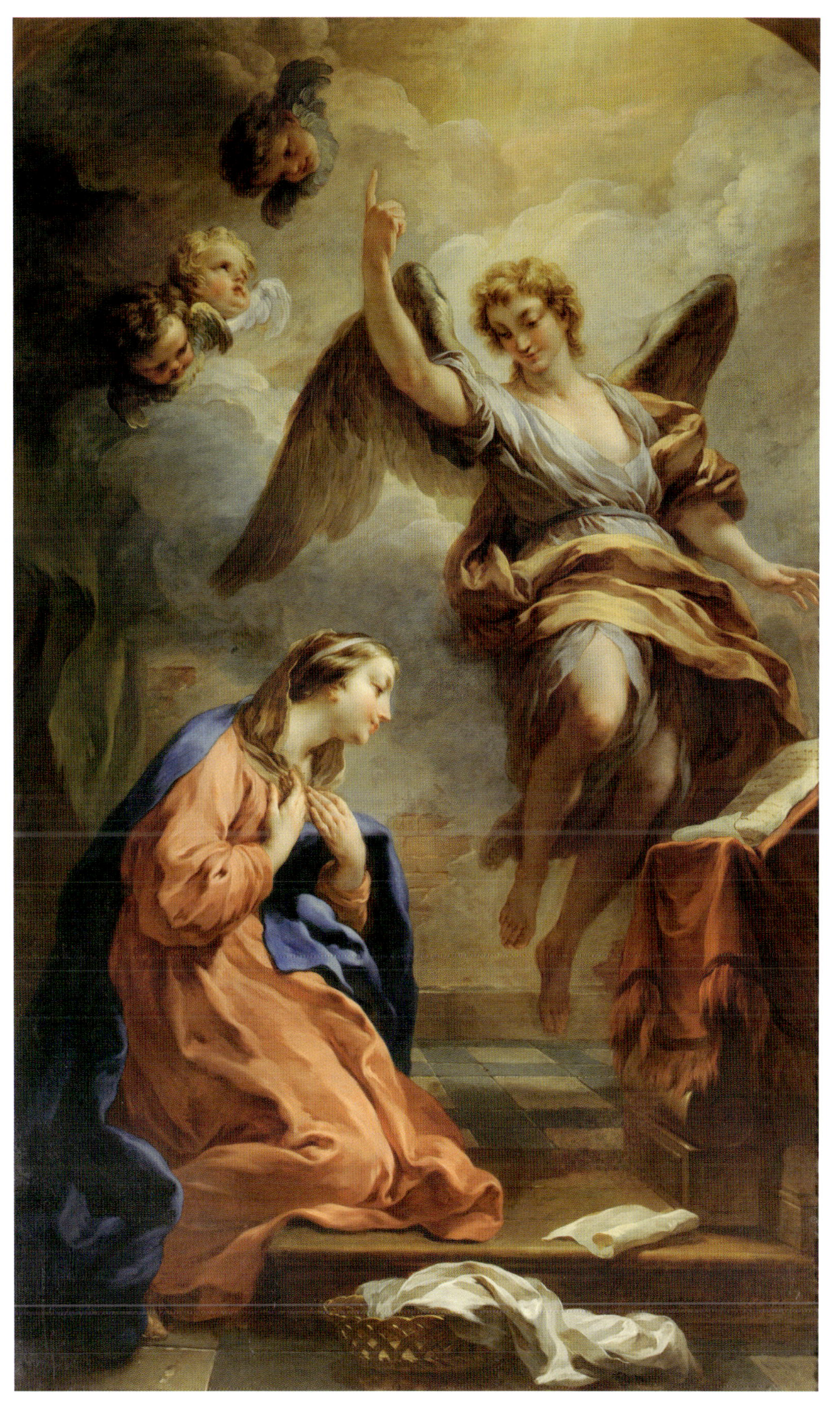

Qing Dynasty Bat Bowl, 1720s–30s

Porcelain with red decoration under a green glaze (D. 15.2 cm)

This eighteenth-century bowl is one of a pair made at the Chinese imperial kilns at Jingdezhen, in imitation of the celebrated celadon wares of the Song Dynasty (960–1279). In the West the term 'celadon' is used to describe porcelain with a green colour, resembling jade. The exact shade varies, depending on how thickly the glaze is applied and the timing of the iron oxide reduction during firing. The pale green of this bowl is similar to that found on the wares made at Longquan during the thirteenth and fourteenth centuries, which were highly prized by collectors in the Qing Dynasty (1644–1911).

Beneath the celadon glaze, an iron-red pigment has been used to paint five bats around each bowl. In this respect these bowls differ from Song celadon wares, which did not make use of underglaze pigments. The word for bat (*fú* 蝠) is a homophone with the word for good fortune or happiness (*fú* 福). This association with good luck has created a plethora of bats in Chinese art, but they are also found in modern China (for example on belt buckles and locks). The colour of the bats also has meaning, as the words 'red' (*hóng* 红) and 'abundant' or 'vast' (*hóng* 洪) are also homophones. Therefore, red bats (*hóngfú* 红蝠) connote abundant good fortune (*hóngfú* 洪蝠). Furthermore, the bowls portray five bats (*wǔfú* 红福), which share a pronunciation with the Five Blessings (*wǔfú* 五福). First mentioned in the *Book of Documents* in the Zhou Dynasty (1046–256 BC), the blessings express the collective desire for wealth, health, longevity, a virtuous life and a natural death. The blessings are still a big part of life today: *Wǔfú línmén* (五福臨門) (the full name for the Five Blessings) is used as a blessing for relatives and *Wǔfú línmén* paper is hung outside homes in an attempt to bring the Five Blessings to families.

On the bottom of the bowl there is a six-character inscription: 大清 雍正 年製. A literal translation of this is: '大 great, 清 Qing, 雍正 Yongzheng, 年 year, 製 produced', meaning: 'made in the great Qing Dynasty under the reign of Emperor Yongzheng'. This mark shows that these pieces were made during the reign of Yongzheng (1723–35) in the imperial kilns at Jingdezhen, which produced the finest porcelain in the world. The Emperor Yongzheng oversaw a period of experimentation and refinement at Jingdezhen. Potters developed new techniques, such as *fěncǎi* (粉彩) enamels, which made available a wider range of colours. They also made superb copies of the celebrated wares of earlier periods. This elegant bowl shows how accomplished the potters of Jingdezhen were in imitating the techniques of the Song Dynasty.

George Morrison (B, 2014–19)

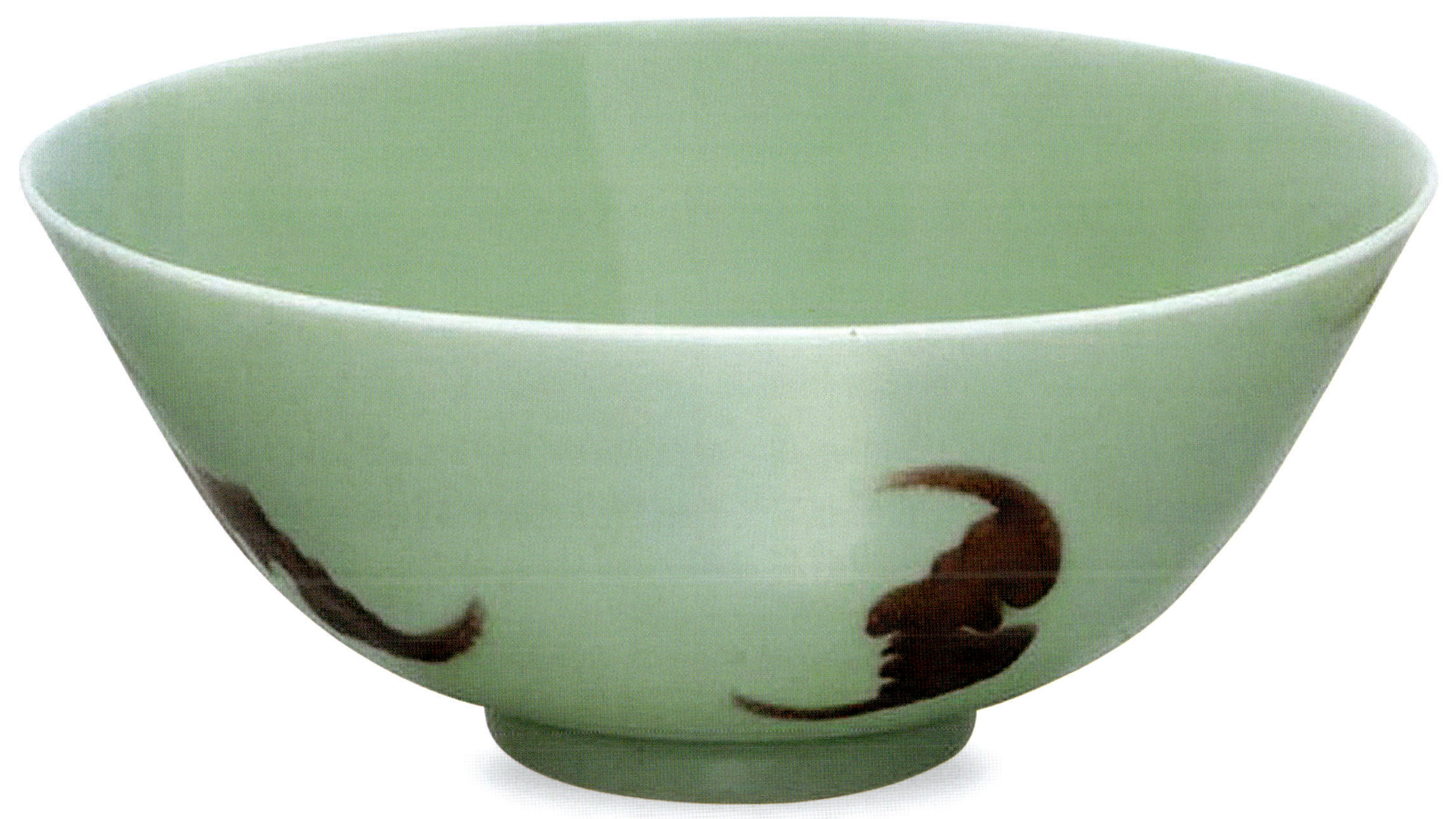

Gentlemen Commoners, 1730s

Oil on canvas in original early 18th-century frames (each approx. 105 × 82 cm)

In the Master in College's dining room, looking down with patrician hauteur from their pedimented frames, hang the portraits of twelve Winchester pupils from rather more rarefied backgrounds than the 'poor and needy scholars' who shared Chamber Court with them. Fee-paying pupils ('Commoners') mostly lodged in town, but Wykeham's statutes allowed for a small number to live in College itself. Their parents must have been glad of the extra supervision – one contemporary memoir of a town-based Commoner describes a riotous lifestyle of gambling and prostitutes. And their boarding fees would have been a welcome supplement to the income of the Headmaster.

Dr John Burton (Headmaster, 1724–66) expanded the number of Commoners, refitting two rooms for those resident in College. It is in one of those rooms that the portraits have hung ever since his lifetime, depicting boys at the school in the 1730s. Nine of them are nobles, a stock which Burton was keen to attract in emulation of more blue-blooded rival schools. Presumably Burton was keen to record the group, although they probably paid for the privilege, anticipating the more famous Etonian tradition by twenty-five years. The set is attributed to Isaac Whood (1688/9–1752), a popular portraitist of the time. Aged eight to sixteen, the boys are dressed in their Sunday finery: velvet coats, satin waistcoats, powdered wigs and one fine red suit embroidered with silver (John Wynne, perhaps showing off his family's new money). Indeed, the fabrics are more successful than the faces, which are suspiciously uniform, and combine rather bulbous eyes with an early-onset stubbly look to the cheeks.

Some of the surroundings are generic elements – pilasters, urns, marble-topped tables. But others are more specific to the sitter: Lord Brooke's background contains Warwick Castle, which he had recently inherited; the Hon. John Bulkeley Coventry is depicted with a warship, perhaps a nod to his ancestor who fought in the Anglo-Dutch Wars; Lord Ossulston, presumably a keen huntsman, appears before horse and hounds in pursuit of a stag. Only three have the scholarly props one might expect in schoolboy portraits: Charles Tryon has inkpot and pens; the Hon. Burlace Wallop a large text on a stand; Lord Brooke a book marked 'ΔHM', presumably a text of Demosthenes. Nevertheless, the pupils' later biographies make clear that Burton's tutelage did much good: several became patrons of the arts who remodelled their country houses with fine taste; Fulke Greville published a book of *Maxims*. Lord Drumlanrig was not so successful: his burgeoning military career was cut short when he accidentally shot himself while travelling.

Dr Burton's Commoners are probably Whood's finest works, but their real value lies in the snapshot they provide of a school evolving from a small medieval charity into a larger, more prestigious institution, patronised by an increasingly national elite. Eleven years after the final portrait was painted, Burton purchased and refitted the medieval buildings to the west of College as a boarding house for all the Commoners. The modern school was on its way.

Tim Giddings (Classics)

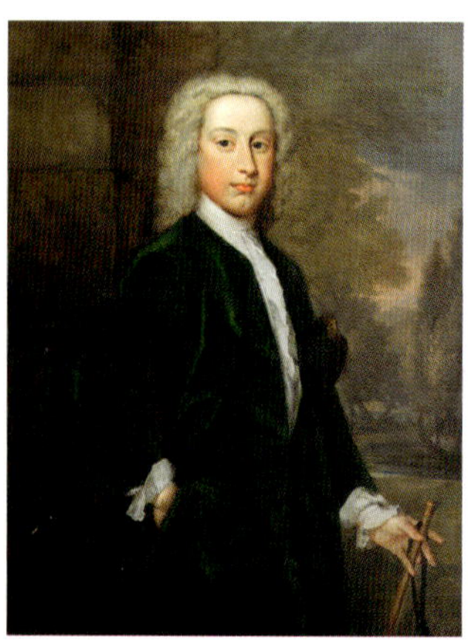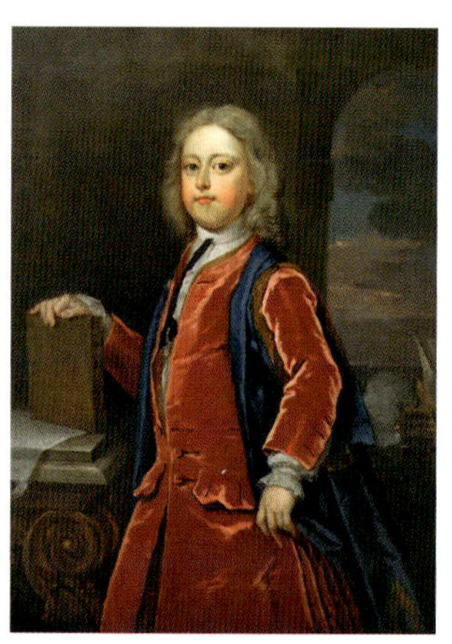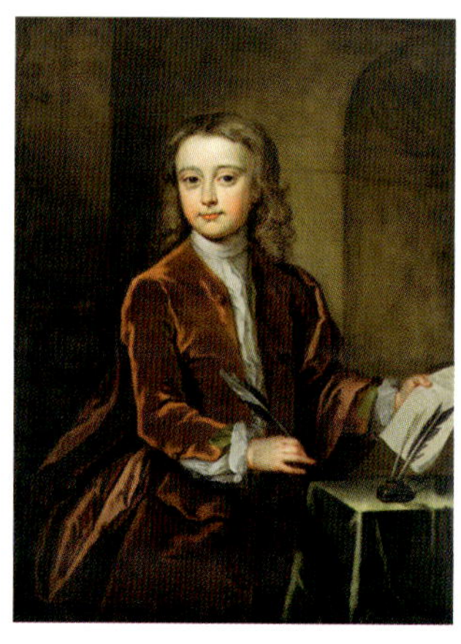

left to right: Sir Robert Burdett, 4th Bt (1731); the Hon. John Bulkeley Coventry (1731); Charles Tryon (1731); opposite: Charles Bennet, Lord Ossulston (1731).

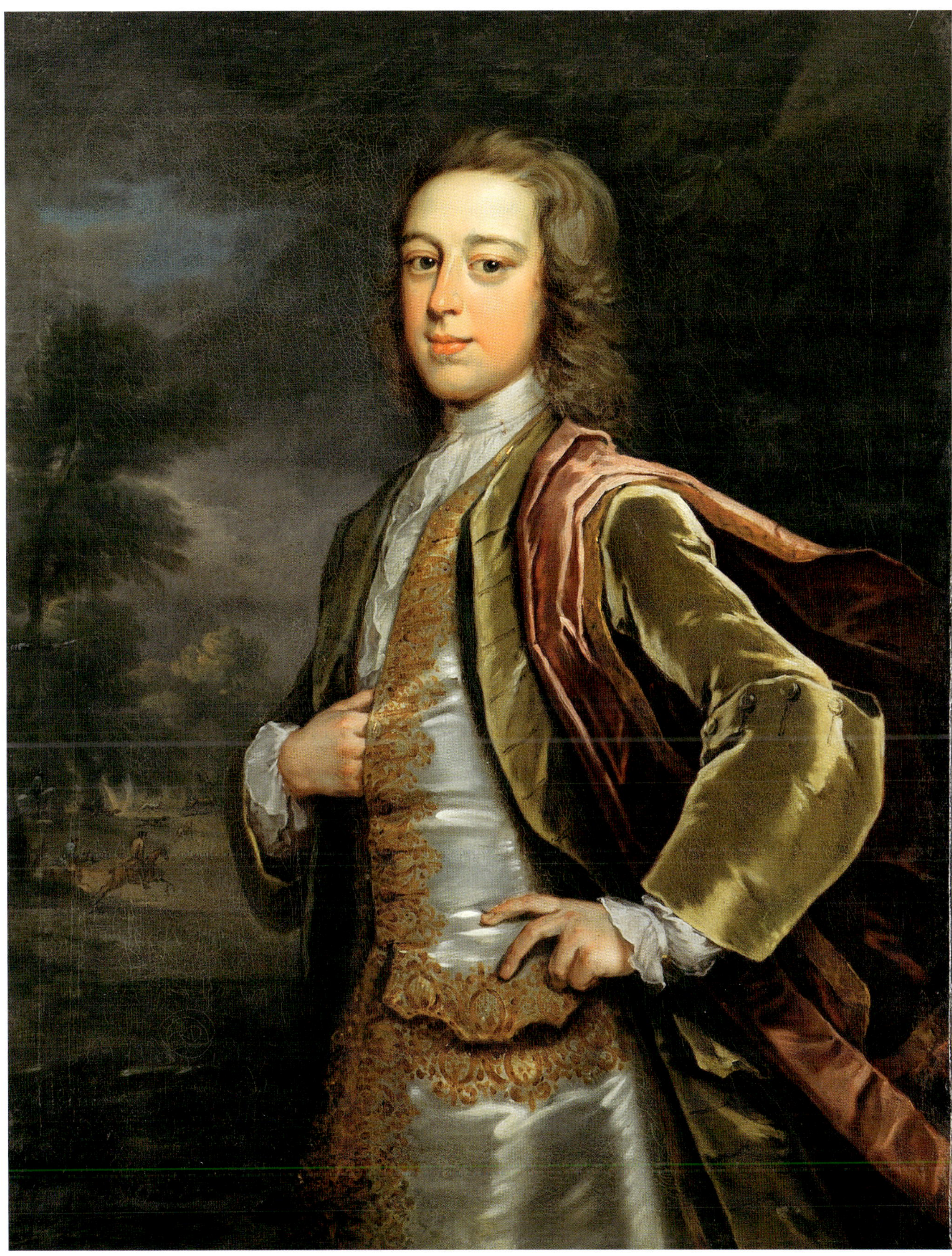

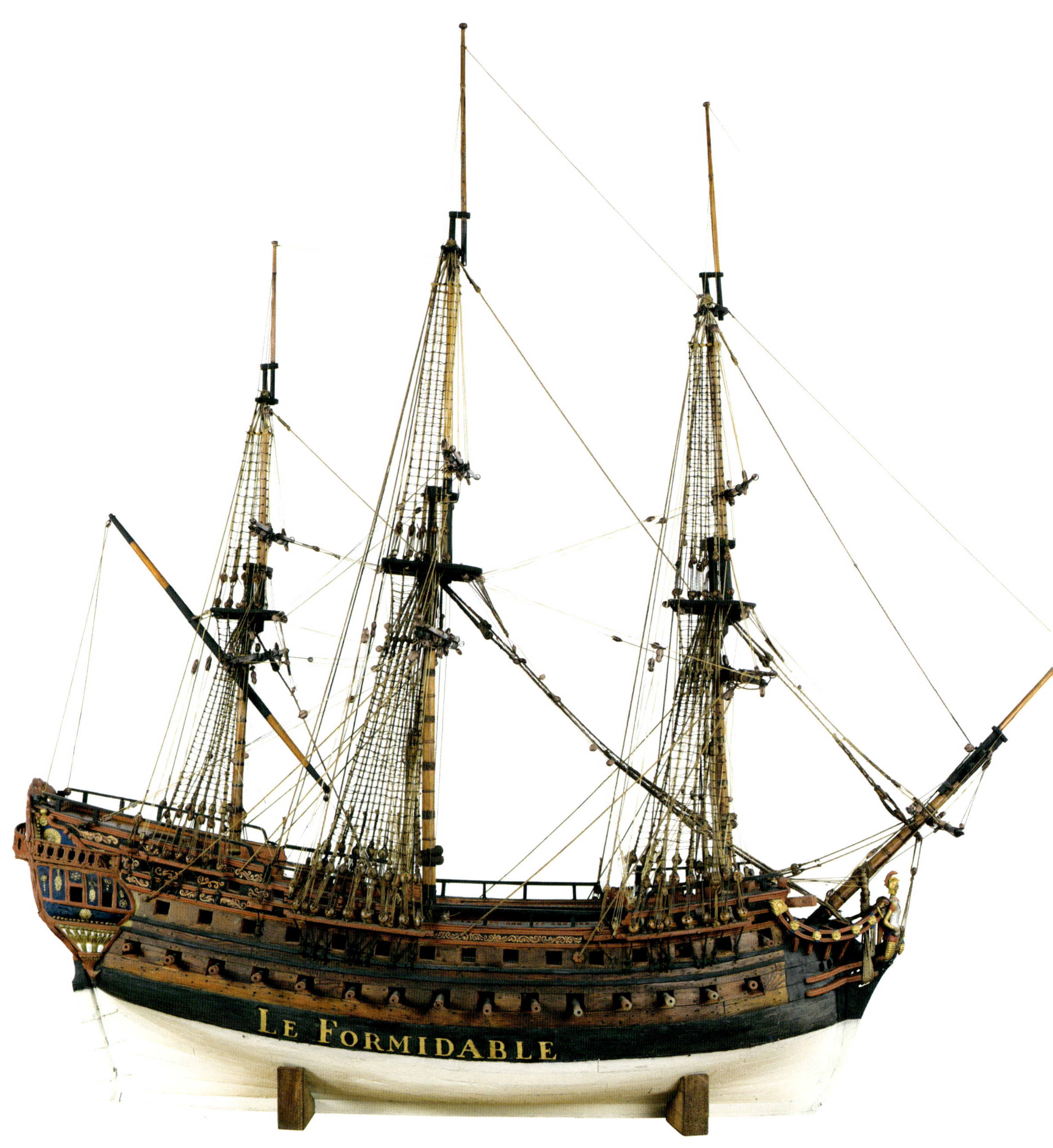
Le Formidable

Le Formidable, 1760

Painted wood (H. 120 cm, L. 140 cm)

This model was made by French prisoners in 1760. It is of considerable historical importance as the earliest prisoner-of-war ship model to survive, and the only one known to have been made in Winchester.

Le Formidable was an eighty-gun ship of the line built for the French Navy in 1751. Under the command of Louis de Saint-André du Verger she took part in the Battle of Quiberon Bay off the coast of Brittany on 20 November 1759. In this battle, the most decisive naval encounter of the Seven Years' War (1756–63), *Formidable* was captured by the English ship *Resolution*. The British destroyed seven out of the twenty-one ships engaged that day and put an end to French plans for an invasion of Great Britain. Some of the crew of *Formidable* were brought back to England as prisoners of war and were incarcerated in the so-called King's House, formerly the site of Winchester Castle.

A faded Latin inscription on the hull records that the model was 'made by French prisoners of war [*Galli bello capti*] in the nearby King's House in 1760', and that it had been presented to Winchester College by Dr John Burton, Headmaster from 1724 to 1766. It is unclear from the records if Burton purchased the model or was given it for some charitable act. The College accounts record a payment of 5 shillings at Christmas 1759 *'ad Incarcerati'* [*sic*] ('to the prisoners').

The model is a plank-on-frame construction made from a variety of woods, presumably whatever the prisoners could get hold of. The decks are constructed in oak, and the upper deck housing is made from pine and other soft woods. Despite the painted inscription which describes the *Formidable* as a ship of seventy-four guns, the model is pierced for the placement of eighty. Only twenty of the original guns survive and the rest are later replacements. The guns retract inside the hull on a ratchet and pawl mechanism, a very unusual feature associated with later Napoleonic prisoner-of-war work, and then only in models of the best technical quality. The masts and spars are almost completely original, but the rigging was subject to repair work carried out on the instructions of the College Bursar, T.F. Kirby, who rescued the model from being used as a Christmas decoration in Hall during the 1870s. Prior to this, it is thought that the ship was kept in Fromond's Chantry, within the College's medieval cloister.

From 1908 to 1920 *Le Formidable* was loaned to the Royal Naval College at Osborne, Isle of Wight. For the rest of the twentieth century it led an itinerant life, being housed in a classroom, the dons' Common Room and finally the Combined Cadet Force's Armoury. Following extensive conservation the model has now been found a new home where visitors can share this unique memorial to the crew of the *Formidable*, which they themselves created while imprisoned in Winchester.

Rachel Wragg (Curator of Treasury)

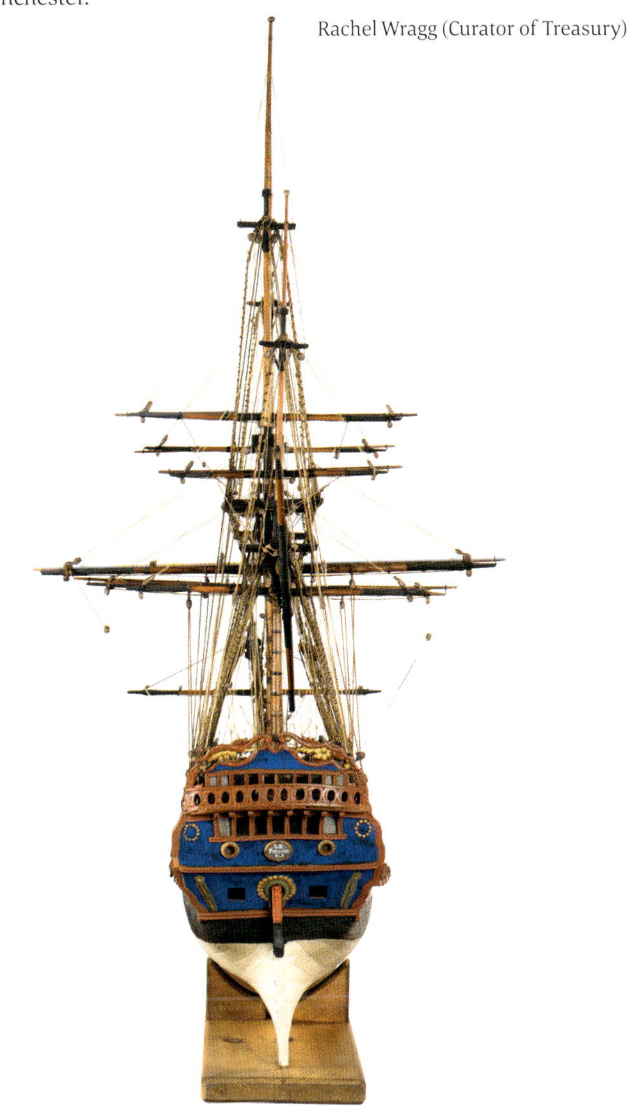

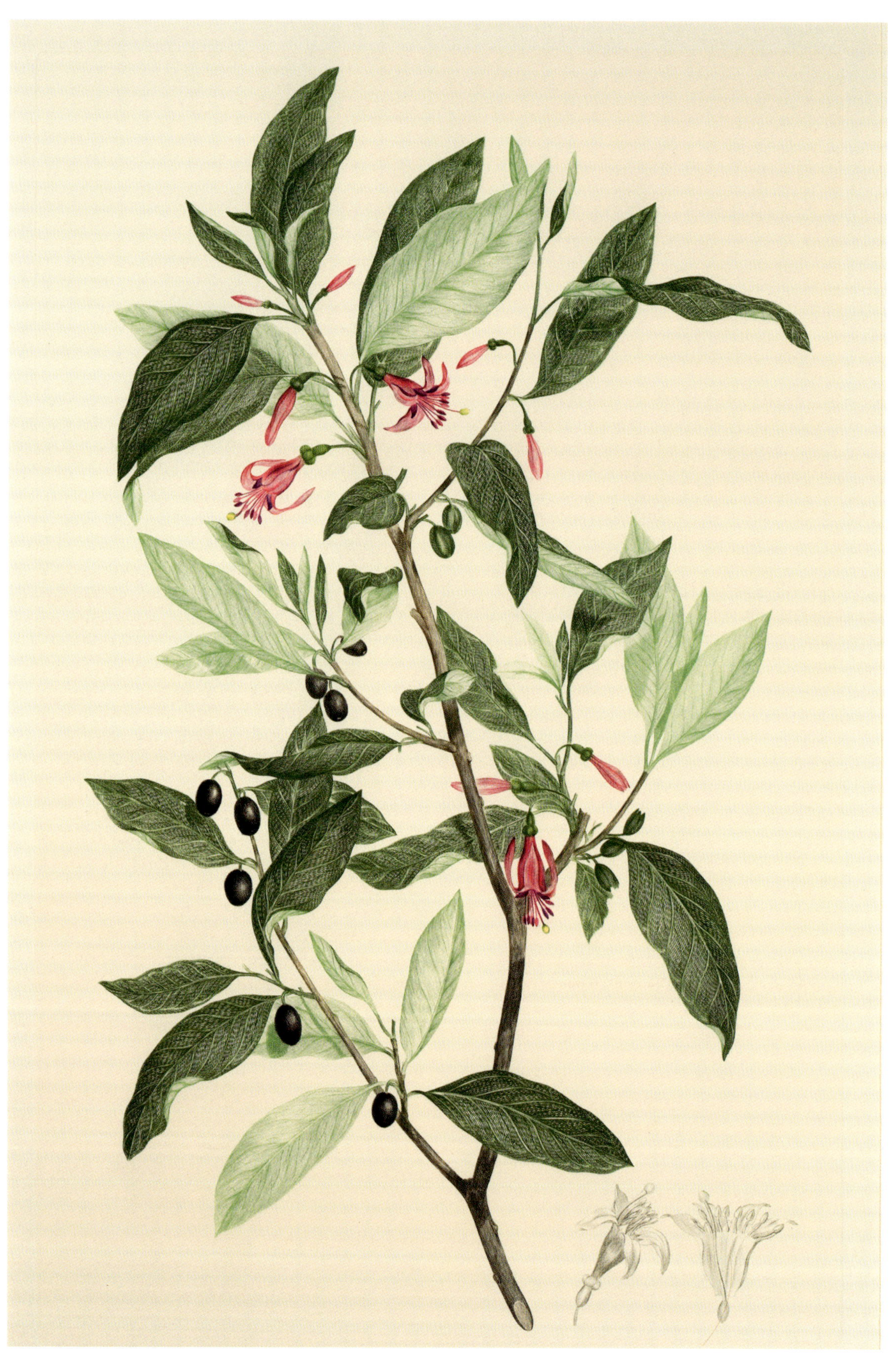

Joseph Banks' *Florilegium*, 1770s

Engravings *à la poupée*, with additional hand colouring (each plate 46 × 30 cm)

Joseph Banks' *Florilegium* is a collection of engravings from plant specimens collected during Captain Cook's first voyage to the southern hemisphere. The work is a unique marriage of Enlightenment art and science with advanced printmaking techniques, and a result of the extraordinary efforts of three remarkable young men: Joseph Banks (1743–1820), Sydney Parkinson (*c.* 1745–1771) and Edward Egerton-Williams (b. 1954).

In 1768 Captain Cook embarked on an expedition to measure the Transit of Venus from Tahiti. He also carried sealed orders from the Admiralty to search for the fabled Southern Continent (*Terra Australis Incognita*). The Royal Society recommended that Joseph Banks join the expedition. With him came Daniel Solander, a distinguished Swedish naturalist who had studied with Linnaeus, and Sydney Parkinson, a talented botanical draughtsman. Over three years of a long and sometimes perilous voyage, Banks and Solander visited Madeira, Brazil, Tierra del Fuego, Tahiti, New Zealand, Australia and Java. They collected nearly 30,000 botanical specimens, from which Parkinson made 280 watercolours and more than nine hundred drawings with colour notes. Banks recorded in his diary: 'We sat across the great table with the draughtsman directly across from us. We showed him how the drawings should be depicted and hurriedly made descriptions of all the natural history objects while they were still fresh'. Sadly, Parkinson died of dysentery on the voyage home.

On his return to England Banks had 743 of Parkinson's plant studies engraved at great expense to himself. The engravings remained unpublished, and nearly a ton of copper plates, still in their eighteenth-century wrappings, languished on the bottom shelf of a cupboard in the Natural History Museum in London. In 1978, more than two hundred years after Cook's voyage, Edward Egerton-Williams, recently graduated from Winchester School of Art, was given some of the Banks plates to 'try out'. After many failures to secure a good print he started experimenting with the seventeenth-century technique *à la poupée*. In this the various different coloured inks are worked into the plate with a twist of cloth, resulting in a beautifully sharp coloured image. The plate is then wiped clean and the whole process of inking up begins again for the next impression. This is a laborious process, sometimes requiring several hours of work for a single impression.

It took over ten years for Egerton-Williams' team to produce the 86,000 prints required for a limited edition of 100 copies, the work being finally completed in 1990. In 2004 a set of all 743 prints was donated to Winchester College by Viscount Gough (G, 1955–59). It is used regularly in teaching by the Biology and Art departments, and a changing selection of prints is exhibited in boarding houses.

Looking back from today we can only marvel at the almost obsessive pursuit of excellence that gave us the *Florilegium*. It brings the eighteenth century vividly to life and still carries with it the shock of the new. What was originally intended as a work of scientific reference has now become the supreme example of botanical painting and the art of printmaking.

Alan Smith, Tim Cox and Lily Livingston (College Gardeners)

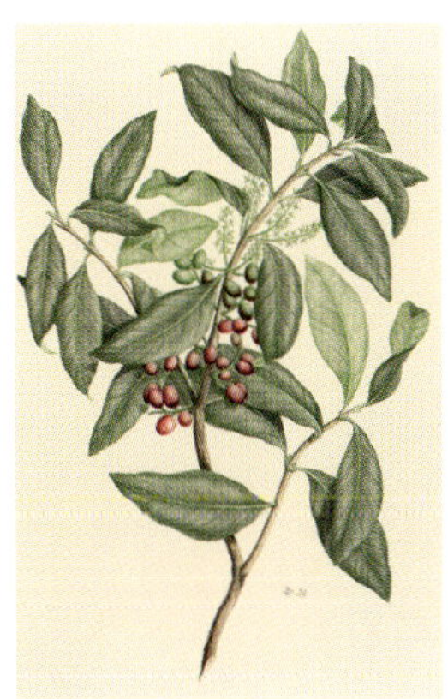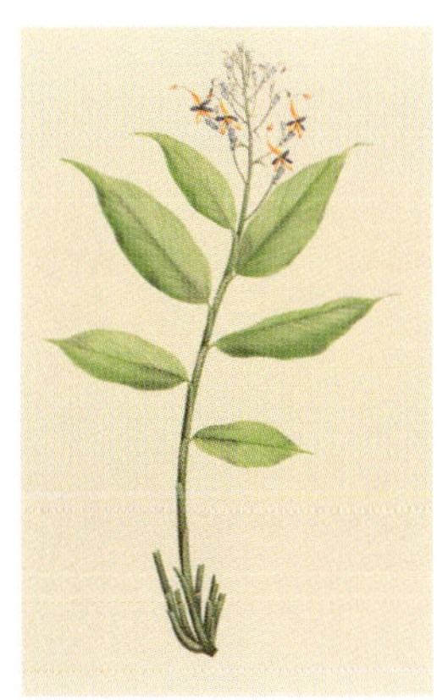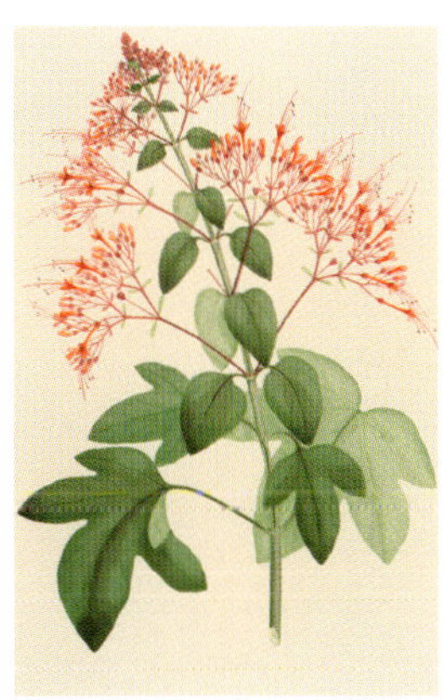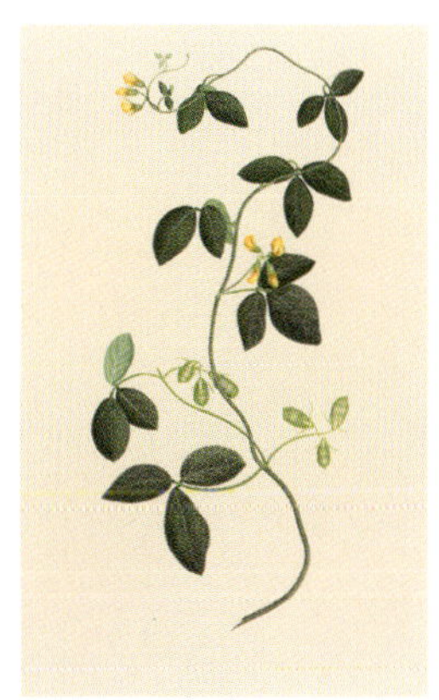

opposite: *Fuchsia excorticata* (New Zealand); left to right: *Nestegis apetala* (New Zealand); *Globba marantina* (Java); *Clerodendrum paniculatum* (Java); *Atylosia reticulata* (Australia).

Jane Austen Manuscripts, early 19th century

Manuscripts on paper (largest 32.8 × 20.3 cm; smallest 19 × 15.6 cm)

Jane Austen died in Winchester, at 8 College Street, and Winchester College therefore feels a particular connection with her. This is enhanced by our possession of four Austen family manuscripts, one in her hand. She is buried in Winchester Cathedral, and three of the four manuscripts commemorate her death: the draft for her memorial, written by her brother Henry, and two copies, in different hands, of her eldest brother James's elegy. The manuscript in Austen's own hand is a copy of a riddle, or 'Charade'. It appears that when the American banker and philanthropist J.P. Morgan was in England in the 1920s purchasing items from the Austen archive, he decided, generously, to give these items to the College, to commemorate Winchester's association with her.

The memorial carved on her gravestone in the North Aisle of the Cathedral is famous – or notorious – for failing to mention any of her works, or that she was a writer at all, although the central paragraph of the encomium lauds the 'extraordinary endowments of her mind', surely a coded reference to the products of her genius. Only some of her novels were in any case published at the time. It also stresses her benevolence, sweet temper, charity, devotion and faith, as does the poem written in her honour by the Reverend James Austen, by then rector of their father's former parish, St Nicholas at Steventon. These seventy-four lines of rhyming couplets scarcely seem today to uphold the contemporary view that James Austen was 'the writer of the family', but they reveal an interesting tension between the unfeminine attributes which he feels obliged in truthfulness to mention, including her 'quick and keen' mental eye, and his insistence that her 'literary taste' has in no way disinclined her to 'share/ The labours of domestic care'. Both poem and inscription, however, exude love, admiration and a strong sense of their loss, 'in proportion', as Henry Austen says, 'to their affection'.

Her death in College Street, in a house now owned by Winchester College, is not the only association Austen had with the city. Her house in Chawton was on the coach road to Winchester, and she was amused by the post-chaises going by, laden, as she said, with 'future Heroes, Legislators, Fools and Vilains', including her own nephews, who were pupils at the College. 'We shall rejoice in being so near Winchester', she wrote in 1807, 'when Edward belongs to it & can never have our spare bed filled more to our satisfaction than by him'.

The Fellows' Library has two Austen first editions: *Emma* (published 1815) and the posthumous edition of *Persuasion* and

Northanger Abbey (1817), as well as this fascinating group of manuscripts. It is frustrating that, unlike Mr Elton, Jane Austen has not written out 'something of [her] own' on this piece of paper. The Charade, 'by a Lady', is the work of Lady Maria Fanshawe; the modern relic-worshipper is therefore reduced to examining the handwriting for clues to Austen's character, just as Emma scrutinises the hand of Frank Churchill. Her writing is firm, clear and orderly, but it would be disingenuous to claim that it was vividly distinctive. Rather, like the existence of Henry's poem, the Charade is a reminder of the extent to which literature was a sociable occupation in Austen's time: the great author was also a participant in family word games and her home life, like that of Emma Woodhouse, was enlivened by fugitive and occasional verse.

Lucia Quinault (English)

Charade by a Lady

Inscrib'd on many a learned Page
In Mystic Characters & Sage,
Long time my First has stood;
But tho' its' Golden age be past,
In Wooden walls it yet may last
Till cloath'd in Flesh & Blood. —

____

My Second is a glorious prize
For those who love their wondering eyes
With curious sights to pamper;
Yet 'tis a sight which should they meet
All impromiso in the Street
Ye Gods! how they would scamper.

____

United, I'm a wandering Throne,
To Woman limitted alone
The Salique Law reversing; —
But when the imaginary Queen
Begins to act this novel Scene,
Her royal part rehearsing,
O'erturning her presumptuous plan
Up starts the old Usurper Man
And she jogs after as she can.

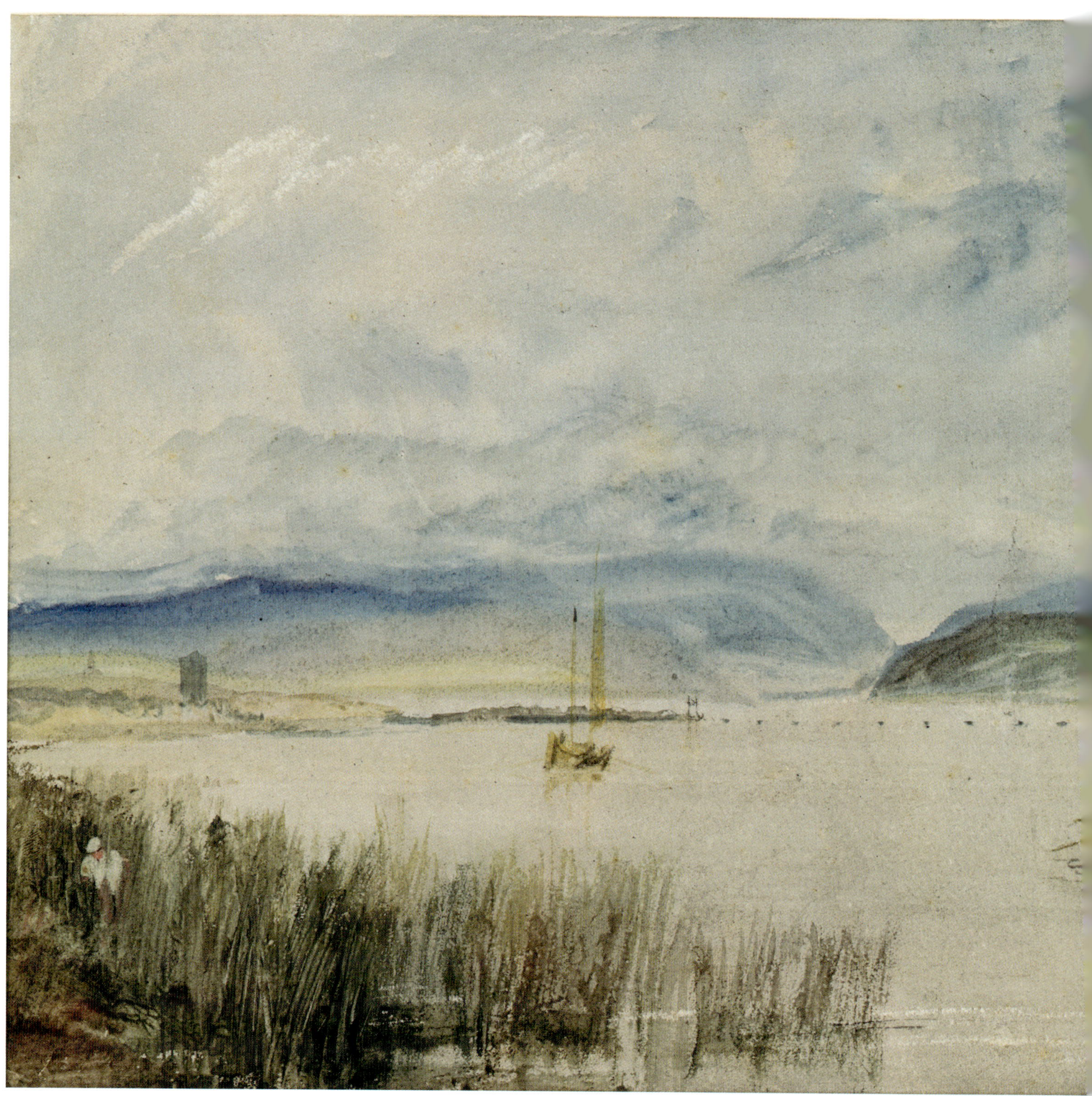

J.M.W. Turner,
Neuwied and Weissenthurm, 1817
Watercolour and bodycolour on paper (19 × 30.5 cm)

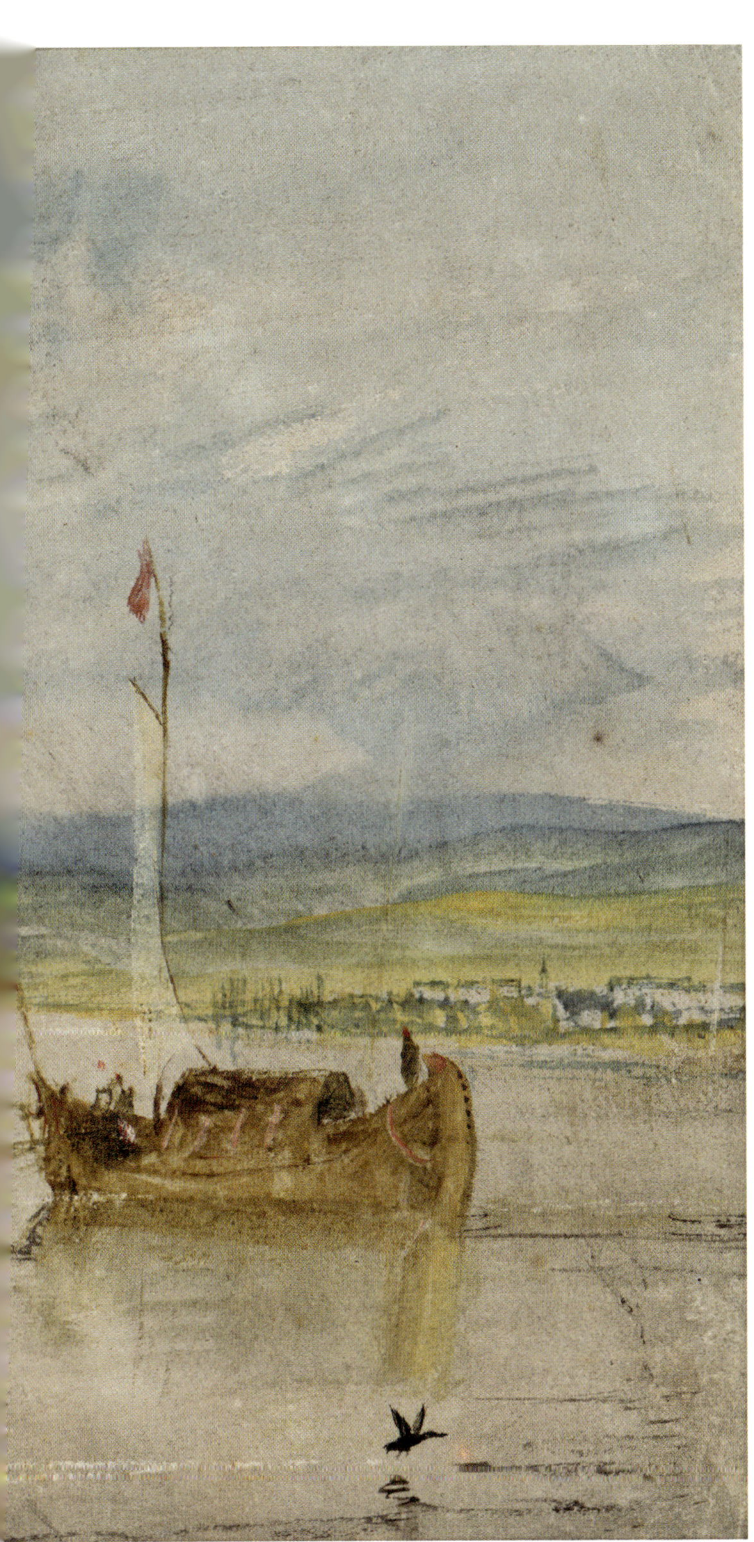

Turner's view of Neuwied and Weissenthurm is part of the College's fine and extensive collection of English watercolours. The subject is the two towns of the title on either bank of the Rhine, which are linked by a low bridge, looking downstream towards Andernach. In the near foreground is a sharply delineated duck exiting right, and in the lower left-hand corner a reedcutter is at work. Beyond the detail of the two towns is a wonderful rendering of the hills on each bank, with the strong blues of distant ground, and a well-worked skyscape.

Clearly, this is a sketch. In the early nineteenth century a sketch was often a rough, unfinished drawing, and so worthless. But this is a Turner sketch, one of fifty-one views on the Rhine, purchased by his patron Walter Fawkes for the large sum of £500 in the autumn of 1817. Fawkes recognised that this watercolour sketch was a work of art in its own right. He understood Turner's innate skill, his assured draughtsmanship, his harmonious composition and his ease of execution.

Turner did not paint this watercolour *en plein air*. He worked from a pencil drawing in his tiny pocketbook (6 x 7½ inches when open), in which he captured, for information rather than effect, the scenes before him as he walked, sometimes twenty miles or more in a day, between Cologne and Mainz in August 1817. Turner valued these pocket sketchbooks so much that he held them tight in his lifetime: happily, they are now in the Tate. The Winchester sketch, in turn, was the basis for a more fully finished watercolour: *Neuwied and Weise Thurn, with Hoch's Monument on the Rhine* (1819), part of the Vaughan Bequest at the National Gallery of Scotland, one of only three views later worked up by Turner from the group of watercolours bought by Fawkes.

Neuwied and Weissenthurm was given to the College in 1940 by Harry Collison (1869–1945), along with more than 100 English drawings and watercolours, including works by Paul Sandby, Thomas Girtin, John Sell Cotman and Augustus John. Collison purchased the Turner in 1926 from Agnew's, who had it direct from Fawkes's descendants. Collison would have been a Wykehamist, but for the illness which prevented him taking up his place in Du Boulay's. Nevertheless, he enjoyed a City career, becoming Master of the Grocers' Company in 1930, and then a proficient and widely exhibited portrait painter. He had inherited a fine collection of watercolours, to which he added a number of works, mostly by contemporary artists. He offered his collection first to Oundle School, who declined, and it would then have gone to Rugby but for the intervention of Dr Rendall, the retired Headmaster of Winchester.

Collison wanted his family collection to be kept together. In a letter to *The Wykehamist* of 9 July 1940, he said: 'I was looking for a place where amid beautiful surroundings and features of historical interest, students would be led to admire works of art in the original and by using their own eyes, gain help and inspiration. What I wanted, I discovered at Winchester.' He would be delighted that each year senior pupils curate an exhibition of watercolours chosen from the school's collection, of which our Turner is a favourite.

Charles Sinclair (B, 1961–66, Warden)

Crimea Scrapbook, 1850s

MS 210: Manuscript on paper, ff. 78, with pasted-in photographs, lithographs and printed maps, bound in 19th-century dark blue crushed morocco over oak boards with campaign medals inset (54.5 × 37.5 cm)

Ely Wigram (1801–1869) was a Lt Colonel in the Coldstream Guards. He retired in 1851, three years before Britain and France declared war on Russia in defence of the Ottoman Empire. After the Peace of Paris (1856), which ended a victorious but largely embarrassing war for the British, Wigram put together an elephant folio scrapbook of the conflict, which he later bequeathed to his nephew, a fellow soldier who had served in the Crimea. The book – given by Monty Rendall to Winchester College Library in 1916 – contains watercolours, lithographs, photographs, military maps, medals and autographs of the leading generals and important individuals on both sides of the war.

The most important photograph contained within the scrapbook is that of Mary Seacole, the Scottish-Jamaican businesswoman who set up (unofficially and on her own initiative) the 'British Hotel' behind the lines at Balaclava. She described it as 'a mess-table and comfortable quarters for sick and convalescent officers'. That Wigram included her photograph (and accompanying signature) is an indication of her importance at the time. Indeed, hers is the only non-combatant photograph in the entire scrapbook. Wigram also highlighted the importance of another woman involved in the Crimean War: Florence Nightingale. The scrapbook includes a letter Nightingale wrote concerning a young private who was her assistant.

There was no great *hero* of the Crimean War. After 1856, the British lauded the abstract common soldier, the brave private. But these were nameless, faceless men. Instead, the Crimean War gave Britain *heroine* outsiders. In the nineteenth century the ideal woman was a domestic rock for her husband and family. Queen Victoria – the wife and mother – was the perfect female model. Religious and classical models shaped ideas of womanhood. These were constructed in writings by men and reflected the male idea of what a woman should be. Women were obscured, omitted and under-written. They were not seen as individuals. History focused on big battles and high politics – spaces dominated and controlled by men. The Crimea scrapbook does focus on powerful men and big battles, but Wigram chose not to obscure Seacole and Nightingale. He stressed their individuality and their importance by including them in his book, albeit one still dominated by emperors, statesman, diplomats, generals and soldiers.

This choice was made ten years before the House of Commons voted for the first time on the question of granting the parliamentary franchise to women. In one sense, Nightingale and Seacole were problematic for those who advocated female enfranchisement. The hospital ward was an extension of the domestic space. Seacole served hot tea and lemonade to soldiers; she comforted the battle-weary. She wrote repeatedly of her soldier 'sons' and of how they called her 'mother'. The writer Elizabeth Barrett Browning saw Nightingale as a throwback and a hindrance to the 'women's movement'.

But Wigram's scrapbook reminds us that Nightingale and Seacole emerged from the conflict as identifiable heroic figures. Nightingale rejected the feminisation of nursing; to her, it was a non-gendered profession. Her aim after the war was the professionalisation of nursing and the improvement of sanitary conditions in hospitals. There was nothing romantic (or overtly feminine) about tending bullet wounds, organising and administering wards or negotiating with generals and the Secretary of State for War. Seacole too defied conventional stereotypes, especially the contemporary one of the 'lazy Creole'. She managed investments in gold-mining businesses and she built and ran a hotel in a war zone. These two women emerged as important individuals in their own right in the ultimate male space. Wigram's scrapbook makes this clear.

Laurence Guymer (History)

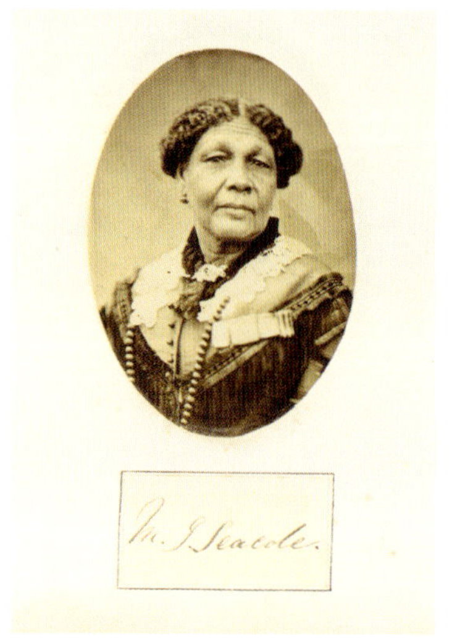

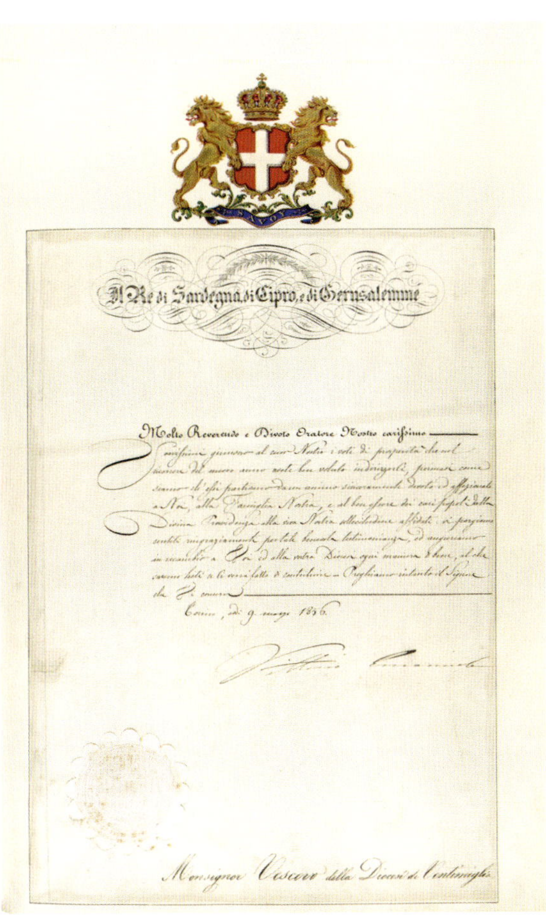

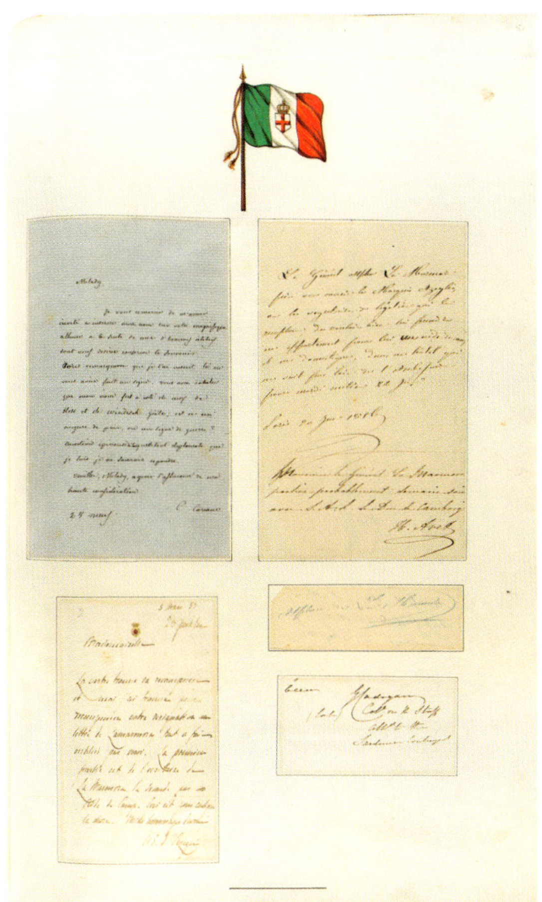

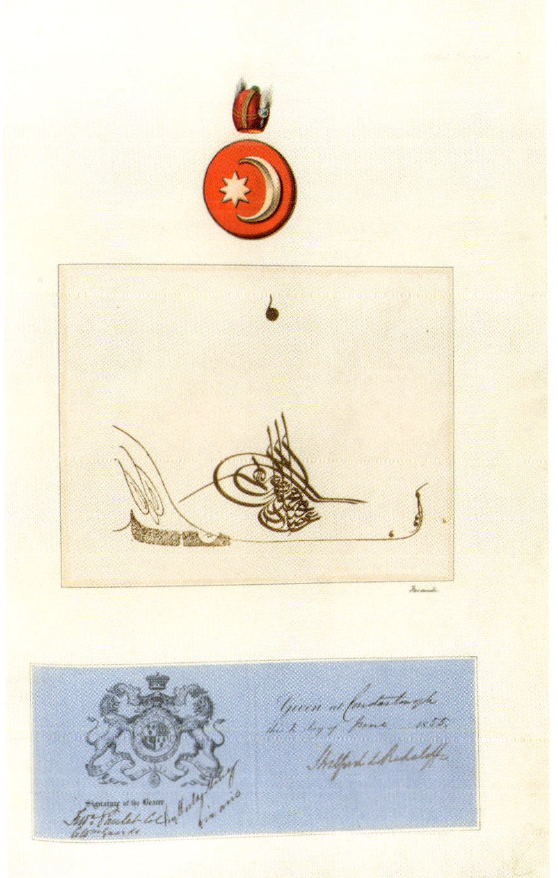

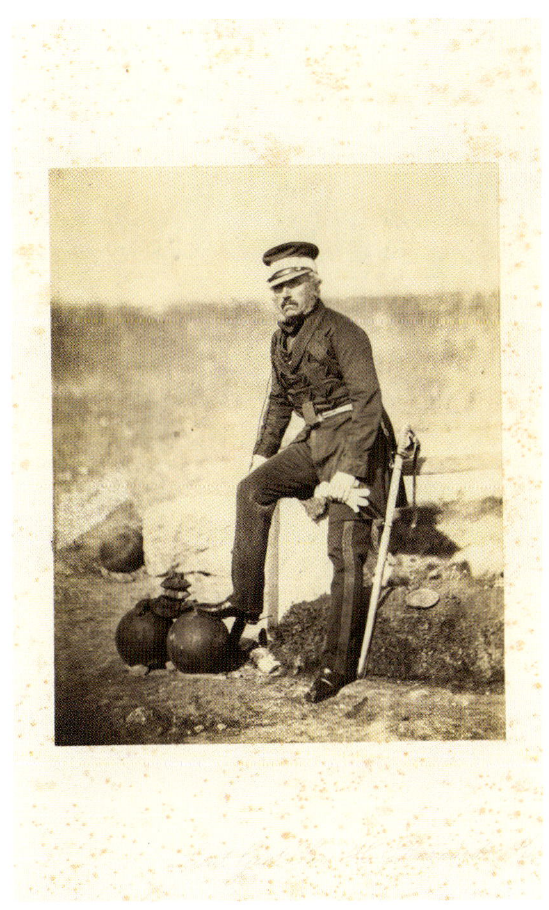

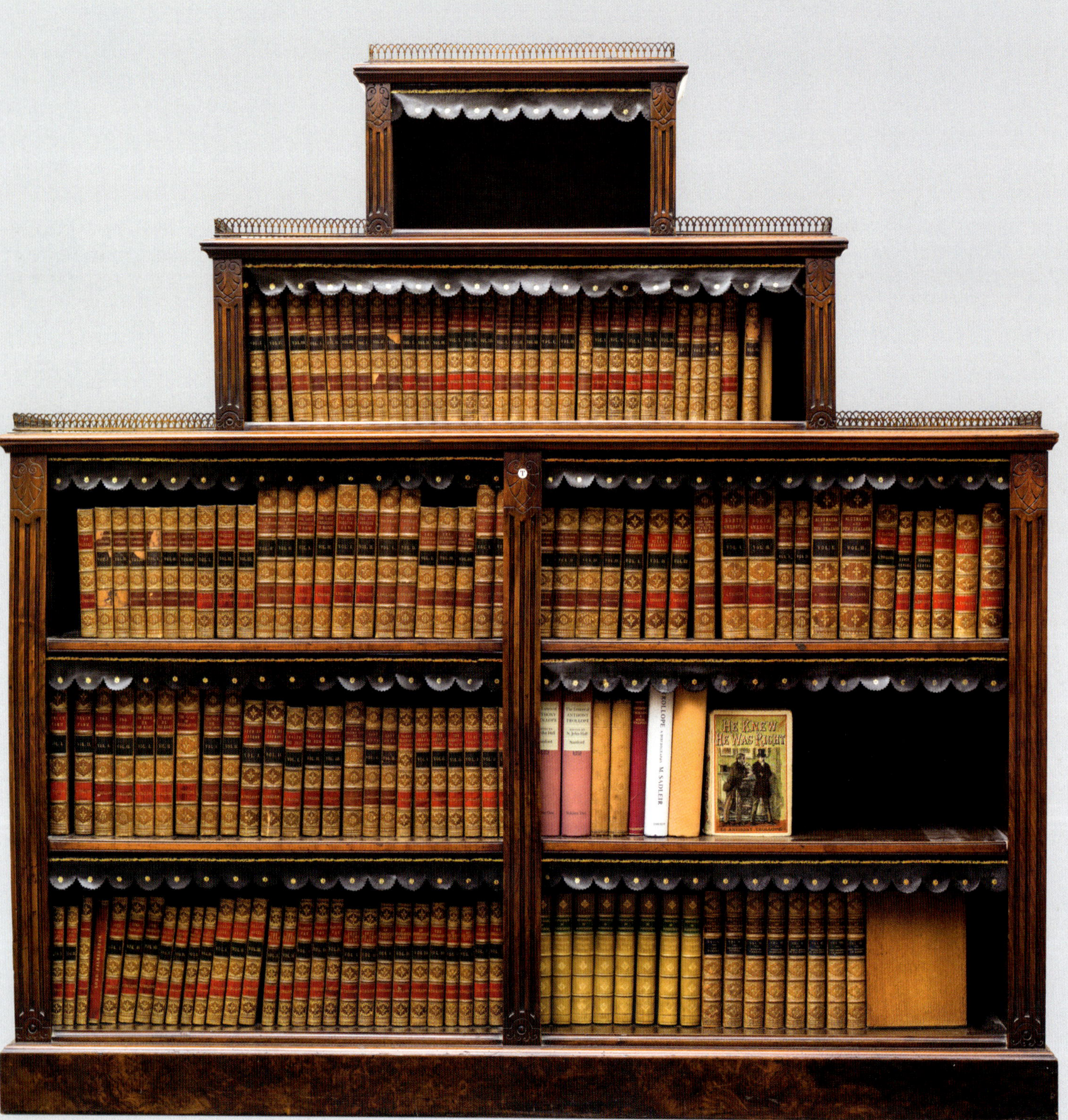

Anthony Trollope, *The Warden*, 1855

Anthony Trollope, *The Warden* (London, 1855), bound in 19th-century calfskin with gilt spine (11.3 × 18 cm)

This first edition of *The Warden*, by Anthony Trollope (1815–1882; College, 1827–30) is part of an extensive gift of Trollope first editions donated in 2007 by Honorary Fellow Al Gordon.

Trollope's father, also Anthony (College, 1785–91/92), wished his sons to follow him to Winchester. All three came; two left their mark. There are graffiti signatures by Anthony on Old Mill, and by his older brother Tom (College, 1820–28) on the banisters of Bethesda. Writing in the *Fortnightly Review* in 1864, Anthony Trollope called public schools 'the backbone of English public and social life.... There we learnt to be honest, true and brave. There we were trained to disregard the softnesses of luxury.... There we became men.' Trollope's *Autobiography* relaxes the stiff upper lip: 'Ah, how well I remember all the agonies of my young heart … whether I could not find my way up to the top of that college tower, and from thence put an end to everything.' Trollope was kept down for lack of academic progress; he left Winchester when deemed unworthy of progression to New College.

Winchester was not in a heyday. George Huntingford, Warden between the years of the French Revolution and the Reform Act, detested the zeitgeist. Described by one historian as 'a bully to the young, a pedant, a liar and a cheat', his mantra was 'No Innovation': pupils twice (1793 and 1818) mutinied in protest. Only with the death of Huntingford and the appointment as Headmaster of George Moberly (a former mutineer), and then George Ridding (son of Trollope's Master in College) could any Winchester reformation begin.

'Is a rude or a refined age more favourable to the production of works of fiction?', candidates for the Chancellor's Medal at Oxford were asked in 1826 (when Moberly triumphed). Reform is indeed one of the grand themes of the Victorian novel: in his first career in the General Post Office, Trollope promoted it, inventing the pillarbox; in his subsequent literary career he chronicled it. *The Warden* describes the controversial modernisation of a medieval almshouse, originally based on the picturesque St Cross, just downriver from the College, and then under investigation for abuse of resources. Thus in title as well as content *The Warden* was close to home.

The banker, benefactor and book collector Al Gordon (1901–2009) worked on Wall Street during the Great Crash of 1929. Like his literary hero Trollope, a man of an industrious energy who refused to bow to adversity, Gordon went on to run the London Marathon aged eighty-one, and died just short of his 108th birthday. Gordon wished to augment the gift of a signed set of the Barsetshire novels made by the author to the College late in life. He therefore purchased an almost complete set of Trollope's titles, originally signed for Trollope's son Henry, and containing marginalia by father and son. The gift was placed in a bookcase once owned by Trollope himself, generously loaned by the Salwey family.

This beautifully bound volume thus serendipitously represents the fortunate accidents of early hardship, subsequent determination and reform, welcome chances, generous donation and successful delivery to a chosen postcode.

Timothy Hands (Headmaster)

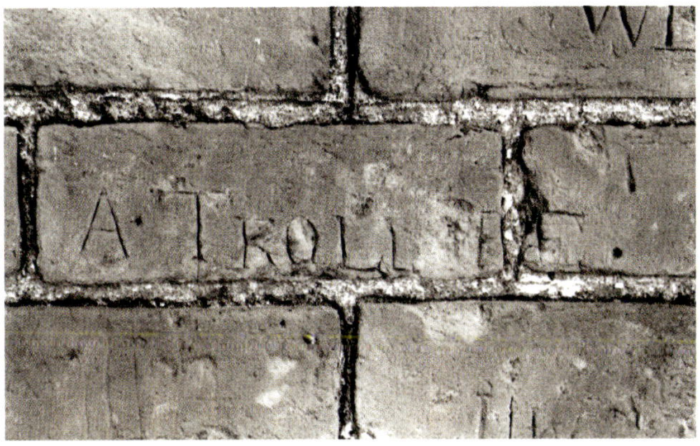

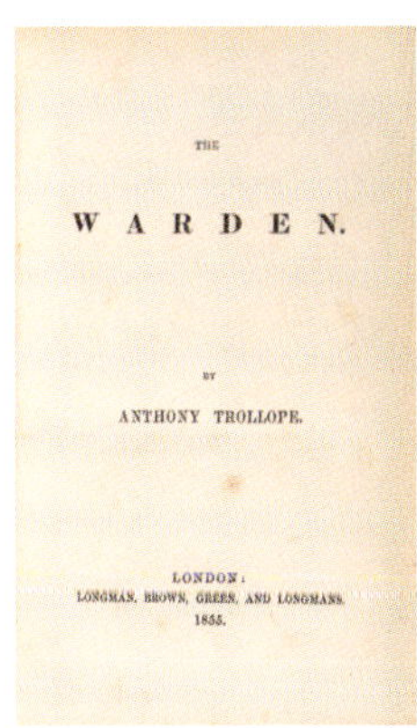

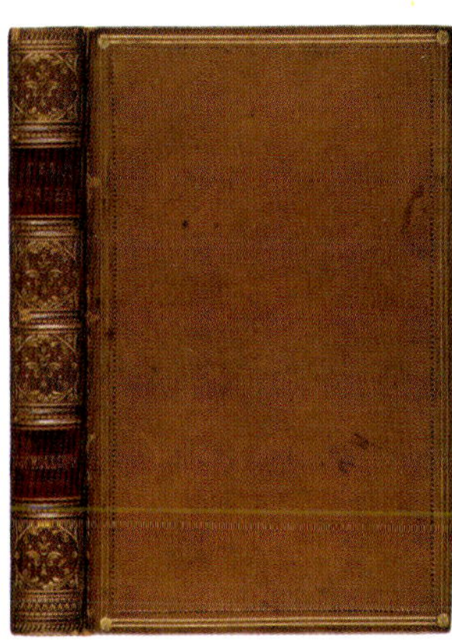

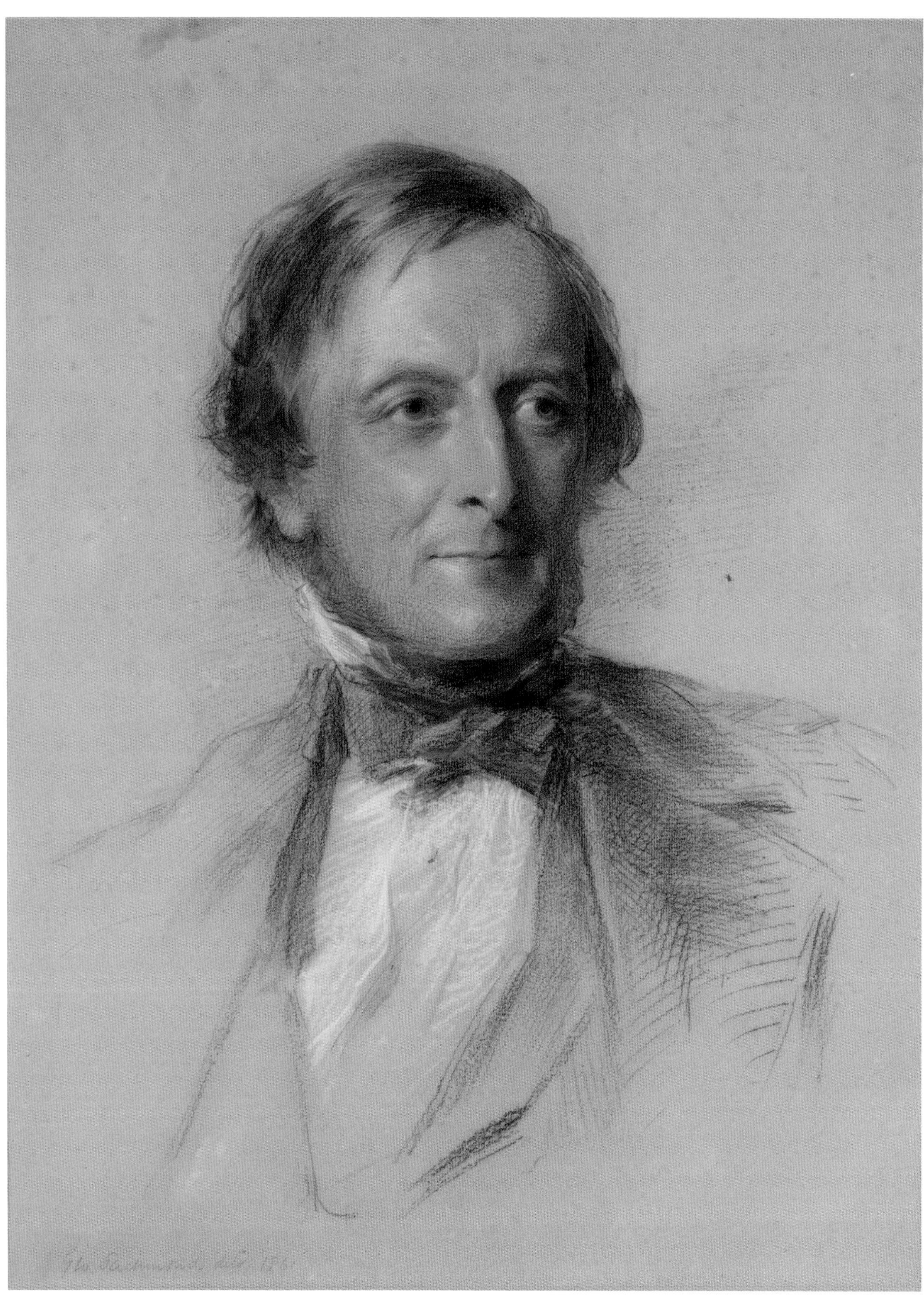

George Richmond, *John Desborough Walford*, 1861

Coloured chalks on paper (59 × 40 cm)

John Desborough Walford is an important figure in the history of Winchester College. A classicist by background, he was appointed to the staff in 1834 as the school's first dedicated Mathematics teacher. He held the post for almost forty years and for much of this time undertook the task alone. In the nineteenth century the school curriculum was dominated by classical languages and literature. Otherwise reluctant Wykehamists were eventually persuaded by the novel discipline when marks in Mathematics counted towards the final orders; moreover, there were significant end-of-year prizes to be won (among them the Duncan Prize, first awarded in 1841, which continues today). Institutional recognition for Mathematics came in the form of 'Walford's', an extension (now demolished) built onto School, in which took place the singular pursuit of mathematical teaching. On his retirement in 1873 Walford was succeeded by the Cambridge Mathematics graduate 'Dick' Richardson (after whom another prestigious Mathematics prize is named). In the early twentieth century the brilliant and prolific C.V. Durrell maintained the momentum of Walford and Richardson, elevating Winchester Mathematics to national importance.

This portrait of Walford was bequeathed to Winchester College by Helen Walford, a descendant of the sitter, in 1974. The artist, George Richmond, was a highly successful portraitist and landscape painter. As a young man he was profoundly influenced by William Blake. In old age he was a mentor to John Ruskin.

Among Richmond's many surviving works are portraits of Samuel Wilberforce (1834), Bishop of Oxford and Winchester, and Charles Darwin (1839). His portraits may flatter, but Richmond said that they were 'the truth lovingly told'.

Richmond concentrates here on the sitter's head, with only indistinct reference to his subject's sartorial elegance, or lack thereof. Emphasis, therefore, is gently towards the action of the mind, drawn out by a subtle play of light on Walford's forehead. There is a suggestion of comfortable scruffiness about his clothes and hair. His indirect gaze seems intensely thoughtful, as if in the act of forming an eloquent admonishment to cajole a wayward pupil. Walford was a strict yet kind teacher and he possessed a quick wit. It is recorded that on one Christmas Eve a boy asked him if goose was to be served on Christmas Day. Walford replied: 'You will get the *anser* tomorrow'.

A modern-day teacher would be delighted to compose a play on words of such quality, and there is indeed something contemporary about Walford's prototype and example. His name was kept alive as a 'notion', part of the private language of the College. 'John Des' is white, unruled, acid-free Heritage Bookwhite paper, expressly guillotined by Wells' Bookshop's bookbinder and, until about fifteen years ago, a bestseller among Wykehamists. Even in our digital age the light tools of pencil and paper remain the favourite for mathematical exploration.

Peter Cornish (Head of Mathematics)

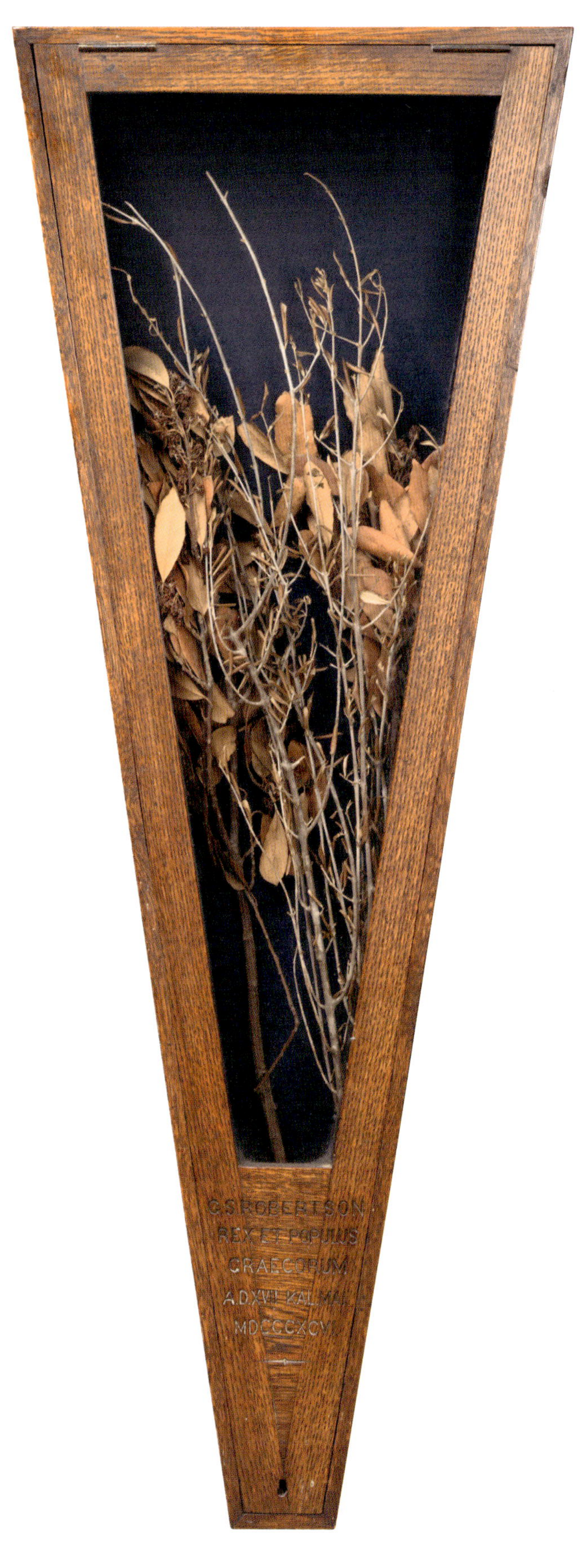
G.S. ROBERTSON
REX ET POPULUS
GRAECORUM
A.D. XVI KAL MA.
MDCCCXCVI

Olympic Prizes, 1896

Olive and laurel leaves in an oak case (H. 98.5 cm)

The twenty-first-century iteration of the Olympic Games is a temple to single-minded sporting obsession. No stone is left unturned in the quest for that extra tenth of a per cent on a four-year pilgrimage to potential Olympic glory. Nothing else matters but the hope of capturing that elusive marginal gain in your chosen discipline. This attitude is quite far from the breadth and balance characteristic of the education young Wykehamists receive. Although sporting excellence is certainly a part of the school's culture today, there has also long been a concern with seeking 'the best for the average games player', as Monty Wright (Second Master, 1924–52) once wrote. In contrast to several other public schools, none of Winchester's nineteenth-century headmasters placed a high premium on physical prowess.

It is perhaps surprising, therefore, that George Robertson (College, 1884–90) was among the select few winners of Baron de Coubertin's inaugural Olympic Games, held in Athens in 1896. On closer inspection, however, Robertson was not quite the mean machine we might readily assume Olympic champions to be. His winner's wreath and garland, the only surviving prize of its kind from the 1896 Games, was not even won for his sporting endeavours in the Athens arena.

Robertson was the ultimate Wykehamist: a Collegeman, he won the prize for best in his div (form) nearly every term. He went on to become the top scholar at New College, where he was made a Fellow in Classics at the age of twenty-three. He was also a brilliant athlete. He was an outstanding exponent of Winchester's own distinctive version of football, playing as a 'kick' in the College VI and XV. At New College he was three times victorious in the Varsity athletics meet.

In 1896 Robertson travelled to Athens to compete in the hammer throw, his favoured event. On his arrival he discovered that the hammer was not actually on the programme, and so he tried his hand at the discus instead. Entries were open to all comers until the evening before the first discus was flung. Robertson was a welcome addition, but he came a disappointing fourth out of five competitors. One observer described his action as 'neither elegant nor successful'. Rather than blaming his result on the total absence of any kind of preparation for his event, he complained that the discus was of a different form from the one that the ancients threw. As he was a classical scholar, this lack of attention to detail from the

Greek organisers clearly offended his sensibilities; he mentioned it again when interviewed by BBC radio at the age of eighty-eight.

In an unusual twist of fate, the king of Greece received word that Robertson was a fine classical scholar, and asked him to compose and recite a Pindaric ode for the closing ceremony. By all accounts, the king was greatly amused by this and rewarded Robertson for his efforts with a laurel branch and a wreath of wild olive brought from Olympia. 'Wot larx!' *The Globe* reported of the episode the following day. Baron de Coubertin founded the modern Olympics in the spirit of having a go, getting stuck in and not worrying too much about who won what. If anyone typified this spirit, it was Robertson.

George Nash (K, 2002–07)

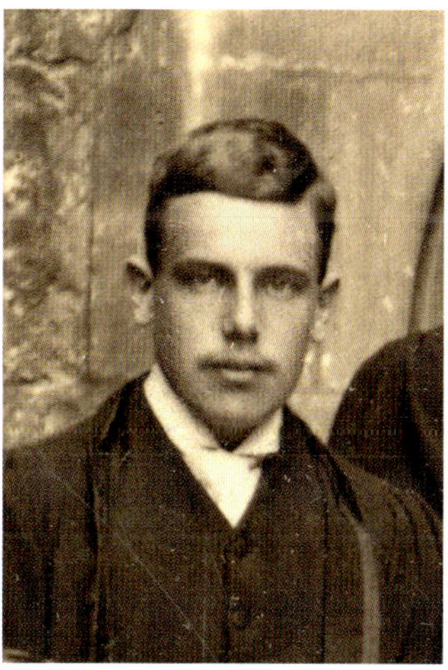

George Robertson as a Scholar at Winchester, 1888.

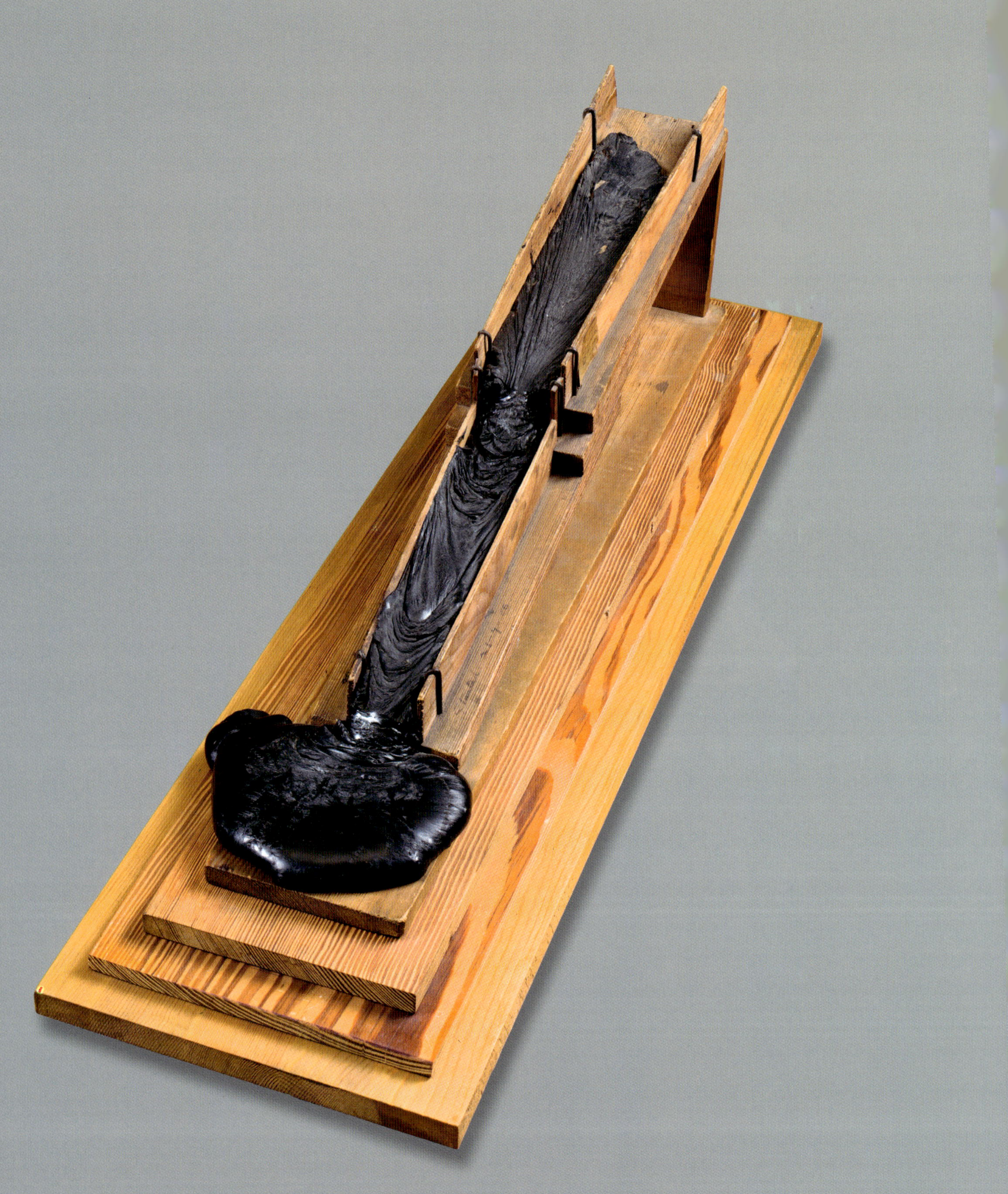

Pitch Flow Demonstration, 1906

Wooden trough with commercial pitch (L. 69 cm, W. 20 cm)

William Bleaden Croft was appointed by Headmaster Ridding to teach Physics and Mathematics in 1874. He was one of the first graduates in Natural Philosophy (Physics) from the new Clarendon Laboratory in Oxford. The scientific community at that time was tiny and Croft, with his laboratory in Winchester, was able to carry out research and keep up with the great advances in physics in the late nineteenth century, bringing them to the notice of his pupils.

Alpine mountain climbing was a popular pursuit of the young gentlemen in this period. The Alps contained many glaciers and the first measurements of the flow of glaciers were made in the 1870s. The mechanism by which glaciers flowed was not well understood, but it was often likened to viscous flow, which had been modelled by Newton in the seventeenth century (in fact, the movement of glaciers is now known to involve several processes of which viscous flow is only a minor one). The flow of pitch, a coal-tar derivative, is an example of viscous streamline flow, and Croft used it to create a simple demonstration experiment to explain the phenomenon to his pupils. His technician, Walter Abley, constructed the apparatus which consists of an inclined wooden trough down which the 'pitch glacier' flows.

The 'pitch glacier' was set up in 1906. It was started on 21 July when a block of commercial pitch was placed against two nails at the top of the incline. Over the years the pitch block has slumped and flowed down the trough, spilling out at the base. In doing this the experiment purports to show the motion of a glacier down a valley. The viscosity of Newtonian fluids falls rapidly with increasing temperature. The improvement in the central heating in the Science School over the past seventy years will have increased the rate of flow of the 'pitch glacier' far more than global warming. Over time, the apparatus has been modified in order to contain the flow of pitch. Since the experiment began in 1906 there have been just four Physics technicians at the school, each of whom has added a plank of wood to the base of the glacier.

Interestingly, the *Guinness Book of Records* cites 'the longest-running experiment' as being a 'pitch glacier' experiment set up by the University of Queensland, Australia, in 1930. Their flow rate has been measured and recorded regularly ever since. Although our demonstration has been flowing for a quarter of a century longer, the historic records are lacking.

Martin Gregory (Physics, 1962–99)

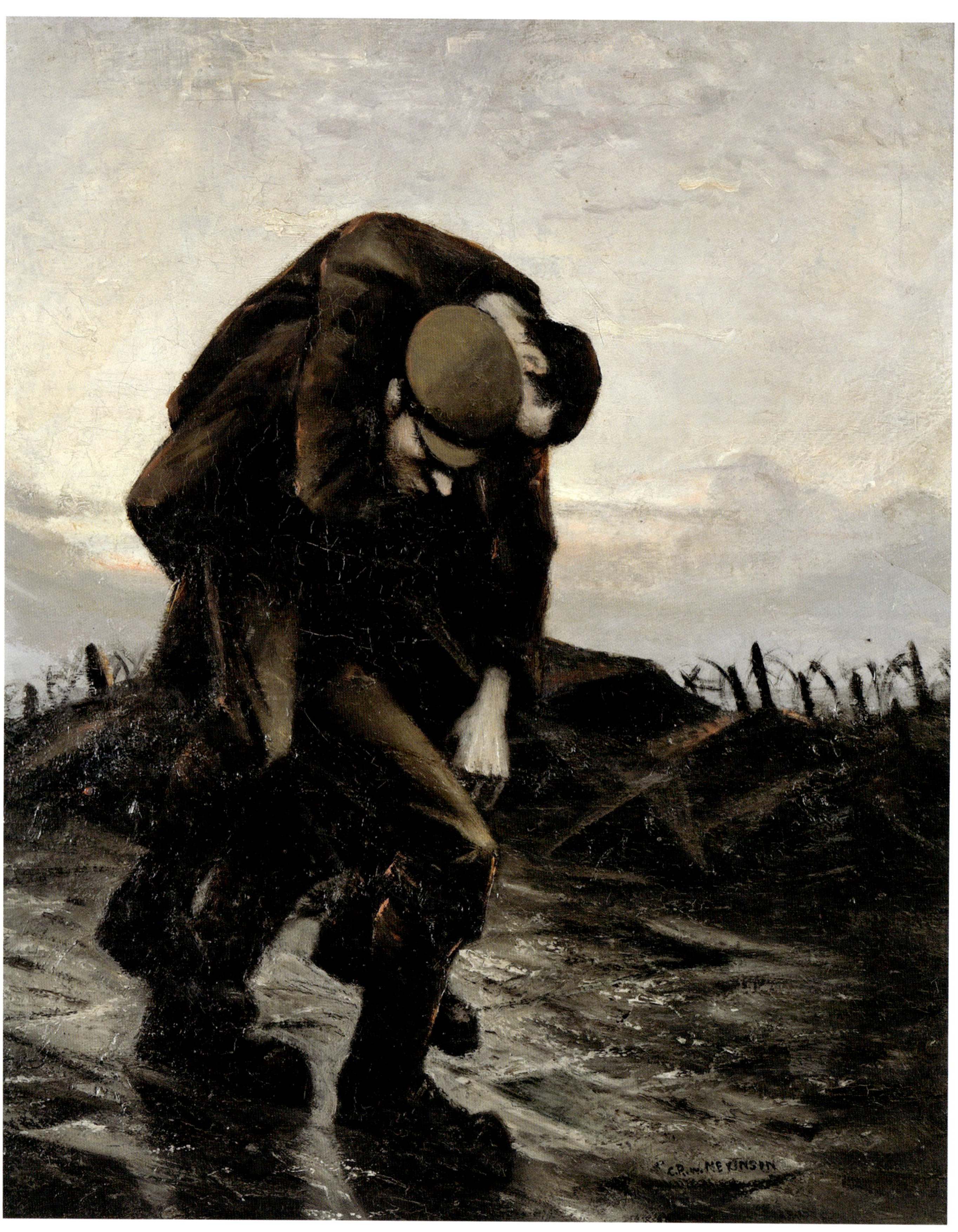

C.R.W. NEVINSON

C.R.W. Nevinson, *Twilight*, 1916

Oil on canvas (53 × 45 cm)

C.R.W. Nevinson's haunting painting of a wounded soldier being carried across the battlefield has belonged to the College since 1951. It was part of the bequest of Monty Rendall, Headmaster from 1911 to 1924. To understand Rendall's acquisition of the painting, and its poignancy within a Wykehamical context, it is important to know something of Rendall, who was Headmaster throughout the Great War. Between 1914 and 1918, 2,418 Wykehamists served in the armed forces. Of these 513 died. Although by no means unique to the schools and universities of that time, Winchester's losses were among the highest in absolute numbers and in percentage terms. It was the equivalent of the whole school roll being wiped out over four years. One can imagine the emotional toll on Rendall announcing these deaths in Chapel on a daily basis. It marked him deeply.

By late 1917 Rendall had come to the decision that this loss, already by then some four hundred Wykehamists, must be marked. After a dinner held in the blacked-out city of Amiens on 17 November, attended by Rendall and sixty-eight Wykehamist officers, the concept of War Cloister was born. Designed by Sir Herbert Baker and completed in 1924, it is the largest private war memorial in the United Kingdom and an incomparable monument to those who fell. Rendall's faith is echoed in the Christian and Marian iconography throughout. Profound grief at the loss of 'his boys' is palpable in every stone and flint, as is his hope in the Resurrection, evoked by Alfred Turner's slender cross at the centre of the cloister.

It is not known when Rendall purchased Nevinson's *Twilight*. The painting was first exhibited at the Leicester Galleries in London in 1916, where it appears as No. 1 in the exhibition catalogue. The subject derives from Nevinson's experiences during 1914 and 1915 in France as orderly and driver with a Friends Ambulance Unit, and subsequently with the Royal Army Medical Corps. Nevinson, a volatile character himself, witnessed particularly in Dunkirk much suffering and horrendous wounds. In January 1916 he was discharged from the RAMC with psychotic rheumatic fever, which would today be recognised as a mental breakdown. Nevinson's pre-war Cubist and Futurist influences are seen in many of the paintings exhibited in 1916. *La Mitrailleuse* (1915) depicts French soldiers behind a machine gun: man and murderous machine are melded into one searing image of pure lethality. *Twilight* is a very different kind of war painting. The sun is setting behind the figures and the light is disappearing into the darkness of the rear trench areas. We see the weight of the wounded man in the bowed head and deeply flexed knee of the orderly. Together they form one whole of succour and suffering. One sees how this would touch Rendall and lead him to bequeath it to the school.

Michael Wallis (Modern Languages)

Gleadowe's Stained Glass, Chantry, 1930s–1951

Stained glass with added paint (400 × 400 cm)

R.M.Y. Gleadowe (Art Master, 1922–39) is not as well known as some other Winchester artists, but his imprint is widespread: the angels with 'loud-uplifted trumpets' on the gates of War Cloister (sadly now replacements after the theft of the originals in the 1980s) and the lettering of its inscription; the stained glass in College Hall; the west window of Fromond's Chantry; Frazer Tent, and the wrought-iron gate from Meads into the Warden's Garden.

While teaching at Winchester, Gleadowe acquired a national reputation for draughtsmanship and design in metal, stone and glass. He was appointed Slade Professor of Fine Art at Oxford (1928–33), and his most famous commission was the Sword of Stalingrad, a gift from George VI to honour the city's resistance to Hitler. The College owns several pieces of silver designed by Gleadowe, including an elegant lily-form cup (pictured), commissioned with a legacy from Sir Oswald Simpkin (Warden, 1932–36).

Warden Simpkin's legacy also enabled an ambitious project to provide a new scheme of stained glass for the west window of Fromond's Chantry, a chapel built within the cloister garth of the College in the early fifteenth century. It was decided that the window should be *en grisaille*, as the effect of the surrounding cloister on stained glass had been to make Chantry too dark, and that its themes should be worship and creation. Gleadowe began by designing the lower part of the window, with the sea at the bottom, and above it the earth with lilies and roses. The window remained unfinished when Gleadowe died unexpectedly in 1944. The College turned to his former pupil, Kenneth Knowles (College, 1921–27). After much searching, it was realised that Gleadowe had destroyed his drawings for the tracery lights, bitterly dissatisfied, but Knowles found a glass angel produced to Gleadowe's design that gave a clue as to his intentions: the heavens, represented by the nine orders of angels, and stars. Knowles then produced the striking array of angels, crowned by a lyrical tableau of the Annunciation, the inspiration for which may be Gleadowe's angels with feathery wings, playing violins in the south-east window of College Hall.

Gleadowe came to Winchester College at the invitation of Monty Rendall, who was himself passionately interested in art and regularly gave lectures on the Italian Renaissance, illustrated by his own photographs. The art master of the time, however, lacked Rendall's energy (Kenneth Clark reported finding him asleep) and pupil numbers dwindled. Nearing retirement, Rendall turned to the talented Gleadowe, a former pupil (College, 1901–07). After a First in Classics at New College, Gleadowe had worked as a civil servant before becoming Assistant to the Director of the National Gallery. In 1922 he was persuaded by Rendall to return to Winchester. Their shared dream, Chaplain Budge Firth commented, was to bring art teaching 'to a new pitch of glory'.

Both were disappointed. Gleadowe never found fulfilment as a schoolmaster and not many pupils came to his new art school on the top floor of Chantry. Rendall defended him from his critics in a highly charged sonnet written after his death. Although it fell to Gleadowe's successors, Sthyr and Drew, with different personalities, to increase pupil enthusiasm for art, Gleadowe made a magnificent contribution to the creation and appreciation of the beauty which Wykehamists are so fortunate to experience daily.

Jane Hands

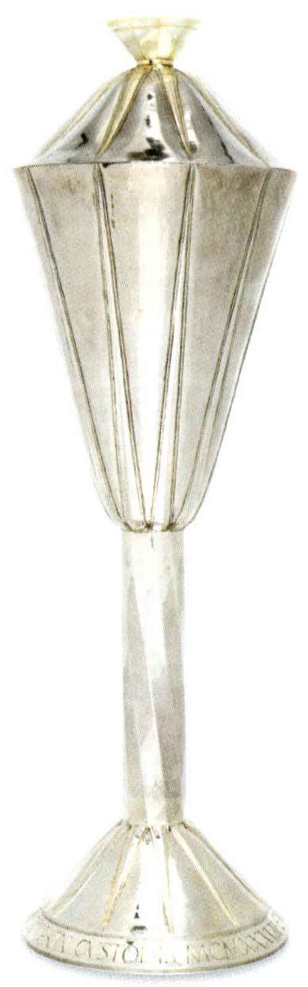

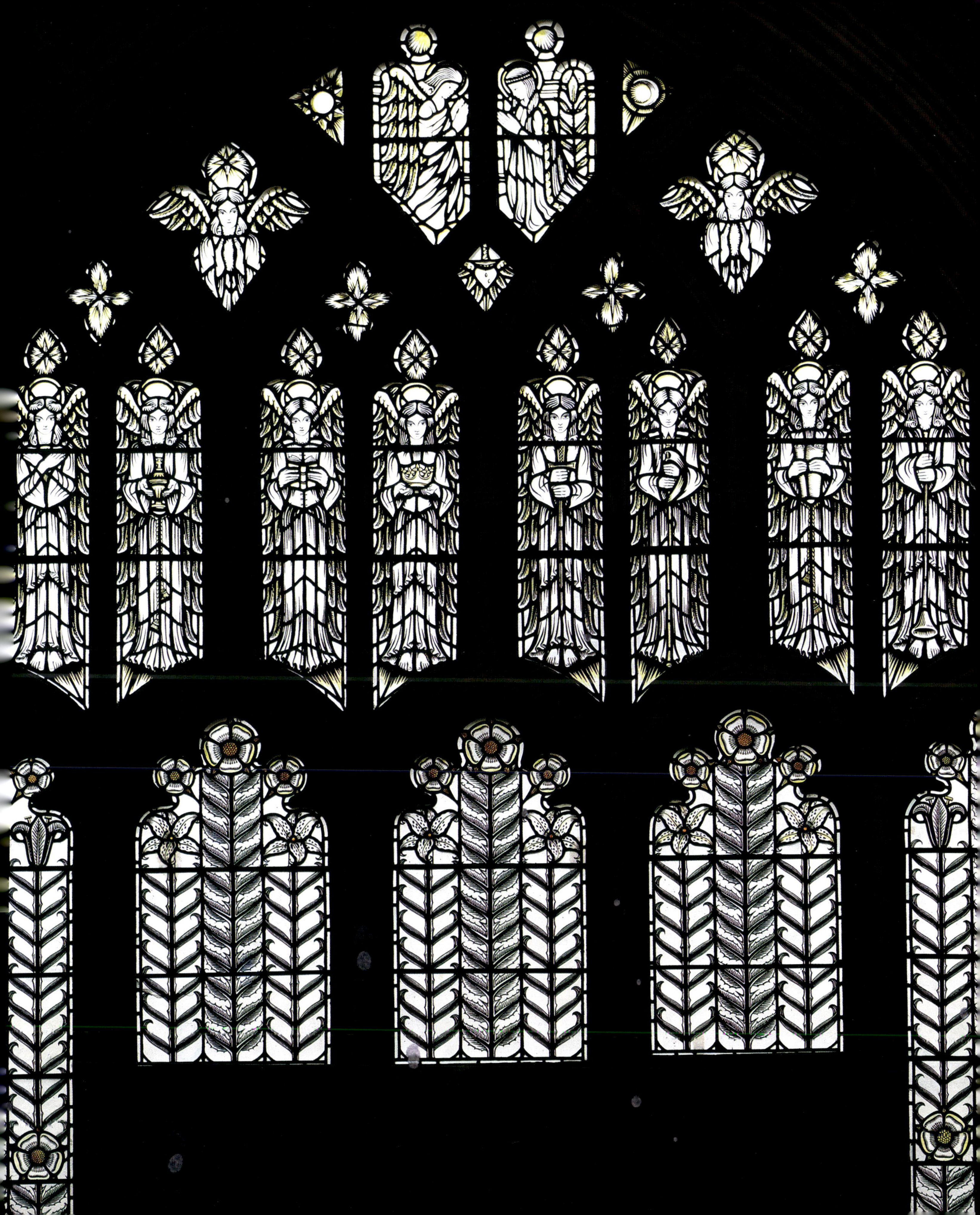

Adonis Blues, 1930s

In an early 20th-century specimen drawer (each butterfly *c.* 1.6 × 2.5 cm)

Some eighty years after they succumbed to the vapours in a Wykehamist's killing jar, these Adonis Blue butterflies still shine like pixels of the brightest blue summer sky atop a steel pin. They sleep, peaceful and unknowing, in their white-papered casket, as today's pupils pass by. They are a reminder of the mixed fortunes of this species in the intervening years and the anthropogenic changes that have driven them, but also of our more profound relationship with the species that live here.

In 1933, when the first of these butterflies was captured, the Adonis Blue was rare, not as rare as it is today, but as a species on the northernmost edge of its distribution, it would have always been on the ecological back foot. It seeks out the suntraps and the hotspots, mainly the short sheep-grazed folds of the chalk downland of southern England. One such place is St Catherine's Hill, a small but spectacular chalk mound that forms a backdrop to the east of the College. In the 1930s this hill would have held an irresistible draw for the boys of the school. This azure-winged male butterfly would have been one such reason to climb it, to catch a butterfly and possess a shard of the purest essence of summer.

A close engagement with local wildlife was encouraged by the College's Natural History Society, founded in 1870 and still going strong today. Among the Society's activities in earlier periods was the enthusiastic collection of insect specimens from the hills, woods and water meadows that surround the College. There is no evidence to suggest that such 'country pursuits' have led directly to extinction, while the experiences and knowledge gained could arguably be greater than the loss of a few individuals taken as treasure. Our collector would have known a St Catherine's Hill that was very different. There were almost certainly more butterflies than there are now, painting the summer with their wings. Some of those species are long gone: Duke of Burgundy, Marsh Fritillary and High Brown, all butterflies which would have been well known in the 1930s, but that have vanished from many of their former haunts, and some even from the county.

The Adonis Blue disappeared from the slopes of St Catherine's Hill in the late twentieth century, seemingly gone forever. If I had been asked to write this a few years ago, the story would have had a very different ending: a sad, often-repeated tale of local extinction, leaving these dry specimens as a shadow of a time now gone. However, in recent years they have returned – nobody knows how. A maverick reintroduction perhaps? A natural recolonisation from nearby? A response to the favourable management of the slopes by the Hampshire and Isle of Wight Wildlife Trust? We do not really know, but to me it does not matter. In a world of negative news, this insect represents a little bit of hope. The fact that this dazzling butterfly has returned is a symbol of nature's resilience and ability to rebound when given a chance. Maybe, we too will open our eyes, recalibrate our definition of progress, and start to become aware of the intrinsic value of sharing our space with creatures like these.

Nick Baker (Duncan Stewart Fellow of Natural History)

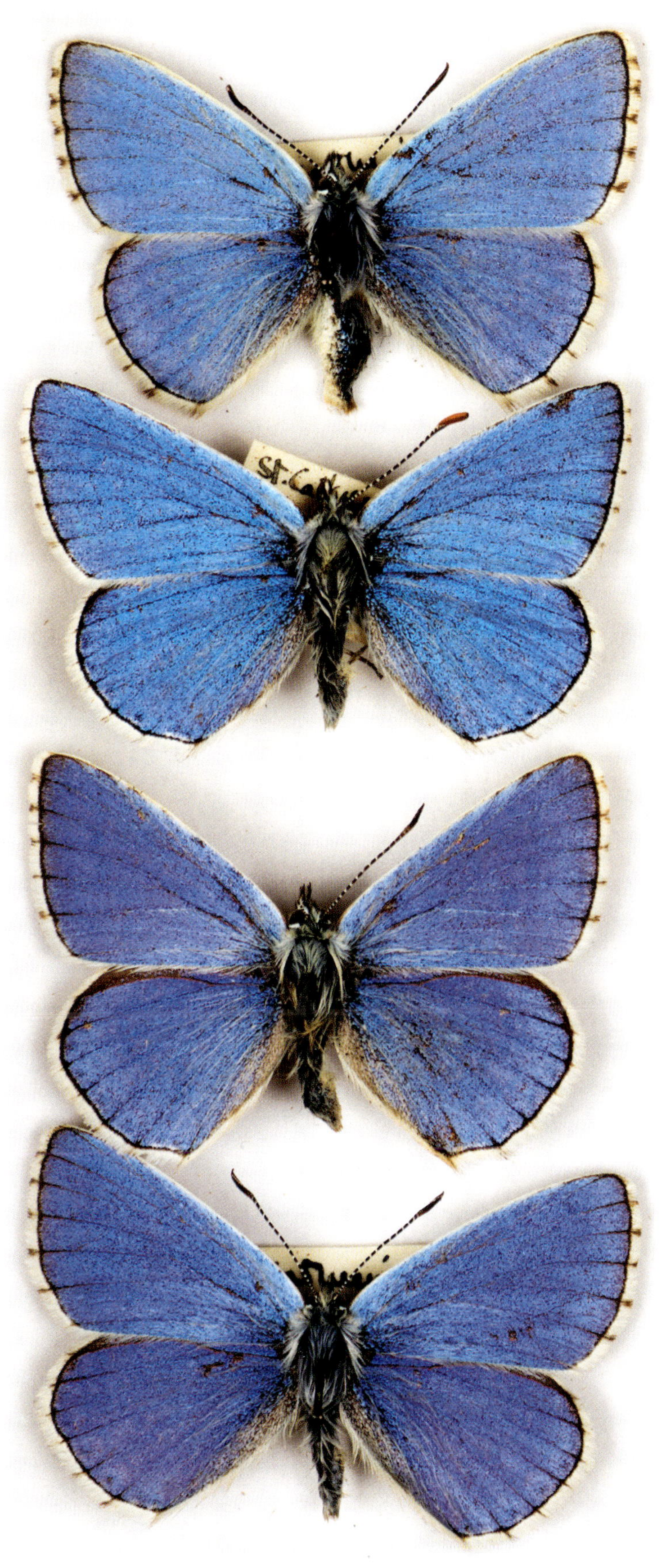

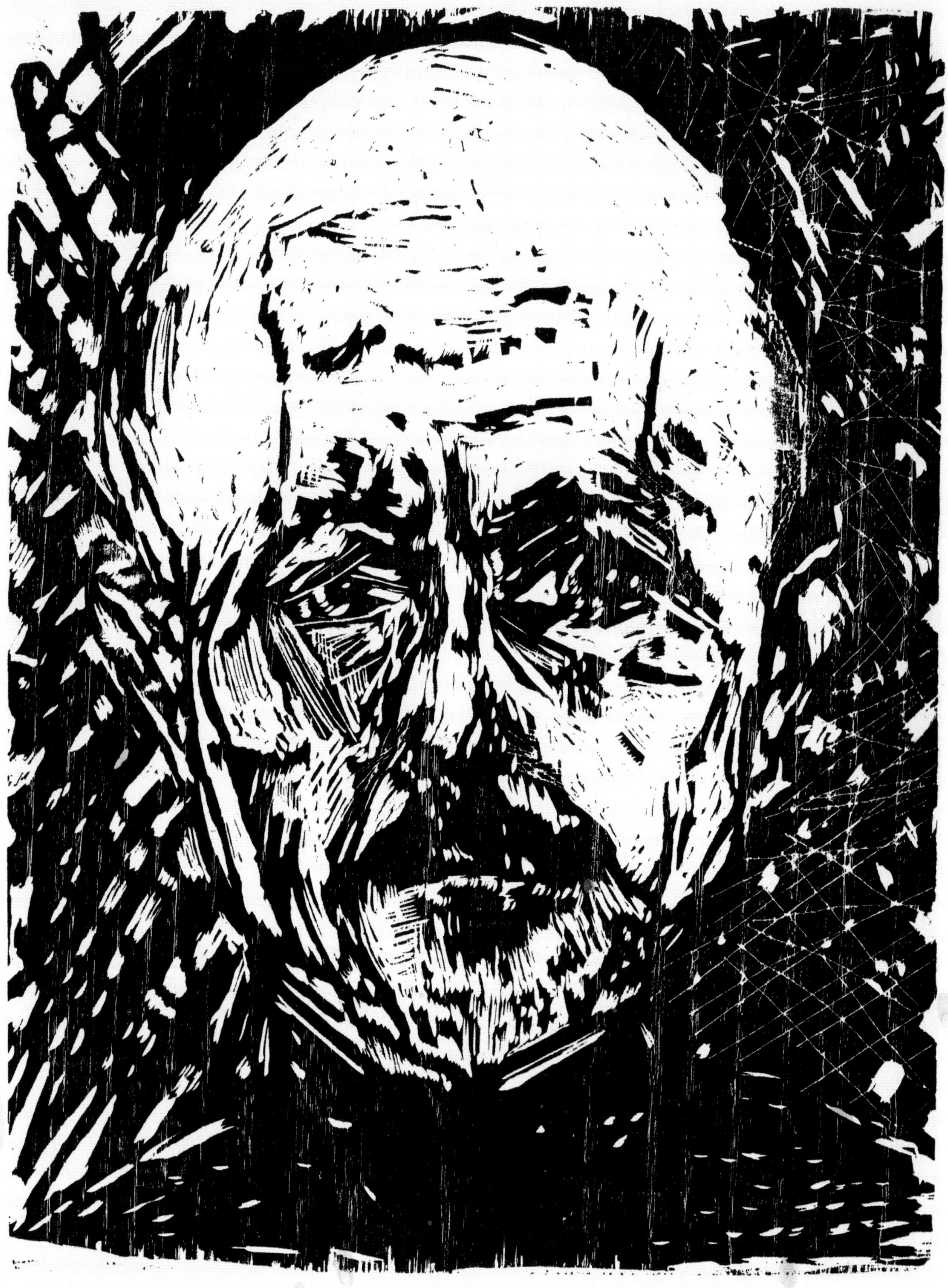

Jim Dine, *The Apocalypse*, 1982

Jim Dine, *The Apocalypse: The Revelation of St John the Divine* (San Francisco, 1982),
bound in quarter pigskin over wooden boards (38 × 27 cm)

In 1994 Viscount Eccles (G, 1918–23) donated his collection of artists' books to the College. It includes work by many of the leading printmakers of the twentieth century, from Paul Nash to Henry Moore. The collection is regularly used as a source of inspiration for pupils studying Fine Art, and it continues to grow through the acquisition of new publications by contemporary book artists.

In later life Eccles spent time in the US, and American illustrated books of the 1980s are a particular strength of the collection. There are several examples of the work of Jim Dine, including *The Apocalypse* (1982), which brings to life the ominous text of the Book of Revelation through a series of twenty-nine dramatic woodcut prints. Dine rose to prominence in the 1960s. As well as a painter and sculptor, he continues to be a passionate and prolific printmaker. He has developed a recognisable visual vocabulary with which he routinely depicts familiar objects and motifs that include hearts, bathrobes, trees and hands. The opening illustration of *The Apocalypse*, entitled 'Artist as Narrator', is a self-portrait, and here Dine introduces himself and the dramatic graphic quality of his work and the technique. The sombre expression captures a sense of anxiety that is heightened by the frenzied and expressive marks that create the background. The mark of the artist is embedded in the surface of each woodblock. Using a variety of gauges and chisels, Dine draws directly with the cutting tools onto each plate, leaving behind gestural marks and cuts that are exaggerated by the qualities of the material, as it tears and splinters with each pass of the cutting tool. The sense of drama is underlined by the stark contrast of black ink on white paper.

Dine's symbolic references are predominantly figurative. Animals, skulls, gates, candlesticks and wings are among the many familiar motifs that he uses to describe key characters and events in this ultimate battle between good and evil. 'The Bottomless Pit' visually describes the turbulence and ferocity of the seven years of Tribulation in a swirling cyclone of marks and shapes, and 'Feet As If They Burned in a Furnace' graphically cements the vision of Hell on earth. The lattice pattern describing the skin on the coiled snake entitled 'That Old Serpent, Called the Devil' is replicated in several images, thus stressing the evil forces that are at work. Symbolic references to vengeance and salvation are equally bountiful, and Dine is successful in generating a sense of redemption. 'Morning Star' illuminates the page with the central image radiating bright rays in a festival of directional cuts, and in 'Behold a White Horse' Dine floods light into the image by carving the majority of the block away to leave a very linear image in relief. The majestic and triumphant stance of the animal leaves the viewer in no doubt of the victor, but its scars indicate a hard-fought battle.

This *livre d'artiste* is an appreciation and acknowledgement of the long tradition of illustrating the Apocalypse and the partnership of image and text. It is a celebration of the book in this digital age, and an artwork that serves to inform and inspire experimentation in the creative process of woodcut printmaking.

Alex Forsyth (Art)

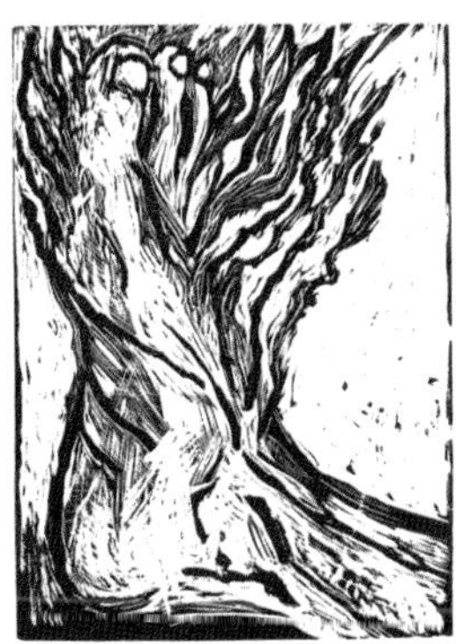

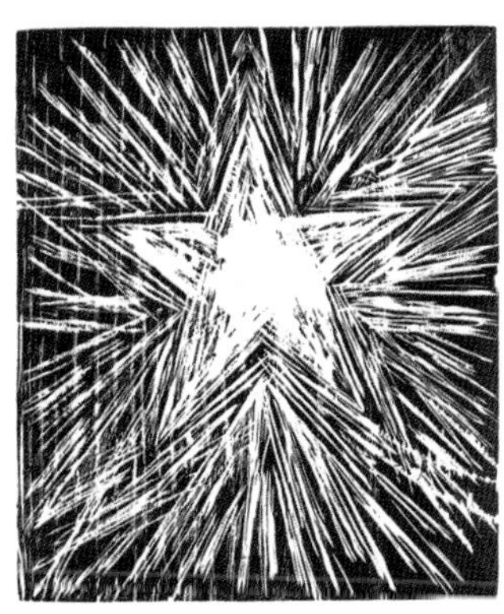

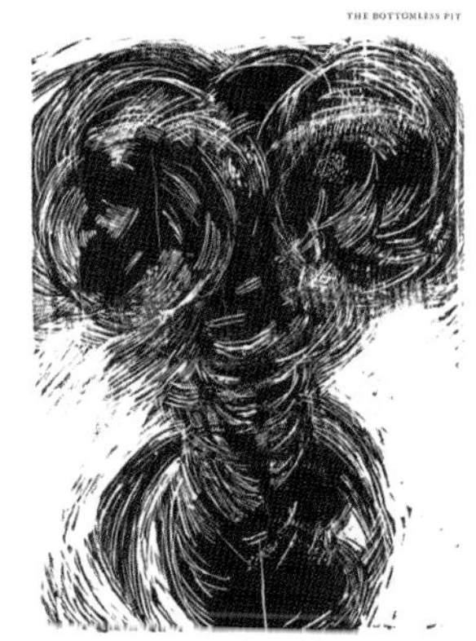

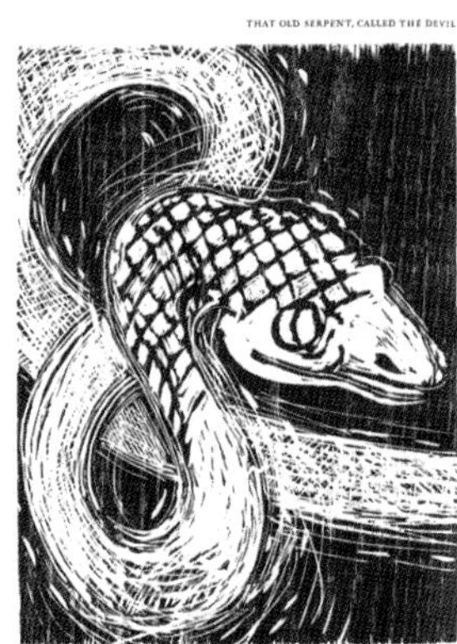

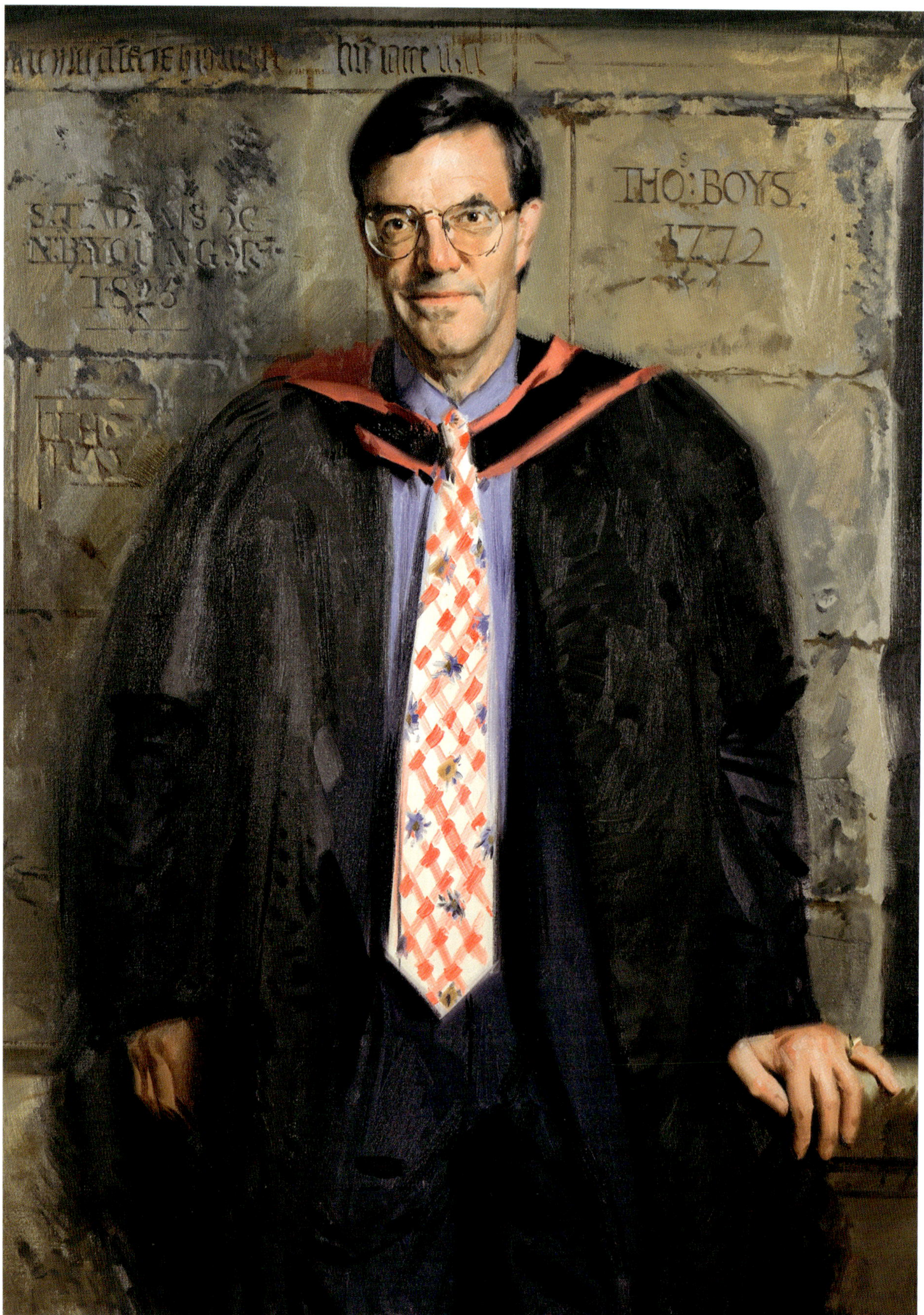

THO: BOYS
1772
S.T.ADAMS OC
N.BYOUNG
1825

Andrew Festing, *James Sabben-Clare,* 2000

Oil on canvas (104 × 78 cm)

James Sabben-Clare stands in the Cloisters, against a wall that is actually a composite of two separate buttresses. In addition to being a brilliant schoolmaster and Headmaster, he was a talented actor, comedian and sketch-writer. With his rather quizzical smile, he gives the viewer the impression that he is about to crack a wry joke. The graffiti in the background create the sense that the sitter is surrounded by the ghosts of past generations of Wykehamists.

Apart from a spell teaching at Marlborough College, including a year as a Visiting Fellow of All Souls, Oxford, Sabben-Clare spent nearly all his professional life at Winchester. He was born in 1941, the son of Ernest Sabben-Clare, Headmaster of Leeds Grammar School. In 1954, having won the top scholarship, he came to Winchester and, finishing his schooldays with a year as *Aulae Prae* (Head Boy), went on to study Classics at New College, Oxford. He eventually returned to Winchester as a don in 1968, and just a year later became Head of the Department of Classics. From 1979 he was Second Master, and in 1985 was appointed Headmaster. He retired in 2000 and died aged seventy-five in March 2017. In addition to compiling an ancient history sourcebook, *Caesar and Roman Politics 60–50 BC*, he produced a translation of Aesop's *Fables* and wrote a new history of Winchester College.

This painting is part of a substantial collection of portraits at Winchester, most of which hang either in the building known as School or in the Warden's Lodgings. Apart from various representations of William of Wykeham, including a contemporary copy of the painting by Sampson Strong (1550–1611) at New College, the oldest surviving portrait in the College's collection is that of Thomas Bilson, Headmaster from 1572 until he became Warden in 1581. He went on to become Bishop of Winchester in 1597 and his wife had the distinction of being the first female resident in College. Other portraits include that of Joseph Warton (1722–1800), one of the school's less successful Headmasters, but an outstanding poet and literary critic, and that of his successor as Headmaster, William Goddard (1757–1845), who revolutionised the way the school was administered after a rather unstable period in its history, which included a serious rebellion by the pupils. There is also Glyn Philpot's fine portrait of Monty Rendall (1925).

In the lead up to his retirement Sabben-Clare had seen examples of Andrew Festing's work at the National Portrait Gallery, and in 1999 asked him if he would paint his portrait. His choice was strengthened by Festing's father, Field Marshal Sir Francis Festing, having been at Winchester between 1916 and 1920. Sabben-Clare spent time in London getting to know the artist, and Festing came to Winchester on a couple of occasions to get a feel for the school and to choose a background. By nature a shy man, Sabben-Clare nonetheless had a strong penchant for bright ties, and for one of the sittings he turned up wearing that depicted in this portrait, a very bright and eye-catching specimen with red diamonds and blue cornflowers, one of the College's emblems. He said later that he thoroughly enjoyed the sittings: certainly his warmth and humour are apparent in the portrait, which is also an extremely accurate likeness.

Jane Boyles (Keeper of Paintings and College Plate)

Contributors

Henry Berry was a pupil at Winchester from 2012 to 2017. In his final year he wrote an extended essay on the Winchester Painter. He is now reading *Literae Humaniores* at Oxford.

Sarah Harden joined Winchester College in 2013 and has been Head of Classics since 2017. She studied at Oxford and wrote her D.Phil. on Greek poetry. Before coming to Winchester she was a lecturer and Director of Studies for Classics at Trinity College, Oxford. She has published several articles on Greek literature in academic journals, and is the author of an A Level Greek textbook published by Bloomsbury.

Alfred Deahl is in his final year at Winchester, studying History, Art History and Classics. He is a keen collector of ancient coins and founded the school's Numismatics Society.

John Nightingale (D, 1973–77, Fellow, 2002–17) is the senior tutor in History at Magdalen College, Oxford, where he has been a Fellow since 1986. His teaching, research and publications are on early medieval European history.

Anthony du Boulay (C, 1943–46) joined Christie's in 1949, where he was Head of Ceramics (1956–80), and President of Christie's Geneva (1967–80). He was an honorary adviser to the National Trust (1981–2011), and is a Fellow of the Society of Antiquaries. He has published two books and numerous articles on ceramics.

Peter Cramer taught History and History of Art at Winchester College until 2018, and was Housemaster of Moberly's (2000–07). Before coming to Winchester in 1993, he studied at Cambridge and Sheffield, and was then Research Fellow at Wolfson College, Oxford. He published a book on medieval baptism, and since then has been writing mainly on twelfth-century subject-matter.

Nicholas Townson teaches History and Div at Winchester College. Previously he was a doctoral student, teaching assistant and postdoctoral research fellow at the University of York, where he worked on academic thought and Italian communes in the thirteenth century.

Magnus Ryan was a pupil at Winchester (G, 1980–84) and is currently a Fellow of Peterhouse, Cambridge. He has held positions at the Warburg Institute, All Souls College and St John's College, Cambridge. His PhD was on Roman law and feudal law; he works on law and political theory in the later Middle Ages.

Malcolm Hebron joined the teaching staff at Winchester College in 1992. He has taught English and History of Art and was Head of Drama (2013–18). His publications include *The Medieval Siege* (OUP), *Key Concepts in Renaissance Literature* (Palgrave) and *How to Read a Poem* (Connell). He edits the English Association journal, *The Use of English*.

Nick MacKinnon has taught at Winchester since 1986 and been Housemaster of Chawker's (1996–2009) and coach of OTH since 1993. He read Maths at Oxford, was editor of the *Mathematical Gazette*, and has been the most prolific setter of the *Sunday Times* Brainteaser for thirty-five years. His poem 'The Metric System' won the 2014 Forward Prize.

Liam Dunne joined Winchester College in 2013 to teach Philosophy & Theology, French and Div, after many years as a lay brother with the Dominicans in France. He has studied at the University of Oxford and the Institut Catholique de Toulouse.

Nicholas Ferguson CBE is a Wykehamist (C, 1961–66) and a member of the Governing Body. He has been collecting medieval sculpture, mainly Romanesque, for forty years. His career has been primarily in private equity. He was Chairman of Sky Plc and is currently Chairman of Savills Plc. He is a Fellow of the Scottish Society of Antiquaries.

Suzanne Ceiriog-Hughes teaches Art History and is also Deputy Librarian at Winchester College. She studied at the Courtauld Institute, specialising in the medieval period, and completed her Master's degree at University College London. She spent twelve years as a Housemaster's wife in Fearon's (1998–2010) and has been part of the Treasury team since its opening.

Nicholas Wilks was Master of Music at Winchester College from 2004 until 2015 when he took up his current post of Second Master. He was a Quirister between 1970 and 1973, read English at Oxford and studied conducting at the Royal Academy of Music. He teaches Div and English, and is the conductor of the Winchester Symphony Orchestra.

Steven Little is Bursar and Secretary to the Governing Body at Winchester College. He read Classics at Cambridge before training as a chartered accountant and working in public practice in London, Sydney and Winchester. He joined the College in 1999 as Chief Accountant and in 2014 became Bursar.

Chun Cai began teaching Chinese and Div at Winchester in 1994. Before joining the College he read English at Jilin in China, studied and taught Politics at Regina in Canada, and studied and taught International Politics at Lancaster in the UK. He wrote his PhD on Chinese foreign policy since 1949, and has published books on classical Chinese culture.

Michael Bruzon is an artist and educator who has exhibited internationally and throughout the UK. He joined Winchester College in 2014 where he teaches painting and is Head of Art School. He has studied at Chelsea College of Art, Oxford Brookes and Goldsmiths, and holds a degree in Fine Art, a PGCE and an MA in Art Education.

Sam Baddeley teaches Classics and Div, and is Head of Drama. He arrived at the College in 2016 after teaching at Solihull School and Eastbourne College. He studied *Literae Humaniores* at Oxford. He has contributed to a GCSE Ancient History textbook and is currently completing a commentary on Sophocles' *Ajax* for an A Level Greek publication.

Ian Fraser is the Master-in-College, responsible for selecting and looking after the seventy Scholars of Winchester College. He also teaches Biology and Div, and is in charge of the Expeditions Society. He has a degree in Microbiology from the University of Birmingham, and interests in adventure travel, drama and art.

William Poole is a Governing Body Fellow of Winchester College, and Galsworthy Fellow in English of New College, Oxford, where he is also Senior Tutor and Fellow Librarian. He studied at Oxford, where he wrote a D.Phil. on the poetry of John Milton. He is a bibliographer and intellectual historian, and also co-edits the Bibliographical Society's journal, *The Library*.

James Webster has taught History, Div and Classics at Winchester College since 1992. Previously he studied at Oxford and Harvard. He has been Head of History, Undermaster and Director of Studies at Winchester, and currently holds the position of Director of External Affairs.

Andrew Leigh has been teaching Latin and Greek at Winchester for over three decades. He read *Literae Humaniores* at Oxford. He is the author of the *Winchester Latin Course*, and his textbook on Latin prose composition will be published in 2019.

Suzanne Foster has been College Archivist since 2005. She joined Winchester as Deputy Archivist in 1999, having previously worked at Hampshire Record Office. She studied History at the University of Nottingham and Archive Administration at the University of Liverpool.

John Falconer taught Classics at Winchester College from 1978 until his retirement in 2014. As curator of the College Treasury from 2001 he played a major part in creating the new museum in the Warden's Stables. He is co-author, with Thomas Mannack, of the publication of the College's Greek vase collection in the *Corpus Vasorum Antiquorum* (2002). He studied Classics at Cambridge.

David Thomas read Music at Oxford. In a teaching career spanning over thirty years, he has held posts at several leading schools in the UK, including fourteen years as Headmaster, first at Reigate Grammar School and subsequently at the Purcell School. He is a singer, organist and conductor and has been Master of Music at Winchester College since September 2015.

Simon Thorn (D, 1979–84) teaches Biology and is Foundation Chaplain at Winchester College. He studied Physiology at the University of Bristol (BSc, PhD). After teaching at Glenalmond, in 1997 he became Head of Biology, and latterly Head of Science, at Radley College. Ordained in 2009, after training at Cuddesdon, he was appointed Chaplain at Downe House in 2011, before returning to Winchester in 2015.

Robert Wyke joined the Winchester Common Room in 1985 as Head of English; in 1990 he became Housemaster of Turner's; he then served as Second Master from 2001 until his retirement in 2015. He was educated at Cambridge and at the University of Durham. He is Chairman of the Laurence Sterne Trust.

Joseph Scull was elected to Winchester College in 2014. He is currently in his final year in College and is studying English, Russian and German.

Richard Foster teaches History and Art History at Winchester College. He joined the school in 2012, and since 2014 has been Keeper of Collections and Fellows' Librarian. He studied at Oxford and the Courtauld Institute. At Oxford he wrote his D.Phil. thesis on the Church of England in the seventeenth century. He has published research on early printed books and the history of collecting.

Geoffrey Day started teaching at Winchester in 1989 and retired as Eccles and Fellows' Librarian in 2014. He has published on a wide range of seventeenth- and eighteenth-century topics, and his most recent book, *John Harmar: Translator*, a biography of the Warden of Winchester who was a principal figure in the translation of the New Testament for the King James Bible, appeared in 2016.

Rachel Poole joined Winchester College in 2011 and teaches Biology and Chemistry. She studied Biochemistry at Oxford, graduating in 2008. She completed a Master's by research in Radiation Biology, also at Oxford, looking at the effect of hypoxia on p53-dependent apoptosis.

Andrea Thomas has been a tour guide at Winchester College since 2016 and previously taught History at many leading independent schools. She studied at Oxford and the University of Edinburgh. She wrote her PhD on the culture of the court of King James V and has published two books and several essays on the Renaissance in Scotland.

Jeremy Douglas was in College from 1988 to 1992. He returned to teach at Winchester in 2004 and is currently Head of Physics and a Div don. He studied Physics at Oxford, Computer Science at Imperial College, and Education at the University of Leeds.

Christopher Rowell (K, 1965–70) studied at Oxford and the Courtauld Institute. He is Furniture Curator of the National Trust, Chairman of the Furniture History Society and a member of the UK Reviewing Committee on the Export of Works of Art. His publications include articles on Lemoyne's Winchester altarpiece and Isaac Whood's portraits of 'Dr Burton's Commoners'.

George Morrison is a pupil in his final year at Winchester College and hopes to read Chinese Studies at university.

Tim Giddings teaches Classics and Div at Winchester College. He was the College Tutor for six years and is currently Housemaster-elect of Morshead's. Before joining the school in 2009 he studied at the universities of Bristol and Oxford. He edits one of the school magazines, *The Trusty Servant*.

Rachel Wragg joined Winchester College in 2012 as Museum Development Manager. Since 2016 she has been the Treasury Curator. She studied at the universities of Nottingham and Leicester. She has had an extensive career in museum management and was previously the Senior Curator at the River and Rowing Museum, Henley.

Alan Smith, Tim Cox and Lily Livingston care for the gardens and grounds of Winchester College.

Lucia Quinault has taught English and Div at Winchester College since 1999. She read English at Oxford, and is currently writing a PhD thesis at Queen Mary University of London on the circulation of eighteenth-century poetry manuscripts. She has published on poetry's role in the history of the emotions, and on manuscript miscellanies, including examples from the Fellows' Library.

Charles Sinclair CBE (B, 1961–66) has been a member of the Governing Body since 2010 and was elected Warden in 2014. He studied PPE at Oxford and taught in the Zambia Forestry Department. He has been a director of various public companies and latterly Chairman of Associated British Foods. He is a descendant of Joseph Wright of Derby and a Newlyn School collector.

Laurence Guymer teaches History and Div at Winchester College. He came to Winchester in 2010 having received his PhD from the University of East Anglia. He writes on British diplomatic history in the nineteenth century. His latest article is on Anglo-Russian relations in the aftermath of the Crimean War. He is a Fellow of the Royal Historical Society, and is Housemaster-elect of Kingsgate House.

Timothy Hands became Headmaster of Winchester College in 2016, having previously been Headmaster of Portsmouth Grammar School and Master of Magdalen College School, Oxford. He studied at London and Oxford universities and has published four books and several articles on Victorian literature, the first article forming a study of one of Trollope's Winchester contemporaries.

Peter Cornish is Head of Mathematics at Winchester College. Before joining the school in 1987 he read Pure Mathematics at the University of Birmingham, and Education at King's College London. In 2002 he completed a PhD at Royal Holloway University of London entitled 'Conception and Enactment in Musical Performance'. He studied the clarinet with Alan Hacker and has given numerous lecture-recitals on twentieth-century clarinet music at various UK universities.

George Nash (K, 2002–07) is one of Winchester College's most successful Olympians. He won bronze in the coxless pair at London 2012, and gold in the coxless four at Rio 2016. He read Engineering at Cambridge and was President of the University Boat Club. He is now the technical director of a mechanical engineering firm.

Nick Baker joined Winchester College in 2016 as the first Duncan Louis Stewart Fellow of Natural History, a position created to enthuse and engage pupils and staff in the rich natural resources of the College. He works closely with the College's Natural History Society and the Biology department. He is also a naturalist, broadcaster and author.

Martin Gregory taught Physics at Winchester College from 1962 to 1999. He studied at Oxford and has a D.Phil. in nuclear physics. He has written several textbooks on physics and electronics and served as Chief Examiner and Chair of Examiners for A Level Physics. In retirement he mills flour and works on preserved steam engines.

Michael Wallis teaches French, German and Div. He joined Winchester in 1985. He has been Assistant Head of Modern Languages, Head of Div for the top two years, Commanding Officer of the CCF for sixteen years, and was Chairman of Common Room for six years. He is now Don Associate and Director of the Friends. He recently published a small monograph on the architecture of War Cloister. He was educated at Edinburgh and Oxford.

Jane Hands read *Literae Humaniores* at Oxford and worked for Slaughter and May for nearly thirty years, as a solicitor and more recently as Partnership Secretary. She is married to the current Headmaster.

Jane Boyles was educated at La Sagesse Convent, Romsey, and joined Winchester College in 1972 as Bursary Receptionist. She has been Assistant Bursar's Secretary, Works Bursar's Secretary, and Estates Bursar's Secretary. Since 2013 she has worked on the cataloguing of the College collections, and has special responsibility for the oil paintings and College silver.

Alex Forsyth joined Winchester College in 2018 and teaches Art. He studied printmaking at Duncan of Jordanstone College of Art and Design in Dundee.

Acknowledgements

I am grateful to the Warden and Fellows of Winchester College for their generous funding of this publication, and to the Headmaster who has given enthusiastic support throughout its preparation. Suzanne Foster (Archivist), Rachel Wragg (Curator of Treasury) and Amber Davenport (Chief Science Technician) shared their knowledge and provided a great deal of practical assistance. Justine Potts gave much invaluable advice. Stephen Anderson (College Editor) assisted with the copy-editing of the text.

Richard Foster

Illustration credits

Rob Fry: pp. 15, 17 (left), 18 (bottom), 22, 26–41, 44–50, 54–69, 72–99, 103, 106–22, 126, 129–31; Chris Andrews: pp. 2–3, 10 (top), 12, 13, 14, 17 (right), 21 (top right); Gordon Plumb: pp. 9, 42, 53; Andy Sollars: pp. 8, 16, 18, 19, 20, 21 (bottom), 70–71, 100–01, 104–05, 124, 127, 132.